*OPEN
EDUCATION
AND THE
AMERICAN
SCHOOL*

OPEN EDUCATION AND THE AMERICAN SCHOOL

by Roland S. Barth

Foreword by Joseph Featherstone

AGATHON PRESS, INC., NEW YORK

Distributed by

SCHOCKEN BOOKS, NEW YORK

For information address:
Agathon Press, Inc.
150 Fifth Avenue
New York, N.Y. 10011

Distributed by:
Schocken Books Inc.
200 Madison Avenue
New York, N.Y. 10016

Library of Congress Catalog Card Number: 72-80265
ISBN 0-87586-036-2
DESIGNED BY PAULA WIENER
Printed in the United States of America

Second printing, 1973

Contents

To Joanna

Foreword

Roland Barth's *Open Education and the American School* is a timely book. For one thing, Barth has chosen to influence change as a working school principal. Next to children and parents, the people least heeded in our endless discussions of education are practitioners—teachers and principals. So it is refreshing to hear from an articulate and thoughtful practitioner. For another thing, Barth is a practitioner with a profound interest in theory: the first part of this book, in many ways the most useful part, is an account of children's learning and some of the theoretical assumptions that ought to underlie work in open or informal schools. There are clear discussions of such complex matters as the nature of knowledge and a good long chapter on the role of the teacher in the open classroom.

Few new ideas are revealed, but as a sensible general synthesis of a large inchoate body of thought, *Open Education* is helpful. Much of this body of thought is still hypotheses and guesses; one of the strengths of Barth's book is that it points to many contradictions, ambiguities, and unresolved issues. This sort of basically friendly, yet probing and skeptical treatment may yet make "open" education a serious movement.

Barth's invitation to practitioners to begin seriously reflecting on the theoretical implications of their practice is essential: without an ongoing interplay between theory and practice, without thought about children's thinking on the part of classroom teachers and principals, much of the current wave of interest in informal practice will turn out to be just another empty fad. Barth is an effective antidote to those who imagine that good informal practice disregards skills or discipline.

I'm growing wary of slogans like open education. So is Barth. I think they may do more harm than good. Currently I'm seeking to enlist everybody in favor of open, informal schooling into a movement whose one slogan will be a demand for decent schools. I know I can count on Barth's support for this movement, because in a way the middle portion of this book—a participant's case study of a misguided attempt to introduce open classrooms into two schools in an Eastern city—bears on much wider issues than open or informal education. Barth's chronicle of racial suspicion, bureaucratic ineptitude, and purblind reformism suggests that there was much more wrong with the educational climate in that city than the lack of informality in classrooms.

The basic issues ran much deeper. There was the tension between schools and parents. There was the unprofessional—one might say anti-professional—system of priorities which almost seemed designed to undercut the work of practitioners, depriving teachers and principals of support and autonomy. There was the standard pattern of "innovation" from the top down, reforms imposed by outsiders with little consideration for regular administrators, teachers, or parents. This last problem was compounded by two things. One was the folly of the project's awkward administrative structure, which linked together two quite disparate schools, took away the principals' authority, and put it into the hands of an assortment of ill-matched subadministrators. And the other was a crew of reformers—young, relatively inexperienced university-trained educators—whose philosophy, clothes, and general way of working were not likely to be approved of by other teachers, administrators, or parents.

The oldest response of city school systems to complaints is

to do nothing at all. The second oldest response is to grind away at the Rube Goldberg machinery of innovation—programs which make no sense, and which are imposed on schools with no consultation of administrators, teachers, or—heaven forbid—parents. Those interested in open schools must try not to get lured into playing the game. Open education will never amount to real change if it is shoved down people's throats. Barth is saying that the standard American patterns of educational reform—more money, more people, more pointless gears churning away—are often antithetical to creating schools where people are treated as human beings. This is not an argument against more money and more people; it is, among other things, a reminder that the occupational disease of reformers is blindness to the limitations of the conventional patterns of reform.

So there seem to be immense difficulties in getting from the vision of Barth's early pages to good, open schools in real cities like the one in Chapter 3. That is the principal lesson of this distressing case study. I wonder how much it says about the response of parents in general, and black and minority parents in in particular, to open education. Any concerned and thoughtful parent in almost any situation would have been appalled at the slipshod, chaotic way this project seems to have been conducted, no matter what it was labeled. Yet, as Barth says, this is, routinely, the way our schools "innovate," and there is every likelihood that we will all see much more of the same kind of thing.

Barth is pointing to some gloomy lessons about the obstacles to change in our schools in general; he is not saying we will never get decent urban schools. One of the things I hope Americans are learning is to mistrust stereotypes about ourselves—the sort of pop sociology that tells us what blacks as a group believe, or what blue collar workers as a group believe, or what the suburban white middle class as a group believes. We are all tired of being labeled. Over the doors to every newspaper, sociology department, and school of education the following warning should be inscribed: "Differences within groups are usually more interesting and important than differences between groups." This holds for our stereotypes of people's response to informal schools. For good reasons of their own, as Barth says, inner city residents are apt to be particularly concerned about skills and discipline; nobody educating their children can ignore these concerns. I don't think this is so strange. As Barth says, no teacher should ignore parents' concerns for skills and discipline. To me it's interesting that many of the private, parent-run ghetto schools have tended to move in an informal direction. Schools like Boston's Children's Community Schools, the East Harlem Block Schools, some of the parent-run Headstart centers, have emerged as examples of good open practices. In fact what distinguishes the best of these ghetto ventures from the many chaotic and shoddy "free" schools one encounters is a clear interest in uniting informality and active learning with discipline and competence. More of this kind of work on the part of committed black and white teachers may keep open education from being what it often seems to be, a white fad.

Another bad habit Barth is urging us to give up is the premature obituary. Many people by now are ready to recognize that the grandiose claims made on behalf of each new educational fad are usually ridiculous. What we have to learn next is that most of the bitter "lessons" we draw from the failures of these fads are also pretty silly. The Lincoln-Attucks program in its first year was plainly a shambles, as Barth shows, yet he also points out that four years later "interest in and successful movement toward more informal classrooms now characterizes both the Lincoln and the Attucks schools."

What we have to learn is that there is no recipe to be imposed on people from the outside. There is no class of educational saviours with magical knowledge and special powers. There are very few parents who are going to accept reforms unless practitioners can persuade them that the reforms are good for their children. And there are relatively few of our school systems whose workings really provide a proper framework in which teachers can develop.

All this goes, as I say, much farther than the issue of open schools. Exploring the possibility of open education in American schools today is like turning a searchlight on the underlying structures in our schools and in the society that prevent schools from being decent places, no matter how teachers teach. In particular two sets of structures stand in the way. The first is the pathological professional structure within schools which undercuts the work of practitioners and in no way promotes the growth of good practice. The second set of structures is the hostile relationship of schools to parents, especially poor and minority parents. Both these things are more fundamentally important than specific questions of classroom style, be it formal or informal. Neither gets addressed by conventional school reform.

The next to last part of Barth's book discusses one element in the kind of professional structure necessary for growth within schools: the principal. He is right to insist that principals are vital in promoting the kind of school where children and teachers thrive and parents have confidence in what's going on. Barth's description of what a good principal does clashes with much of the conventional role of American principals. Generally—of course there are exceptions—our principals do not act as the heads of a teaching staff, supporting teachers' work, and operating in classrooms as good examples of ways of teaching and working with children. It is not common for them to do much with parents. Good principals in our school systems are the first to complain that most of the job's pressures push one toward thinking of oneself as an administrator. The educational opposition movement in America needs to understand that principals are crucial, and that at present the system is not organized to get good practitioners as principals. This is one of the depressing reasons why, although you see many scattered open classrooms in America, you rarely encounter a situation where the staff of an entire school is working together to create a good informal environment.

In education there are what I call macro and micro issues. The macro issues are the big political problems: inequality, race, finance. The micro realm is the sphere of teachers and children working in classrooms: materials, pedagogy, learning, the subtle human encounters that defy the pronouncements of planners, experts, politicians and community leaders. It is important always to keep both macro and micro realms in mind, not to lose sight of one in dealing with the other. In many cities, I would guess, the macro issue of race is so important that to promote open classrooms without dealing with the racial climate of the schools is futile. Macro issues can decisively limit the possibilities for decent practice. At the same time, the micro realm, the realm of teaching practice, has an autonomous validity of its own. With brilliant, scattered exceptions, there has been a tendency for movements like community control to skimp on the micro sphere. The community control movement has at times found itself so embattled over macro issues of power and control, usually on a district-wide basis, that it has neglected children and the importance of pedagogy, even to the tragic extent of treating classroom teachers as the enemy. Most readers of *Open Education and the American School* will share my difficulty in relating the first part of the book—the good discussion of the micro theory of open education—with the disheartening macro realities of public schools in the inner city, but the connection between macro and micro realms has to be forged if we are ever going to get decent schools.

Meanwhile Barth is reminding us of important points that simply have to be repeated over and over again: change should come from teachers, from the development of their own philosophy and their own pedagogical experience; skills—in read-

ing, writing, math, and the arts—are important, and a movement that does not consider them so will fail; classroom work
needs a lot of support; good informal practice requires a lot of
materials; change ought to be slow and orderly.

Barth would like to find ways that our monolithic schools—
which exist in suburbs as well as in slums—could give parents
and teachers options, and I would too, although I have the
feeling that when Americans are talking about options they are
often less concerned with educational practice or the philosophy of education than with exploring whether in this divided
and suspicious society there can be any basis for mutual trust.
There ought to be more of a question about anybody's right to
impose an educational program on the children of parents who
find the program philosophically repugnant. This is one theme
in Barth's last chapters. He doesn't settle it; nobody else has,
either. I think he may be on one promising tack when he talks,
as a principal, about encouraging different varieties of good
practice within the same school. To promote that kind of diversity, a school would have to abandon all orthodoxies, even
open education, in favor of a common, yet diverse, pursuit of
good learning. This common, yet diverse, pursuit is in fact
what the best informal, open practice already is.

JOSEPH FEATHERSTONE
March 1972

Author's Preface

I first visited the Elementary Science Study, then at its prime, in 1965. As a 5th-grade teacher in the California public schools I brought with me many questions. I was pleased with few answers.

For what grade levels are these materials and units appropriate?
They can be used over several age and grade ranges.

Can I see a copy of your K-6 curriculum guide that shows scope and sequence?
We have no curriculum organized in this way.

How does one unit follow from the previous and prepare for the next?
Each unit and set of materials stands alone; children can explore it and learn from it without reference to what comes before or after.

Can I see the lesson plans for one unit?
We have none.

How does a teacher teach without plans?
You put the materials out and see what children do with them. When children ask a question or need something, you help them.

How do you evaluate what the students are learning?
We have no instrument. You can tell by watching them.

I left ESS puzzled and disappointed with what appeared to be a random, sloppy, haphazard bunch of people and curriculum materials. They clearly had little to offer me as a teacher or my students, let alone the parents and administrators I had to work with. But the responses to my questions at ESS so jolted and violated my concepts of teaching, learning, and curriculum, and were so contrary to what other curriculum designers were saying, that I did not forget them.

Two years later as a doctoral student at the Harvard Graduate School of Education, I read in one of those mimeographed weekly calendars—upon which the lives of universities seem to depend—that "Mr. Roy Illsley, Headmaster of Battling Brook Primary School in Leicestershire, England, will attend a sandwich seminar and talk about the 'integrated day in British primary schools.' " Because "Leicestershire" had become something of a code word among a few educators in the Boston area, and at that time had little meaning for me, I decided to eat my sandwich with Mr. Illsley. I have before me some notes I scratched on the back of an envelope that day:

"Children learn from other children, from materials, from experiences in the real world *as well as* from 'teachers.' "

"Schools are better organized to serve the needs of adults than of children."

"If children are really engaged in and having fun with an activity, they are learning."

"Schools are institutions; people are real."

"Our methods of teaching are ineffective, because we don't know how people learn."

"Learning implies the right of each individual to fail and to admit failure; to succeed and to communicate success."

Coming on the heels of five years of less than satisfactory and satisfying experience trying to "learn" 4th, 5th, and 6th graders, I found these now familiar ideas pretty heady stuff. I thought about the ESS visit and some connections were formed. But lots of pieces seemed missing—in my thinking and, it appeared, in the thinking of others. This confusion and dissonance provoked Chapter 1, *Assumptions About Learning and Knowledge*, which I prepared in 1967 as a qualifying paper at Harvard.

In the preparation of that paper my understanding of and enthusiasm for the ideas of Illsley and ESS grew. I began to think in terms of implementation as well as research; of practice as well as theory. This led to Chapter 2, *The Teacher and the Open Classroom*. The following year I accepted a position as principal of an inner-city elementary school, determined to explore the benefits for children of more informal approaches. This experience revealed the likelihood of resistance to change in the direction of open education more than its effects upon children. Hence Chapters 3 and 4.

The names of people, places, and institutions in the case study are fictitious; otherwise, the situation was real. I have changed names and disguised the locale to eliminate concern with "who" and "where" so that the focus can rest where it belongs—on what can be learned from this experience. It is my hope that by describing and analyzing in detail my bloody nose, other educators who are beginning to explore and implement ideas and practices of open education (and the children, parents, teachers, and administrators with whom they work) may be spared bloody noses of their own.

I am only one contributor to this work. I would like to acknowledge again the inspiration of Roy Illsley, who introduced me to the ideas of open education; the Milton Fund of Harvard University, which supported my study of primary schools in England; members of the Leicestershire Advisory Center and the Elementary Science Study, especially Edith H. E. Churchill and William Hull, who so completely shared their resources; David Purpel, Maurice Belanger, and Israel

Scheffler, who helped give form to my ideas; Barbara Powell, Susan Schacher, and Faith Dunne, who helped transform ideas into prose; Anne Smith and Peggy Newman, who, rather than making either coffee or policy, typed; the many classroom teachers who have had the courage to pursue the ideas of open education; and finally Beth, whose personal and professional counsel shines through this book.

ROLAND S. BARTH
Newton, Massachusetts

*OPEN
EDUCATION
AND THE
AMERICAN
SCHOOL*

Introduction

The development within each human being of intelligence, self-esteem, and personal dignity is, I believe, crucial to the quality of life. Each individual should be instrumental in affecting important aspects of his life—things, ideas, relationships with others, education—and capable of perceiving, reflecting on, finding meaning in, and enjoying the many dimensions of his existence.

Open education offers practices and assumptions about learning and knowledge significantly different from those found in most schools. Although there is little hard evidence, in theory or in practice, that open education is good for children; although these ideas have been tested by few teachers with few children in few schools for few years; and although it is not clear that children who attend open classrooms develop these and other important qualities in ways which are superior to those who do not, nevertheless, I am convinced that open education both places priority on these qualities of human life and can provide the means most likely to result in their development. By and large, I support the beliefs of open education presented here; furthermore, I believe that it is possible for these assumptions and practices to be introduced into school systems and be accepted and valued by children, teachers, parents, and administrators.

A prevailing climate exists in this country which is potentially hospitable to fresh alternatives to our floundering educational establishment. In this climate, open education may have the opportunity to prove itself in the U.S. school systems.

However, implementing foreign ideas is a precarious business, and I fear this opportunity may be abused or missed. Indeed, many attempts at implementation have already died and been buried, and are marked by such epithets as "sloppy permissivism," "chaos," "communist," "anarchichal," and "laissez-faire." An even more discouraging, although not surprising, consequence has been to push educational practice further away from open education than was the case prior to the attempt at implementation.

It is my conviction that the success of the present opportunity to implement open education in American schools depends upon the thoughtful, simultaneous development of an essential body of information and experience. We must reach a clear, conscious understanding of what we as proponents of open education believe about children and knowledge. This is the intent of Chapter 1. We must have a clear idea about the role of the adult in children's learning (Chapter 2). We must implement open education in a variety of settings and be sensitive to sources of resistance from children, teachers, parents, and administrators (Chapter 3). We must have access to alternative means of working through this resistance and an understanding of the appropriateness of each. We must understand how we can best contribute to positive educational change; Chapter 4 addresses these questions. We must carefully consider open education in the larger context of the crisis now facing our public schools. The final chapter addresses this issue. It is my hope that this work will lead to an elaboration in these important areas that will enable the fate of open education to rest more on its lasting effect upon children than on the momentary reactions it elicits from adults.

The literature of open education considered here is confined to writers of the last decade whose primary inspiration has been innovations in British schools. Neither British education nor the literature, however, has emerged from a vacuum. No one today can think about learning, knowledge, and education without being influenced by those who have preceded him. The current wave of thought and practice I have called open education has emerged from fertile soil, tilled and harvested frequently during 4,000 years of educational history. Many historical, philosophical, and epistemological antecedents have contributed to open education's distinctive character.

Open educators' assumptions about learning and knowledge both parallel and intersect a vast literature of educational thought that I have not examined here. In particular, it is important to acknowledge three bodies of literature which have had an important, if indirect, influence:

Learning theory. Open educators cite their indebtedness to Piaget, but they are not independent of other learning theorists as well. For instance, open educators' emphasis on the interaction of the child with his environment seems closely related to psychoanalytic theories of Freud and Erikson which stress the interaction of a person with his environment in forming his identity. Open educators' ideas about the child learning from a total experience rather than in successive, discrete steps are akin to Tolman's emphasis on the gestalt, or the primacy of a totality of perception and experience. Even behaviorists such as Watson and Skinner have helped clarify the thinking of open educators—if only by providing a foil against which to react.

History of education. While open educators occasionally refer to Friedrich Froebel and Susan Isaacs, the contribution of other important figures in the history of education is seldom explicitly acknowledged. For instance, the philosophy of pragmatism—Peirce, James, Mead—finds expression in open educators' emphasis on the methods of science, the consequence of an action in modifying subsequent behavior. Open educators' child-centered curriculum is reminiscent of Dewey's progressive philosophy. Many have even called open education a neoprogressive movement (although its emphasis on the cognitive development of the child, upon a rich availability of materials, and upon the complex, difficult role of the teacher distinguishes one approach from the other). Rousseau's belief that the learning process of each individual is idiosyncratic is also clearly reflected in open education, as is the work of Maria Montessori, the outstanding observer and diagnostician of children's behavior whose ingenious educational materials have had an unmistakable influence on the equipment that open educators are introducing into their classrooms.

Organizational theory. Finally, open educators' ideas about the teacher's relationship to children, the organization of the classroom, and strategies for changing teachers, parents, administrators, and schools are related to a more recent literature of organizational theory. In addition to the work of men such as Getzels, Halpin, Hemphill, and Lewin, who concentrated on analyzing the structure of organizations, the efforts of current theorists such as Argyris, Bennis, Miles, Morris, and Rogers, who emphasize the personal and interpersonal components of organizational change, should be acknowledged.

In short, the sources of information I have relied upon in this work are limited. In the sense that they represent direct reflections of contemporary thinking about open education, they are primary sources. But in another important sense, my reference to literature is parochial and secondary, in that it omits the important primary sources of the past. That I have made no attempt to relate or assess the contributions of antecedent learning, of organizational or educational theorists, to open education is not to deny the past nor the significant influence of the past on the present. It remains for other investigators to explore these important relationships.

1*

Assumptions About
Learning and Knowledge

INTRODUCTION

In education, as in other domains, practice frequently precedes theory. To the extent that practice helps generate theory, this is a healthy and even desirable sequence. To the extent that practice without an accompanying theory is random, disordered, and misunderstood, practice may become weak and even unproductive.

The present practice of what I have chosen to call "open education" reflects both of these conditions; it is helping to give rise to a coherent educational theory, but at the same time it has been handicapped by the lack of an apparent underlying rationale. Most accounts of open education have been anecdotal and descriptive, painting for the reader a picture of what is happening to the child, to the teacher, and to the curriculum in open classrooms. Reports abound of children making important decisions each day affecting their learning and education; of children posing, solving, and verifying their own problems; of an environment rich in materials and activities; of a teacher who is no longer in the center ring, but in a role supportive of

* Other versions of this chapter have appeared in references 81, 102, 103, and 106 in the Bibliography.

7

the children's concerns. Yet for all the growing literature on open education, few accounts have attempted anything approaching a systematic analysis of the important assumptions upon which these practices are built.

Endemic to education and to educators is a disposition to search for the new, the different, the flashy, the radical, or the revolutionary. Once an idea or a practice, such as "team teaching," "nongrading," or "paraprofessional," has been so labeled by the establishment, teachers and administrators are quick to adopt it. More precisely, educators, who are quick to assimilate new ideas into their cognitive and operational framework, often distort the ideas or practices from the original conception without recognizing either the distortion or the assumptions violated by the distortion. This seems to happen partly because the educator has taken on the verbal abstraction of a new idea without going through a concomitant personal reorientation of attitude and behavior. Vocabulary and rhetoric are easily changed, while practices, people, and institutions often remain little affected. If open education is to have a fundamental and purposeful effect on American education and if changes are to be consciously made, then the important theoretical assumptions which underlie these practices need to be exposed and analyzed. Description without analysis will not suffice.

I hope my exposure of some of these assumptions will move advocates of open education farther away from the realm of ideology, cult, mystique, or technique (which permits one proponent to say, "If I have to explain it to you, you'll never understand") toward the more rational realm of a coherent theory or philosophy. Until an explanation is offered, most educators will remain puzzled, if fascinated, by open education.

SOURCES OF INFORMATION

The history of open education in this country is a recent one.
In 1961 William P. Hull [1] traveled to England to observe the
work of Z. P. Dienes (25).* "Dienes said that I couldn't understand what he was talking about unless I saw it in operation.
He was right." [2] Hull was impressed with what Dienes was
doing and with what he saw happening in a few British primary schools.[3] As a result of his enthusiasm, visits by interested
American educators to England increased remarkably. In addition to Hull's report (48), a substantial literature of "journals"
of these visitors has accumulated (10, 36, 96, 128, 134, 174,
179, 189). The educational practices observed in England have
been labeled in various ways: "free day," "integrated day,"
"integrated curriculum," "child-centered classroom," "developmental classroom," "Leicestershire plan," and "Leicestershire method." The last two terms are identified with a particular county in England because it was in Leicestershire that
Hull happened to have his first look at British primary schools.
In this discussion I have chosen to use the more neutral term
"open education."

Interest in open education—and consequently, sources of
information about it—has been limited primarily to England
and the United States until now. Although open education is
by no means synonymous with British primary education, a recent study (79) estimates that one-third of the schools in England at this level can now be so characterized. As interest has
grown, more and more relevant documents and periodicals
have been published in England by public education agencies
and by private publishing houses. Two such British sources
merit particular attention:

* See Bibliography.

Children and Their Primary Schools (79, 80) offers the most thorough presentation of the ideas and practices of open education to date. The Plowden Report (as it is also called, after Lady Bridget Plowden, chairman of the Central Advisory Council for Education, which conducted the study) was commissioned in 1963 by the British Ministry of Education ". . . to consider primary education in all its aspects, and the transition to secondary education."

Another important British source of information has been the National Froebel Foundation, which publishes pamphlets on a variety of topics related to open education.

In the United States there is a rapidly growing—even exploding—interest in open education. In the 1960's the Education Development Center (EDC) in Newton, Massachusetts, was unquestionably the unofficial center for thought, dissemination, and implementation of open education. Within EDC, the Elementary Science Study (29) was the primary contributor. Through ESS, an informal, remarkable sharing of people, ideas, and materials took place between England and New England. Until recently, ESS served not only as the American outpost of interest in British primary education but also as a travel bureau for Americans visiting British schools.

It was not by chance, for instance, that William Hull was on the staff of ESS; that Madison Judson, the former director of the Fayerweather Street School in Cambridge, Massachusetts (one of the first schools in this country to emulate the primary schools in England), was formerly with ESS; or that Leonard Sealey, who played a central role in the training of teachers for open primary schools in Leicestershire, became the director of EDC's Regional Educational Laboratory Program in 1968. As early as 1965, *The Educational Services, Inc. Quarterly* (EDC's predecessor) included such articles as "Mathematics Reforms in English Schools," "Science Teaching in England," and in 1966 "Learning from Leicestershire" (134).

In addition, frequent unpublished, informal mimeographs representing both momentary thoughts and reasoned positions of the ESS staff document the rich evolution of thought about open education which took place within the Elementary Science Study. ESS's prevailing philosophy can be traced to the influence of two Americans: David Hawkins, a philosopher (141–146), and Philip Morrison, a physicist (165–168), two of ESS's early leaders whose ideas about learning and children coincided with those proliferating in England.

Today, interest in open education is much more widespread. When, in 1971, ESS closed its doors for lack of funds, the EDC Follow Through Program (197), assumed much of the momentum and employed the English infant school as a model for helping to improve education in over 90 elementary classrooms in ten school districts throughout the Eastern half of the United States. An "advisory center," modeled after similar centers in many British school district authorities, is a distinguishing characteristic of this program.

Several state departments of education, such as those in New Jersey (233), New York (133, 169), Massachusetts, and Vermont (92), are showing considerable enthusiasm (and allocating funds) for open education, as are many federally funded Follow Through programs. In addition, teacher-training institutions all over the country, such as those at Leslie College, Wheelock College in Boston (122, 140), the University of North Dakota, the University of Connecticut, and Harvard, are devoting considerable attention to open education. The National Association of Independent Schools (87, 96, 97, 98, 191) has made open education felt in scores of private schools. It is not surprising, then, that the number of individual teachers and schools throughout the country exploring these ideas and practices is expanding at an astonishing rate.

Contemporary interest in open education in the United States can also be related to several recent occurrences centering in New York City: publication of Charles Silberman's

Crisis in the Classroom (89), strongly advocating methods of British primary schools as an antidote to the ills of American education; Harvey Scribner, whose *Vermont Design for Education* (92) reflected a strong sympathy with the rationale behind open education, was appointed School Chancellor for the City of New York; Albert Shanker, President of New York's American Federation of Teachers, responded in a positive and thoughtful way (182) to the opportunities and pitfalls that open education presents to urban schools; Lillian Weber's "open corridors" approach (189) in several New York City public schools has met with increasing success and publicity.

Undoubtedly, growing interest in open education has been related to the upsurge in attempts all over the country to find "alternatives" to the status quo of public education. Such innovations as "free schools," "storefronts," "day-care centers," and "schools without walls" are proliferating. The "free school" movement merits special mention here because it has frequently been coupled in an unclear way with open education. Several distinctions between the two seem important. The origins of the two movements are quite different. The free schools have grown in large part out of the free university movement. Often students who were disenchanted with the remoteness and formality of the large university, or those who gained satisfaction from a more personal commitment to a small college, became the very same parents and teachers spearheading free schools.

Whereas the *methods* employed in some free schools and the methods advocated by open educators may frequently intersect, the reasoning through which these methods evolved is quite different. Free schools have usually been established to provide an alternative to the cultural setting characterizing most public schools. In free schools, diverse styles of life are explored with the purpose of permitting and encouraging alternatives to flourish without restrictions from past, or even present, cultural norms. The methods of open education, on the other hand, are rooted in public education. They stem from the observation of children in educational settings (i.e., schools). The focus is on the pedagogical domain of thinking and learning. Decisions are made on the basis of insights from developmental and cognitive psychology, with the overriding concern being to help children learn more effectively and to give them easier access to their own abilities.

Despite the profusion of information accumulating around open education, there is still virtually no rigorous research concerning its effects upon the development of children's thinking, attitudes, and behavior as compared with the effects associated with more traditional forms of education. There is, however, a general feeling among proponents that if careful studies were carried out comparing the attainment and attitudes of children in "traditional" schools with that of children in more informal or "open" schools,

. . . children allowed to be active and companionable would prove more lively and inquiring, more inventive and enterprising, more resourceful and co-operative than the others. But no one could say *how much more*. And it might be true that those who were persuaded to toe the line would appear to do better in those subjects of formal learning by which the Infant School still so commonly seeks to justify itself.[4]

Because Miss D. E. M. Gardner has been the only educator to investigate this hypothesis seriously, her work merits special attention. In 1942 she published *Testing Results in the Infant School*:

. . . an inquiry into the attainments and attitudes of children who had received their education in Infant Schools in which spontaneous activity was the keynote and learning through play characteristic, as compared with those of children in good but "traditional" schools where the curriculum was entirely planned by the teachers. . . .[5]

She found that

> . . . not only had the children not suffered from the more free and "child-centred" type of education but in some respects had done better.[6]

In 1950 a second report was published, *Long Term Results of Infant School Methods*, which

> . . . followed up the children from the two types of Infant Schools into the Junior Schools, most of which were still at that time on the whole traditional. Again I found that the results of the children who had received their earlier education in the experimental Infant Schools tended to be superior to their controls when measured at the age of ten.[7]

Gardner's most recent study, *Experiment and Tradition in Primary Schools* (38), is the only contemporary attempt[8] to compare over a long period of time (1951–1963) the attainment and attitudes of children in schools tending toward open education ("experimental") with those attending more traditional schools ("controls"). She examines the performance of children (age 10) in twelve matched pairs of primary schools on a variety of measures. A "summary of results at the junior school stage" [9] reveals:

(1) Tests in which the experimental schools are undoubtedly superior:

> Listening and remembering
> Neatness, care, and skill
> Ingenuity
> Free drawing and painting
> English (both papers and original composition)
> Interests

(2) Tests in which the experimental schools, though less superior, are

nevertheless ahead in half or nearly half the tests, while controls
are definitely less than this:

> Social situation
> Concentration on an uninteresting task
> Moral judgment
> General information
> Reading
> Handwriting

(3) Results which show no significant difference between experimental and control schools:

> Concentration on task of own choice
> Social distance scale
> Moral conduct

(4) Tests in which control schools are superior in five or six pairs of
schools (i.e., half or nearly half):

> Arithmetic, mechanical (six pairs)
> Arithmetic, problems (five pairs)

From this study Gardner concludes:

. . . it does appear that, other things being equal, the type of education more definitely oriented towards the purposes and interests of
the children [open education] has had a very favorable effect in these
respects.[10]

Although her conclusions consistently appear to reflect favorably on open education practices, one must interpret them
with considerable caution. For a generation, D. E. M. Gardner
has been a strong advocate of these practices, and her research
has the flavor less of objective comparison than of an attempt
to justify the kind of education she supports.

When experimental groups outperform control groups, it
appears to be the result she expected. When control groups

excel, she attempts to rationalize the discrepancy. Her sampling procedure is open to serious question. No systematic means is used to differentiate those schools designated as "control" from those labeled "experimental"; she selects schools for inclusion in the control group (conventional schools) at random from a large number. The experimental schools are far fewer, and each is something of a special case. It *is* an experimental school usually because of an innovative leader, carefully selected or trained teachers, and the availability of a rich supply of materials. Nevertheless, Gardner assumes that the random group of control schools is "matched" with the random group of experimental schools with respect to the important variables in question. The instruments Gardner uses to measure skills and attitudes of children in the two groups are established ones and apparently valid. Her method of statistical analysis of the scores is, however, unsophisticated. She compares mean performances of entire school populations on each measure, never reporting range or standard deviation of scores. One suspects that there may well be children in experimental schools performing at a low level—perhaps lower than that of some children in control schools—but this data is not reported. Tests of significance are not carried out, nor are confidence levels established. Rather, only gross differences in raw scores are used to support the conclusions. For these reasons Gardner's research, although attempting the important task of comparing performances of children in experimental schools with those in "control" schools, is closer to a sample survey with subjective interpretations than to careful research. One can admire her intention, but it is impossible to accept her conclusions with great confidence.

OPEN EDUCATION: ASSUMPTIONS
ABOUT LEARNING AND KNOWLEDGE

What is it that Americans see in British primary schools? What fosters such excitement and fervent conversion? What has led several educators to attempt transplants to the United States? Open education has generally been thought of and written about as a collection of practices. Individual impressions and descriptions dominate the literature. I have suggested the importance in educational innovation of theory attendant on new practices and the danger, and perhaps futility, of introducing new ideas without a supporting theory.

To be successful, an educator need not be, and seldom is, conscious of all major suppositions which underlie his professional behavior. It is only the exceptional educator who is aware of the relationship between his assumptions and his practices. However, if educators wish to influence and be understood by others, an attempt to relate the practices to the premises is no mere academic exercise. Underlying the more or less clearly circumscribed set of practices associated with open education, there is, I believe, a set of assumptions—a rationale —which contains the germ of a theory.

There are many dimensions along which an educational point of view such as open education might be examined. I have chosen to emphasize two: the process whereby a person becomes educated (learning), and the nature of that which is learned (knowledge). My purpose here will be to make overt and to organize a number of covert assumptions about children's learning and the nature of knowledge which underlie the practices and statements of open educators. What follows, then, is a taxonomy of assumptions made by open educators with respect to the nature of learning and the nature of knowledge. Classification will be generative; that is, each assumption will be based to some extent upon those which have preceded it and will give rise to some extent to those which follow.

Though I realize that not all these assumptions would be acceptable to every advocate of open education, they do, I believe, reflect the thinking of most. In fact, I have "tested" these assumptions with over a dozen British primary teachers, headmasters, and inspectors at an in-service workshop for teachers offered by the Leicestershire Advisory Centre and with a number of American proponents of open education at EDC and elsewhere. To date, although many qualifications in language have been suggested, there has not been a case where an individual has said of one of the assumptions, "No, that is contrary to what I believe about children's learning or about knowledge."

It should also be made clear that, while I personally share many of these beliefs, these are assumptions which I attribute to open educators. It will not be my purpose to assess their validity or to answer the question "How does one *know* that the practices related to these assumptions are in the best interest of children?" I shall not attempt to evaluate open education; rather, my concern will be to uncover and analyze what I see to be its salient features and to point out some of the perplexing questions associated with the assumptions. The format for this discussion will be (1) a statement of the assumption, (2) a sample of open educators' thinking which both exemplifies and gives rise to the assumption, and (3) my own reactions.

Assumptions About Children's Learning

Motivation

ASSUMPTION 1: *Children are innately curious and will explore without adult intervention.*

Young children display a natural curiosity about their environment which provokes them to explore and to ask questions.[11]

The child appears to have a strong drive, which shows itself at a very early age, towards activity and the exploration of the environment. . . . As far as can be judged, this behaviour is autonomous since it occurs when there is no obvious external motivation such as hunger.[12]

A little child's motives for learning come, in the first place, from his own nature, from his innate impulse to achieve, to find out, to master his own body and his environment.[13]

. . . the most powerful learning mechanisms available to us are built in biologically rooted mechanisms of search and exploration, relatively separate from the primary biological drives of hunger, sex, and the like.[14]

The child has the capacity not only to initiate exploration for himself but also to sustain such activity over a long period of time.

ASSUMPTION 2: *Exploratory behavior is self-perpetuating.*

. . . explorations carried on in any consecutive direction can always be turned into a self-rewarding, self-extending, self-multiplying process.[15]

The concept of motivation has always had a prominent place in theories of learning. Since such theories are man-made constructs, it is not surprising to find the intervention of adults commonly associated with the learning of other organisms. The pigeon pecks at the light, and the adult human dispenses the pellet or arranges to have the pellet dispensed. The child submits a perfect paper, and the adult supplies the "A." In these views of motivation we find the adult placing himself in a position of both importance and control with respect to the learning organism. This seems to be a place of some comfort.

Open educators question whether motivation generated and

manipulated by the adult results in greater learning or just in increased production. They also question whether the adult's intervention is essential for the child to be motivated and to learn. Thus, the assumption that children are innately curious and predisposed toward exploration and are not dependent upon adults, for either the initiation or the perpetuation of learning activities, seriously challenges much conventional learning theory and raises some important questions.

The assumptions discussed here about motivation point toward an underlying sense of *trust* in the innate abilities of children, in their capacity to energize and direct their own exploration, and in their wanting to explore and learn. This implies the existence of an inner motivation on the part of the child and a hands-off, "don't meddle" role for the adult.

A closer examination of these assumptions about motivation suggests another component as important as the autonomy of the child's motivation. Children may have in and of themselves the *capacity* for motivation, but motivation is realized only through the relationship of the individual to something outside himself, to other persons or to bits and pieces of the world. That is, one is not motivated in a vacuum; one must have something to be motivated about. The source of motivation resides neither in the child nor in the external world, but in the *interaction* of one with the other. It is only through the interaction of the person with what is external to him that motivation comes to exist and to energize learning. One has only to imagine withdrawing all external stimuli from a motivated child to see the importance of the object of exploration as well as the capacity for exploration.

In contrast to the thinking of many educators and psychologists, open educators do not see adults as the unique suppliers of the elements of the external world which will release the child's potential for motivation. The world is there and children, just by being in and of the world, have their own access to it. They can influence their own motivation and exploration just as much as the adult can. They bring things into the classroom as well as use what is supplied by the teacher.

Motivation, then, which may seem from some of these assumptions to be internal, personal, and autonomous, has an external component over which both adult and child have influence. It remains for open educators to clarify the place of the adult in releasing or activating the child's motivation and to differentiate the child's control from the adult's.

Conditions for Learning

ASSUMPTION 3: *The child will display natural exploratory behavior if he is not threatened.*

. . . exploratory behavior dominates only in the absence of other more urgent needs.[16]

Children can think and form concepts, so long as they work at their own level, and are not made to feel that they are failures.[17]

ASSUMPTION 4: *Confidence in self is closely related to capacity for learning and for making important choices affecting one's learning.*

Perhaps the greatest benefit that time in the infant school gives is confidence in what has been learned. The child's own satisfaction in having really mastered something—whether it be riding a bicycle or telling the time—is important. If the beginnings of school work are only half learned and anxiety ridden, the effects may persist throughout school days. Confidence in the power to learn is vital.[18]

Open educators assume that opportunities to explore, to try and fail in the absence of threat, contribute to a sense of mastery and the development of a child's knowledge. There seems to be some relationship between knowing oneself and self-esteem, and this self-esteem is crucial for learning. Put more strongly, a strong self-concept on the part of the child is the *sine qua non* of open education; if, and only if, the child respects himself will he be able to be responsible for his own learning. Does this mean that schools are in some fundamental way responsible for fostering self-confidence?

Open educators often think of children's potential for self-directed learning not in terms of "smart," "dumb," "fast," or "slow," but rather along dimensions of self-esteem. If the child feels good about himself—if he is self-confident—then he will be capable of initiating and sustaining his own learning. If he doesn't have these qualities, he won't.

But what is self-esteem? What are the minimum components of self-confidence which would permit us to say a child has it? A circular argument underlies the reasoning here: If a child is capable of making important choices affecting his own learning, he has a strong self-concept, and he will be able to make responsible choices. Or looked at in another way: children who are trusted to make choices may develop self-control, but those with self-control are more likely to be trusted to make choices.

Open educators have only touched on children's reasons for making choices. Is choice, *qua* choice, by the child desirable, or only choice out of certain motives? Is the behavior of the child who chooses to swing the pendulum in order to attract the teacher's attention, or to take the apparatus from another child, as desirable as that of the child whose choice is directed by his desire to explore the relationship between the swing of the pendulum and the length of the string? Are the former child's choices as legitimate, whatever his reasons, as those of the latter?

The important point here is that open educators have not yet considered, let alone established, a relationship between development of self-confidence and the ability to make responsible choices about learning. So far, the two are seen as necessary to each other, but the nature of the relationship remains to be spelled out.

ASSUMPTION 5: *Active exploration in a rich environment, offering a wide array of manipulative materials, facilitates children's learning.*

At every stage of learning children need rich and varied materials. . . .[19]

You don't teach children to think; you give them something to think about.[20]

When using any material for the first time, the child will experiment with it, exploring its possibilities.[21]

. . . children come to school already imaginative, curious, and intelligent. But to learn for themselves, they require materials, space, time and other people.[22]

. . . the interest in *things* is a perfectly real, perfectly independent and autonomous interest that exists in young children just as genuinely as the interest in persons is there. In fact, some children are *only* able to develop humanly by first coming to grips in an exploratory and involved way with the inanimate world.[23]

I hear, and I forget;
I see, and I remember;
I do, and I understand.[24]

. . . sound and lasting learning can be achieved only through active participation.[25]

. . . the child must discover the fact for himself in his own time. He will do this if the relevant material is available to him in sufficient quantity and variety, if he is given many opportunities of handling it and trying it out. . . .[26]

One mandate is imperative for our style of work: there must be personal involvement. The child must work with his own hands, mind and heart. It is not enough for him to watch the teacher demonstrate or stand in line to take a hurried glimpse of the reflection of his own eyelashes in the microscope eyepiece. It is not enough for him to watch the skillful classmate at work, not enough to follow the TV screen. He needs his own apparatus, simple, workable.[27]

ASSUMPTION 6: *Play is not distinguished from work as the pre-dominant mode of learning in early childhood.*

. . . play is the natural way of learning for all young things.[28]

In playing with materials children begin also to discover the possibilities and limitations of their own powers.[29]

We know now that play—in the sense of "messing about" either with material objects or with other children, and of creating fantasies—is vital to children's learning and therefore vital in school. . . . In play, children gradually develop concepts of causal relationships, the power to discriminate, to make judgements, to analyse and synthesise, to imagine and to formulate.[30]

The word "water" is learned quite early, but its full range of suggestion can only be learned through play, through having discovered all the things that water can and cannot do and the words: run, soak, drip, boil, freeze, gurgle, splash, etc., which stand for these things.[31]

Children's learning, like motivation, does not occur in a vacuum. Children play *with* something or someone; they do not just play. Exploratory behavior is of little consequence unless there is something to explore:

Children need stuff, all kinds of stuff, bought, found, or made. They need solids, plastics, and liquids. They need tables. Tables that can be moved, shoved, and turned; turned to the wall, to the windows or to a friend. They need surfaces that can be a place to sit, a palette to smear on or a bench to build on. They need tools. They need tools to create, modify and to investigate. Tools that bend, cut, fold, punch and squeeze. Tools to use and maybe to abuse, but not to not use.

They need things in containers and things to contain. They need paper, paper that blots, folds, and repels. They need colored paper, typing paper, newspaper, and any paper. They need nails, bars, boxes and jars. They need rope, cord and thread. They need loads of bones, boxes of rocks, scads of rags, and hoards of boards. They need, in brief, a bizarre bazaar of stuff.[32]

The importance of play in the learning of children has been recognized by many educators ever since Froebel discussed it in *The Education of Man,* in 1826. The word "play" is often used in schools to distinguish activities from "work," but in many open classrooms neither term is appropriate; this distinction has all but disappeared and given way to one between involvement and lack of involvement.

Yet perhaps this distinction should not be dismissed quite so easily. There are many activities in which children engage, such as learning to play the piano, that are tedious, laborious, and even painful. Others such as playing ball are fun, unrestrained and carefree activities for most children. Both may be characterized by active involvement with materials, but they have considerable differences, as any child knows. One appears, from the adult point of view, to be "work" and the other "play." How, if at all, do open educators account for these differences?

Most would admit that there are vast differences in the nature of activities in which children become involved, but that rewards come from participating in and completing the activity and are not dependent on its ease. Hence, the labor in learning to play a musical instrument may well be greater than that of playing ball, but so may be the reward; otherwise, the child would be playing ball, not playing the piano.

One of the problems open educators have in trying to distinguish between work and play or in trying to eliminate the distinction is that they have not been able to separate the adult's view of what the child does from the child's view. Young children are not conscious of a work-play distinction, but become increasingly aware of one as they proceed through the grades. This difference appears to be an adult artifact. Adults have assumed that anything which is productive for children in school is difficult and often painful. If it hurts, there must be something beneficial about it. Conversely, it has been assumed that those things which are fun and pleasurable are unproductive and usually take place in "free time" or out of school. John Holt has put it well:

We're still hung up on the Calvinist distinction between work and play or learning and play. . . . A really healthy, active living person, man or child, lives his life as a whole and if you were to say to him at any second, "Are you working or playing?" he would say, "I don't know." [33]

Open educators have some obligation to make the relationship between play and learning clearer.

ASSUMPTION 7: *Children have both the competence and the right to make significant decisions concerning their own learning.*

ASSUMPTION 8: *Children will be likely to learn if they are given considerable choice in the selection of the materials they wish to work with and in the choice of questions they wish to pursue with respect to those materials.*

ASSUMPTION 9: *Given the opportunity, children will choose to engage in activities which will be of high interest to them.*

ASSUMPTION 10: *If a child is fully involved in and having fun with an activity, learning is taking place.*

The child is the agent in his own learning.[34]

. . . children can respond to courteous treatment by adults . . . to a great extent they can be trained to take the initiative in learning, if choices are real and if a rich variety of material is offered them.[35]

. . . the best materials are ambiguous; they can be used for many purposes. By choosing their own uses, . . . the children learn on their own terms.[36]

. . . the understanding of a subject, the grasp of its structure, comes— in short, learning comes—through a self-directed activity of the child, an activity of inventing and discovering.[37]

When children first come to school they learn most effectively if they choose what to do from amongst a range of materials carefully selected by their teachers.[38]

It seemed to me in watching that even when they were not playing things "straight" (i.e., *our* way) they were learning a great deal, and learning things that they could not learn when we were in control.[39]

Central to open education is the question of agency. Who or what will direct the child's explorations and play? What will be the origin of the problems and materials with which he is engaged?

Many open educators eschew any attempt whatsoever to control or manipulate children's behavior. However, in the act of selecting materials for the classroom, the adult does in fact exercise a large measure of control over the direction of the child's learning and exploration. Ideas and concepts emerge out of activity with materials. Control of materials, then, implies control of experience, which in turn implies control of ideas and concepts. By bringing books into the classroom the teacher makes it more likely that children will want to learn to read. If there were no written words available, perhaps they wouldn't. By bringing a telescope into the classroom the teacher increases the likelihood that children will become interested in the stars and planets.

If open educators really wish to free children from all adult controls, they may have to let children bring all materials into the classroom themselves. They also may have to abandon the institution of school altogether. Still, it is doubtful that even these measures would eliminate adult control of children's activities. At the same time it is questionable whether complete removal of adult control is desirable. Most children do not have access to a wide range of materials they might want to explore; nor do they have at their disposal the time and place which would permit such exploration.

The success of the open classroom would seem to depend not on adults' giving up of control to children but on a deliberate and conscious sharing of responsibility for learning on the part of both child and teacher. The adult, to a large extent, determines the nature of the school environment; the child decides with which of these materials he will work, to which problems he will address himself, for how long, and with whom.

Since the materials for children's learning are so important, criteria for their selection are crucial (see also Chapter 2, p. 76). The teacher in the open school favors materials which are likely to initiate and sustain interest, exploration, and learning. For five-year-olds he might choose a set of blocks rather than a deck of cards, or a picturebook rather than a dictionary. Often his selection is based on a hunch that the materials will be found interesting.

Applied purely, this criterion meets with difficulty. Almost anything might be expected to evoke some interest from some children, sometime—be it a scrap of linoleum, a jar of mayonnaise, or a mathematics text. Saying that children will choose to engage in activities which interest them, then, approaches tautological reasoning, for if children are given the chance, what they choose to do is by definition what interests them. Hence, there is a second criterion often used by open educators: the teacher selects materials which are likely to stimulate a child to explore in a productive way, along a productive course, toward a productive understanding. But what does "productive" mean? It is commonly held that *any* material which fully stimulates a child's interest is productive and leads to productive learning. To the extent, therefore, that "productivity" becomes defined in terms of a child's interest and not the predetermined interests of an adult, this criterion becomes indistinguishable from the previous one.

Thus, we find open educators inconsistent and even somewhat confused on the question of criteria for selection of materials. On the one hand, there is confidence that any activity in which the child is fully engaged and interested is productive and will result in learning; on the other, there is an inclination to make distinctions between "productive" and "unproductive" materials. The former implies a trust in children to choose what is best for themselves, and the latter suggests that adults know what is best for children. We find democratic and humanistic assumptions about children—that the individual regardless of his age and size is master of his own life and mind—contrasted with doubts that the child always knows what is best. This is an area which needs clarification.

Rather than attempting to gain a consensus somewhere on how much to trust children, it might be more useful to ask and try to resolve questions of another sort. What should be the division of responsibility between adult and child concerning the child's learning? What are the kinds of situations in which the older and presumably wiser, more mature adult should prevail, and what are the situations in which the child's judgment should predominate? We need to know, for example, whether the "What am I supposed to do?" syndrome of children is a cue for more adult intervention or an expression of need for greater child responsibility. We need to know whether the fact that children study about the things they know and care most about is a cue to give more external direction and control or an argument for permitting the child to follow his own path. We need to know whether, in being willing to give up control over the content of a child's learning (by letting him choose what to pursue), adults are not often seeking control over his motivation and participation. We need guidelines and statements of priorities which will help adults make decisions. We need to know which of these guidelines are generalizable and which are specific to the child and to the situation.

Social Learning

ASSUMPTION 11: *When two or more children are interested in exploring the same problem or the same materials, they will often choose to collaborate in some way.*

ASSUMPTION 12: *When a child learns something which is important to him, he will wish to share it with others.*

When children explore for themselves, they make discoveries which they want to communicate to their teachers and to other children.[40]

Open educators emphasize the individual: individualized learning, individualized materials, individualized knowledge. There is talk about the interpersonal relation of child with teacher, but very little of the relationship of one child to another; yet children come to school together, sit together, work together, eat together, and learn together. Children are seen as individual learners with unique styles, while in fact they are often members of many groups. What role do other children play in an individual's learning?

The interaction of children within groups has important pedagogical implications. For instance, children learn to talk not individually but through participation in group activities. The development of spoken language is crucial to concept formation. Often children understand one another's problems, interests, and possibilities better than adults do and are able to assist in ways which would be impossible for adults.

Both "family grouping" in England and the "nongraded primary" in this country have shown the potential of flexible grouping arrangements. But open educators only hint at the place other children play in an individual's learning: each child is seen as a potential resource for another, just as the library, the adult, and classroom materials may be seen as resources for the child's learning. However, this view of the other person as a "resource" seems to place him in the position of an animate *object*—a place quite inconsistent with the prevailing humanism of open education.

The dynamics among children are essential to any educational rationale. As yet open educators have not clarified either the meaning for the child or the effect on learning that such interaction might have.

Intellectual Development

ASSUMPTION 13: *Concept formation proceeds very slowly.*

Much learning involves what often looks to an adult like mere play or mindless repetition. A teacher can quicken learning and direct it along more methodical lines by providing suitable experiences and discussion, but children need time and often learn most efficiently on their own.[41]

Piaget was the first to see that the process of forming a concept takes far longer than had been believed, and that much work, seemingly unrelated to the concept, must be done before there is any clue to the direction which the thinking is taking.[42]

. . . all of us must cross the line between ignorance and insight many times before we truly understand. Little facts, "discoveries" without the growth of insight, are *not* what we should seek to harvest.[43]

. . . a great majority of primary school children can't just be told things, . . . they learn basic mathematical concepts much more slowly than adults realize, and . . . the patterns of abstract thought used in mathematics ought to be built up from layer after layer of direct experience—seeing, hearing, feeling, smelling.[44]

. . . what I'm speaking for is a laboratory involvement which may be painfully slow, which "doesn't get anywhere." You don't "cover the material" but you spend a good many hours of the week doing something.[45]

What the children know, they know for sure; they have time in which to establish an understanding of extremely basic things.[46]

ASSUMPTION 14: *Children learn and develop intellectually at their own rate, and in their own style.*

There is an individual pattern of growth for all living things.[47]

In the last 20 years schools have provided far more individual work, as they have increasingly realised how much children of the same age differ in their powers of perception and imagery, in their interests, and in their span of concentration.[48]

[School organization] allows for individual differences, but only as those differences show up on one dimension, a rate of progression . . . we should emphasize individual differences in *all* their qualitative richness.[49]

ASSUMPTION 15: *Children pass through similar stages of intellectual development—each in his own way, and at his own rate and in his own time.*

Although children think and reason in different ways, they all pass through certain stages depending on their chronological and mental ages and their experiences.[50]

. . . children learn by stages and . . . it is no use hurrying them on to later stages before they have mastered earlier ones.[51]

ASSUMPTION 16: *Intellectual growth and development takes place through a sequence of concrete experiences followed by abstractions.*

But if you want truly abstractive learning, then you have to provide something from which the child can abstract.[52]

One of its most important conclusions [i.e., of Piaget's research] is that the great majority of primary school children can only learn efficiently from concrete situations, as lived or described. From these situations, children acquire concepts in every area of the curriculum.[53]

. . . in order to establish a conceptual framework, you have to draw away the true nature of the ideas from direct experience.[54]

ASSUMPTION 17: *Verbal abstractions should follow direct experience with objects and ideas, not precede them or substitute for them.*

In the Garden of Eden, Adam saw the animals before he named them.[55]

Verbal explanation, in advance of understanding based on experience, may be an obstacle to learning, and children's knowledge of the right words may conceal from teachers their lack of understanding.[56]

Students may learn the formal terminology and expand their useful vocabulary, but we hope they will know what they are talking about first.[57]

It is part of the ESS approach to avoid introducing the formal names of things and concepts before the reality is understood . . . we feel it is necessary for the student to confront the real world and its physical materials directly, rather than through intermediaries such as textbooks.[58]

The place for talk about the subject, for verbal discriminations and communication, is late in the phases of learning, not at the beginning, and not all the time; here and there, gathering momentum as interest mounts.[59]

Open educators have been heavily influenced by the work of Jean Piaget, a Swiss philosopher and psychologist. Piaget has written prolifically since the 1930's, and although he has been known to educators and psychologists in England for most of that time, Americans have begun to discover him only in the past decade. Few on either side of the Atlantic read Piaget with understanding, but more and more now invoke his name and his work and count themselves among his followers.

Today Piaget is without question the most quoted, most referred to, and most influential psychologist for proponents of open education. Open educators understand enough of Piaget to find an affinity and complementing support between their ideas and his. Many of the assumptions made by open educators about children's intellectual development mirror Piaget's thinking; indeed, many *are* his thinking. Some of these assumptions have been sufficiently examined empirically to challenge the contention that they are assumptions at all and not established principles.

The elements of intellectual development emphasized by open educators appear to be the following: children need time to learn; they go through developmental stages; their thinking progresses along a sequence from concrete to abstract.

Shortage of time seems to be a necessary consequence of an abundant society, as characteristic of the child's life as of the adult's. Most schools assume a short attention span on the part of children and, to ensure maximum coverage of desirable experiences, allocate, schedule, control, and in other ways fractionate children's time. It is thought that children's intellectual development can be made to follow the convenience of arbitrary adult-made timetables.

Open educators question whether the adult is the best judge of how to organize children's time to ensure maximum intellectual development. They argue that until adults know more about how children think and learn, the child is a better judge of his needs with respect to time than is the adult. Children need varying amounts of time—often quite a long time—to develop concepts. They need time to repeat experiences over and over again, such as lighting a bulb with a battery and wire or measuring volume with a cup. Children's exploration is initiated and directed by materials and interest, and is facilitated rather than controlled by the clock. In short, time is the servant, not the master, of the child.

The fact that Piaget and others have identified and described stages of intellectual development characteristic of most children has great significance for open education and for the schools. Some educators have responded by trying to accelerate children's passage through the stages—an intention which Piaget has deplored, as have most open educators. What the stages imply for open educators is not clear. Although Piaget, like open educators, believes that children need materials in order to develop cognitively, there is some difference between his emphasis and theirs. Piaget has children use materials so that he can see what they are thinking. Open educators encourage children to use materials in the hope that the children will make discoveries. Whereas materials permit Piaget to describe children's thinking, open educators' materials appear instead to prescribe children's thinking. Measuring devices and sand are provided in classrooms with the expectation that children will develop the concept of conservation of volume. But does this imply that all children should be required to play with these materials? Is there an optimal or "logical" sequence of materials which corresponds to the stages of intellectual development?

Open educators distinguish between concrete and abstract; between object and symbol, especially with regard to language acquisition and development. Piaget's research has demonstrated the immense difference between the thought world of the child and that of the adult—quantitatively and qualitatively. What appears to the adult to be conceptual thinking on the part of the child is often verbal association. Consequently, open educators believe that children must go through a physical, kinesthetic experience before they can talk or write about the ideas implicit in the experience. They resist labeling or having children label bits of learning before they have these primary experiences. They feel that if the verbal level of thought is not based upon concrete experiences, words may obscure rather than enhance meaning. One can infer a hierarchy of thought and communication which must be negotiated in some order.

What are the practical implications? For instance, how soon after a child has had a primary experience and under what conditions can he verbalize ideas? Is adulthood seen as a period of abstract verbal thinking based upon the collected experiences of childhood, or does anyone at any age develop his ideas by moving up and down the hierarchy of experience to abstract verbalization? Is it more desirable for the child to operate from the real to the abstract or to move toward the time when he can operate in both modes simultaneously or in alternation? Or is the goal a condition where the concrete is no longer necessary?

These questions are of particular import to the classroom teacher whose concern is teaching reading. To be sure, reading is considered part of the language and general cognitive development of the child, but open educators have been somewhat evasive, offering few specific guidelines which would help a teacher help a child learn to read. The child reads because others do, or because he needs information, or because it is fun. Provide children with sufficient materials which involve looking at words, talking, listening, writing, and reading, and they will somehow evolve their own best individualized reading "programs"; they will learn how to read.

Without more research and a clearer understanding of the relationship between children's reading and their cognitive development, uncomfortable discrepancies will continue to exist between what is thought necessary for classroom teachers to teach reading, what is acceptable to parents, and the more relaxed, informal approach to teaching reading advocated by open educators.

By holding to the premise that intellectual development can be reduced to a sequence of concrete experiences followed by abstractions, open educators ignore an important alternative view: that experience and abstraction, rather than being discrete, ordered, and mutually exclusive in time, occur simultaneously from the moment of first sensory perception—a position which cannot be put aside lightly. Furthermore, open educators have not yet reconciled their view of learning as unique and idiosyncratic to each individual with the uniformity of thinking, or at least of the development of thinking, implicit in the idea of intellectual stages of development. So far, the existence of stages and the flow from concrete to abstract in the development of children's thinking has been of great interest to open educators, but has not led to a theoretical basis from which decisions about materials and activities can be made.

Evaluation

ASSUMPTION 18: *The preferred source of verification for a child's solution to a problem comes through the materials he is working with.*

There is no easy authority; the right answer comes not from the quickest kid in the class but from the apparatus itself.[60]

. . . the only satisfaction, the only reinforcement that counts importantly is that which accrues from discovery, from finding structure and order in our own individual and unique experience.[61]

Open educators believe that appraisal of a child's work is best mediated not by external authorities, be they adults or repositories of knowledge, but rather by the materials themselves. Materials in the classroom enable a child to pursue problems. They also provide information *back* to the child—information which lets him know if and to what extent he has answered his question. If he has a question about how to light a bulb using a battery, wire, and bulb, he tries it. If it lights, he can probably answer his question. If it doesn't light, he can still answer his question. In either case it is the materials, the world around him, which have verified (or failed to verify) his hypothesis. In traditional schools, the child has little responsibility and opportunity for participating in the assessment of his work. Open educators believe that the child should become as independent and as instrumental in assessing his behavior as possible, and as dependent upon the materials and the situation as is necessary.

The problem is not simply one of determining the ultimate source of authority for assessment of the child's learning, but rather under what conditions the adult should become a source of authority for the child and under what conditions the "world" should provide this authority. Obviously there are questions a child may ask which cannot be answered or verified by his direct experience. For open educators, therefore, an important goal is to help the child learn to discriminate between questions he can ask and answer for himself and those for which he must draw upon external authorities. The asking of the question and the assessment of the result, then, are as important to the child's learning as coming up with the answer.

ASSUMPTION 19: *Errors are necessarily a part of learning; they are to be expected and even desired, for they contain information essential for further learning.*

One develops a feel for the kinds of explorations [by children] which are worthwhile by running into blind alleys as well as by being successful. Someone once said that an expert is a person who has made all the possible mistakes in his field.[62]

One difficulty for many teachers is that they set themselves up as guardians of correct science. Believing in the myth of truth, they view it as their duty to enlighten the children and to keep them from error.[63]

. . . error itself is a way of knowing, in some sense the most powerful. The constructive use of error is a characterization of scientific method not worse than the more usual ones. We need very much to learn a tolerance of error, a willingness to try and to fail, and a recognition of the value of first halting steps. The tendency to equate error and defeat is a school trait which is one of the most pervasive.[64]

. . . children who are honestly working on new problems will, like the rest of us, make all kinds of stupid blunders. Growth in problem solving skill requires opportunities for involving children in investigations which they will continue to work on for long periods of time or put aside and come back to at a later time. It requires a climate in which it is possible to benefit from mistakes and not one in which they must be hidden so as to avoid ridicule. A person who takes few chances will make few mistakes . . . but also few discoveries.[65]

ASSUMPTION 20: *Those qualities of a person's learning which can be carefully measured are not necessarily the most important.*

Even in such subjects as the teaching of math and reading where many new styles and innovations were introduced, objective evaluation was almost impossible because the variation of teacher-centered and child-centered variables could never be accurately assessed.[66]

The "objective test" is so completely at variance with all our models of the science classroom that we bridle at the notion of such a means to evaluate a program aimed at ending the monopoly of the word and the tyranny of rote authority.[67]

We therefore envisage that some use will continue to be made of objective tests within schools. Such tests can be helpful—and their norms can serve as a basis of comparison—as long as they are used with insight and discrimination, and teachers do not assume that only what is measurable is valuable.[68]

Objective assessment of factors that really matter would seem to be almost impossible. As a result, things that we can and do measure are often trivial.[69]

. . . there are, arising from an informal approach, qualities which are very difficult to test and define . . . qualities of initiative, independence, social skill.[70]

From an outsider's point of view, one of the most serious problems is the question of evaluation . . . it is difficult to measure the kind of progress the children are making. "You can't prove it . . . sometimes you can't even see it." The Leicestershire classroom tries to encourage qualities like curiosity and creativity, believing that other important qualities will flow from these. And it is very hard to measure such characteristics.[71]

ASSUMPTION 21: *Objective measures of performance may have a negative effect on learning.*

Letter grades and other forms of competitive marking set production goals for teachers and students which have a poor effect on learning.[72]

External incentives such as marks and stars, and other rewards and punishments, influence children's learning mainly by evoking or representing parents' or teachers' approval. . . . The children who most need the incentive of good marks are least likely to gain them. . . .[73]

That side of evaluation—the ranking of individuals—goes on the whole against the tenor of our thinking. . . .[74]

Assumption 22: *Evidence of learning is best assessed intuitively, by direct observation.*

. . . very important things such as a more relaxed atmosphere in the classroom, a sense of fun in relation to learning, and a greater willingness on the part of children to become involved with learning situations and to stay with them, could all be easily recognized without the application of sophisticated testing.[75]

In Leicestershire, evaluation of innovations was seldom attempted. We were content to judge subjectively, to decide by the "feel" of the situation whether or not it was in the best interest of children.[76]

The most satisfying form of evaluation reported to us is a subtle one. Teachers tell us of children's excitement at what they are learning and of their enthusiasm for the ways in which they are learning. . . . To us an interested class is a successful one.[77]

Assumption 23: *The best way of evaluating the effect of the school experience on the child is to observe him over a long period of time.*

Primary schools should hear from secondary schools how their children compare over a period with children from other schools.[78]

Evaluation takes a long time. . . . The only real way to evaluate the effectiveness of the free program is to find out how students perform after they have completed their schooling.[79]

Assumption 24: *The best measure of a child's work is his work.*

. . . in play the child not only eagerly practices skills, gains knowledge, and learns to organize his emotions, but also shows us most clearly what his real problems are.[80]

"You know when you're doing the right thing with children," one of the Advisors told me. . . . "There is a kind of direct human evaluation going on all the time." The Heads and Advisors do not have to look at test results because they have the children in front of them.[81]

[A Head, when asked how a teacher knows what a child is learning, said] she jots. She jots during the day, and she writes it up at the end of the week. She keeps a very comprehensive record about her children, about their characteristics.[82]

If American parents could ever see some of the detailed histories kept of each child's separate path, including his art work, they would feel, quite rightly, that a report card is a swindle.[83]

Before we can learn anything from the systematic evaluation of our work, this evaluation will have to be conducted by means which reflect the nature of the work.[84]

Conversation with the child is more reliable and more fruitful when it is related to experience with adequate material, and when the child, instead of thinking in the void, is talking about actions he has just performed.[85]

Learning may be thought of as the effort to adopt appropriate or "correct" responses to specific situations. A child, in striving toward this end, is bound to make inappropriate or "incorrect" responses (from his or from someone else's point of view). Open educators seek to remove from children's mistakes the moral loading, the connotation of "bad" or "wrong," and instead help them to look at the function their mistakes can serve in directing subsequent learning, in much the same way as a scientist uses his mistakes. One should not teach children to avoid errors, but to utilize the information which errors contain. Thus, it is not only unnecessary but perhaps undesirable for adults to prevent children from making mistakes. Such intervention cuts off avenues of exploration—perhaps blind alleys—and thereby prevents children from discovering for themselves their own limitations as well as their abilities. Presumably, if a considerable element of danger to self or material were involved, the teacher would not hesitate to intervene. But like many others, this is a fine dividing line (i.e., when it is in the child's best interest to ward off a mistake and when his learning is better served by making the mistake) and not one for which open educators have developed guidelines.

Open educators seek to remove the heavy affective loading surrounding children's mistakes so that mistakes can be used productively. They are reluctant to use children's correct and incorrect responses for purposes of placement, promotion, testing, or grading. They feel that to use a child's mistakes in these ways is inconsistent and hypocritical. This points up a serious weakness of open education practice to date: namely, the inability and/or unwillingness to measure in any objective and systematic way important outcomes as a function of children's experiences in school. This reluctance often finds expression in statements of humility and helplessness with respect to evaluation, and a conviction that important things are happening to children which need not and cannot be made known to adults with existing instruments. It is held that such changes will not show up in objective tests over a short span of time. There is a feeling that distilling or symbolizing a child's behavior, accepting any measure of his performance less than his total work, distorts the behavior and perhaps interferes with learning as well. Reluctance to "evaluate" may also be the result of a decision to spend time facilitating behavior, rather than measuring it—if one must choose between the two.

Open educators' ideas about evaluation reflect a profound trust in the human being, in the capacity of one to judge intuitively the performance of another. Evaluation is not distinguished from teaching or learning. There is no special time set aside for it because it is going on all the time; a good teacher cannot absolve himself from it. One can appreciate reliance

upon subjective judgments and the human quality thereby retained, but is it really necessary to collect every bit of data
about a person before one can assess his learning? Is there no
alternative to giving objective tests and recording total behavior?

Although open educators reflect a wide range of viewpoints
about testing and evaluation, they convey little of what evaluation is, whether it is desirable, or how it may be best carried
out. Is testing by any objective means inherently undesirable,
or is it just the imperfect existing instruments which are undesirable? Is the concept of evaluation bad in itself, or is it that
evaluation implies a clear statement of goals and objectives
against which a child's performance can be evaluated? Is such
a statement of objectives unpleasant for open educators because they are not sure they know what their objectives are, or
because their objectives cannot be expressed in conventional
ways? It is clear that open educators are uncomfortable when
talking about evaluation. Unfortunately, their generalized dis-
comfort obscures what it is specifically that they are uncomfortable about.

Assumptions about Knowledge

Traditionally, the goals of education have been abbreviated
and symbolized by the word "knowledge." Implicit in the
ideas of open education are assumptions which bring into
question not only the importance of knowledge *qua* knowledge but also its meaning for the learner. Rather than an end
in itself, knowledge is seen as a vehicle for the development of
processes of thinking such as logic, intuition, analysis, and hypothesis formation and as a catalyst which facilitates the individual's development toward the ultimate goals of education:
self-esteem, dignity, and control over himself and his world.

ASSUMPTION 25: *The quality of being is more important than
the quality of knowing; knowledge is a means of education,*

not its end. The final test of an education is what a man is, not what he knows.

More important than knowledge of the facts of science is the experience of having been personally involved in a search for knowledge.[86]

These children are engaged in living, not in becoming those unfortunate trained animals called students or pupils.[87]

ASSUMPTION 26: *Knowledge is a function of one's personal integration of experience and therefore does not fall neatly into separate categories or "disciplines."*

The particular key which opens a new door for a particular child is not predictable. Therefore our curriculum is not at all to be cut into separate disciplines, fenced off by frontiers of technique and history.[88]

A 9-year-old who writes an account of an experiment in science which has involved some measurement and calculation, does not think: "Now I am doing English, now science, and now mathematics," though all three are involved. . . . The classification is of course useful, but its usefulness is limited, and it may even be a hindrance. . . . Young children simply do not think in this way.[89]

We are striving at present to bring together again, at least on the top levels of education, the different parts of a world which we have allowed to get divided and partitioned; but how much better if we merely made up our minds from the outset always to keep it one, since as one for each of us it begins.[90]

It [a good primary school] insists that knowledge does not fall into neatly separate compartments. . . .[91]

Assumption 27: *The structure of knowledge is personal and idiosyncratic, and a function of the synthesis of each individual's experience with the world.*

The question comes up whether to teach the structure, or to present the child with situations where he is active and creates the structure himself. The goal in education is not to increase the amount of knowledge, but to create the possibilities for a child to invent and discover. When we teach too fast, we keep the child from himself inventing and discovering. Teaching means creating situations where structures can be discovered; it does not mean transmitting structures which may be assimilated at nothing other than a verbal level.[92]

. . . we as scientists would be mistaken to be impressed by the logic and structure of these scientific [chemistry, physics, biology] materials; rather we ought to regard them all as they are seen, experienced, worked on, and evolved by the child and his teacher.[93]

We do not correct any grammatical errors. We write it just as the child says it. . . . Don't attempt to put it grammatically correct, because the child is only going to read what he said. . . . He would read "Me is going shopping" even if you wrote "I am going shopping." [94]

ASSUMPTION 28: *There is no minimum body of knowledge which is essential for everyone to know.*

. . . no real core of knowledge exists that is essential for everyone.[95]

"Do you have any standard that you try to get all the children to do by the time they leave you and go on to the junior school?" "Well, yes, we do like to send every child to the junior school able to attempt reading." [96]

There is no important body of material in science . . . which for conventional reasons must be learned and learned well. The names and sizes of the planets, or the classification of local mammals to the family level, or the parts of the perfect flower, do not impress us as universal nuggets of science everyone must store up. It is equally true that the so-called methodology of science, with its neat hierarchy of observation, hypothesis, test and so on, is a mythology without appeal.[97]

. . . are there certain histories, stories, poems, and myths that continue to illuminate our culture and for this reason belong in the curriculum for all? Can these be left entirely to individual choice? Should intrinsic worth of content be a factor in the selection of materials for study? [98]

ASSUMPTION 29: *It is possible, even likely, that an individual may learn and possess knowledge of a phenomenon and yet be unable to display it publicly. Knowledge resides with the knower, not in its public expression.*

Education must reconcile the two modes of thought, the thought which pertains to the public domain and the thought which is personal, private.[99]

Much less is said in the literature of open education about knowledge than about learning. Perhaps this is because knowledge is seen as an integral part of learning rather than a separate entity. Knowledge is not separated from the knower; the emphasis is on the process of interaction between the knower and what he comes to know. The assumptions made by open educators about knowledge raise profound questions for education: Does no knowledge exist which is external to the idiosyncratic thought of the child? Are there not some things open educators prefer that children learn more than others? Is not knowledge of the spoken and written language, for instance, more desirable than how to pick the lock of an automobile? Can learning take place in an institution where adults have no priorities about what is worthwhile for students to learn?

It is likely that open educators have priorities with respect to knowledge but for some reason are reluctant to make their preferences known. As important as whether adults have or choose to reveal their priorities for children's learning is the fact that children can generally *feel* what adults prefer for them to be doing or learning. In other words, there may well be a "known" which is external to children's idiosyncratic thinking and perhaps even to adults' conscious and deliberate planning, a "known" which is conveyed to children in ways more subtle than knowledge is conveyed in most schools.

If knowledge is acquired and organized in very personal and idiosyncratic ways—that is, peculiar to each individual—can a statement of *goals* or *objectives* in terms of knowledge or content, so common to most educational theories, have meaning?

. . . everyone appears to be working at an individual level, and . . . if you asked the teacher what the aims of this *particular* lesson were, she would not understand the question.[100]

If a particular lesson is too small a realm for goals to be articulated, do open educators have goals for children with respect to larger questions? If so, they have been reluctant to put them forth. For someone to say, for example, that "all children shall have an understanding of the causes of the American Civil War" would imply to an open educator that all children will want to, be able to, and choose to reach this particular understanding through their unique and independent routes, at about the same time—and, once reached, will have personally structured this understanding in a way similar to that of every other student as well as to that of the adult who posited the understanding. Given the foregoing assumptions about learning, such a notion of congruence of method and content on the part of each student and adult is extremely inconsistent. Open educators' assumptions about knowledge suggest that one cannot predict, let alone predetermine, with any certainty the direction or destination of another's inquiry; there is no certain way for one person to pose a question, a problem, or an objective which will be truly significant for another.

That one cannot predict the learning outcome of a child in response to specific subject presentations or experiences does not imply that educators have no priorities of importance with respect to content and experience, or that a child's life in school can be immune from these adult priorities. Learning, then, is perhaps best thought of as neither person-centered nor subject-centered but as an interaction of person and subject.

This is not to say that the educator has *no* influence on the direction or content of another's thinking. If a battery, a bulb, and a piece of copper wire are put before a child, he is unlikely to pursue a sequence of thoughts and actions which will lead him to the causes of the Civil War, but he is quite likely to try to light the bulb and in the course of this experience think about what we might call an "electrical circuit." One cannot be sure, however, that he will "know" what others know about a circuit or will come to know it in the way others come to know it. One student might reach the idea of a closed or complete circuit through a diagram on the blackboard or by visualizing it in his head, whereas another might have used batteries, bulbs, and wire, or a water-and-pump model; and a third might never have grasped it at all.

In open educators' assumptions about knowledge there is the belief that one person cannot program or determine the learning style, or that which is to be learned, for another. One cannot give experiences to another; one can only present opportunities for experience and accept what the student does or does not do with them. This is a devastating realization, for it implies relinquishing the long-accepted immense control of the adult over what the child learns—something educators have always, perhaps mistakenly, believed they possessed.

The instrument whereby knowledge is thought to be conveyed to students is the curriculum. What do open educators' assumptions about knowledge imply for the concept of curriculum? Is there a place for curriculum in open education? What does the word mean? To the extent that curriculum is seen as that which adults deem important for children to know, that which is broken down from simple to complex in a predetermined trail of adult footprints leading presumably from where the child is to where the adult would have him be (i.e., where the adult is)—open education has no curriculum.

What, then, do open educators mean when they say "curriculum"? Is an individual's knowledge so personal that another person cannot influence it? For open educators there is both an adult and a child component to curriculum; the adult selects materials (objects, books, water, tubs, etc.) which on the basis of experience are known to be likely to stimulate the thinking and exploration of children. Experience also provides information about the kinds of things the child will do, and the kind of thinking the child will engage in, with these materials and perhaps a guess about the knowledge which will result from this thinking. This is not to say that children are required or even expected to light a bulb when given the materials (they may make a necklace!), but trying to make the bulb light is what *most* children do under these circumstances. Why they do it or who really controls their doing it are questions yet to be explored.

For open educators, then, curriculum is a joint responsibility, guided by the adult through the selection and construction of materials and determined by the child through his individual response to the materials. Curriculum has the quality both of adult initiation and uniformity and of student initiation and diversity. In a real sense, children's own experiences are the subject matter—the content—of their learning. These experiences are good and bad, productive and nonproductive, pleasant and unpleasant. Open educators worry less about whether a child has had a particular experience than about the quality and meaning for him of the experiences he has had. It is for time and future experience to assess the significance of a student's experience, not for the adult to judge.

One must ask another set of questions of open educators' assumptions about knowledge: Where is the source of continuity? What is the organizing principle, or what are the lenses through which children perceive, focus, and organize their experiences? Is there a logical sequence to knowledge, or only a psychological sequence? Is learning but a series of discrete, random experiences—a smorgasbord—connected and related only by contiguity in time? Will myriads of personal experiences bounced about within a child's head ultimately settle in organized arrangements which have meaning and relatedness? Can random experiences have meaning without some conceptual framework? Who or what is to provide and to be responsible for the integration and organization of experience? Does this happen naturally?

The means commonly used to organize knowledge in schools are the traditional disciplines: math, science, English, social studies, etc. It is assumed that students' experience with knowledge so packaged has permitted them to organize the knowledge in corresponding categories in their heads. Open educators question the usefulness and validity of arbitrary distinctions of subjects; but what, if anything, takes the place of these disciplines in organizing experience and knowledge?

We have noted that a source of great interest in open education in the United States has been the Elementary *Science* Study. This, I believe, is significant, for it is science which to a large extent provides the theoretical and practical rationale that organizes experience and knowledge.[101] It is not the *content* of science, nor perhaps even the so-called "method" of science, but rather what might be called the *culture* of science which provides structure for open educators and for children's learning in open classrooms. The culture of science is nothing less than the conscious, deliberate analysis of experience.

Open educators note important similarities between the exploratory behavior, curiosity, search for explanation, and tendency to reconcile beliefs and assumptions with discordant information of the child explorer, on the one hand, and the behavior of the adult scientist, on the other. Indeed, some argue that the child is not *like* a scientist but *is* a scientist. If one were to examine the spontaneous interests of young children, he would find them asking questions about what things are, what they are made of, where they came from, and how they work. A great deal of their activity resembles what is commonly regarded as scientific inquiry.[102]

Science, for open educators, then, is not a body of knowledge but a way of thinking, of knowing, and of being. It is questioning, guessing, trying and failing, and learning by failing. It is pragmatic. Some things work; others do not. It is these qualities of the culture of science to which Isaacs (53–56) refers when he proposes to ". . . integrate science, in its broadest sense, into its proper place in the education of us all."

But is science the only appropriate and desirable way of knowing for young children? Is only that which can be experienced and learned by the pragmatic methods of science worth knowing? Can scientific methods accommodate all the subjects, feelings, information, and values which are desirable for the enrichment and fulfillment of human life? It is a strange paradox that open education, a very humanistic way of thinking about children, learning, and knowledge, seems to be so dependent upon, and possibly restricted by, the culture of science.

On reflection, it is not surprising that science should have become a point of departure for open education in this country. In fact, the use of science as the vehicle for fostering a more flexible approach to learning may have been somewhat deliberate. Teachers have traditionally been awed and intimidated by science, a subject akin to "truth." Few people are comfortable teaching "the truth"; few teachers have been comfortable teaching science.

One of the objectives of the Elementary Science Study was to remove the "revelation" stereotype from the teaching of science and to transfer the focus to objects of the real world. The American penchant for "gadgets" and machinery undoubtedly contributed here, for gadgets, games, and materials permit the teacher and student to meet on neutral territory; or in

Hawkins' language (145), they provide an "it" which permits teacher and student to have an "I-thou." There is an objectivity in the object which seems to make the learning situation more comfortable for both teacher and student.

American reliance on science as the vehicle to help make classrooms more informal is contrasted with the much greater emphasis in British primary schools upon exploration of art, music, drama, and movement, for it has been through these "subjects" that the transformation of British schools has occurred. In England the arts have now become an integral and influential part of each school day.

Why music and art in the United States continue, even in many open schools, to be taught in another room at another time in another way is an interesting question for speculation. In fact, the entire affective, emotional domain of learning remains underdeveloped in American classrooms. Compared with the British, we continue to be self-conscious, inhibited, and repressed about exposing our feelings either through words or bodily movement. It is noteworthy that the assumptions about learning and knowledge touch so little upon the relationship between emotional and cognitive development.

Although few open educators acknowledge distinctions between subjects or disciplines in the primary schools, they often *act* as if such distinctions existed. Most materials seem to have an explicitness which causes the object to be associated with a discipline. A book is literature; an adding machine, mathematics; a telescope, science. Open classrooms are commonly arranged into "interest tables" or subject corners devoted to math, science, reading, social studies, art, etc. [At a workshop for teachers in Leicestershire (174) a separate *room* was provided for each subject area in which adults were encouraged to explore freely.] Spatial organization by subject area is employed despite the fact that one cannot be certain that a child in the science corner is doing what adults would label "science," or "math" in the math corner, or "reading" in the reading corner. When a child is given freedom to explore materials in his own way, he is likely to be oblivious to the categories in which adults have placed the materials.

A child playing with a pendulum may be engaged in music by beating time with the swing, or in art by making interesting patterns with a sand pendulum, or in math by timing the frequency as a function of string length. But the pendulum is placed in the science corner because the adult, at least, sees it as having intrinsic "science" value. It is puzzling that open educators continue to organize their materials by academic subject when they see such distinctions as having no meaning for children. We are left with an important and, as yet, unanswered question: To what extent and in what ways is it appropriate for the adult to *order* the environment in which children are exploring and learning?

It is quite clear that the subject science can be explored using the methods of science; but what about the other subjects? If children's exploration is dependent on materials, if concrete manipulations are to precede verbal abstractions, how are situations going to be provided in which children might explore the Greeks, the Ten Commandments, or the parts of speech? Some open educators would argue that if you cannot introduce physical, primary source materials which children may investigate, then the topic is not appropriate for the children. The means seem to determine the end; only that which can be reduced to concrete nonverbal materials can be learned. This is too simple and too narrow a view. It implies that that knowledge which can be reduced to and stimulated by materials is inherently more valuable than the knowledge which remains in history, in story, or in abstraction. This is a value judgment based upon expediency which is hard to accept.

This view, nonetheless, has led to some fresh and ingenious thinking about materials in schools. One could fabricate a huge Greek fluted column and place it in the room. From that object, from that material, a child might ask, "What is it? What is it used for? Where can I go to see columns?" All these questions could lead him to filmstrips, related reading, or trips to see local examples of neoclassical architecture. In other words, although it may be difficult, it is possible to place materials in a classroom which will lead to exploration by what are essentially scientific means toward what is essentially nonscientific content. Open educators are doing more and more to explore and exploit the use of materials and primary experiences to initiate *all* of children's learning. Materials such as math blocks, musical instruments, animals, plants, pictures, and tools are being brought into classrooms, and children are being taken out of the classrooms for ever-wider experiences. The limitation of materials as a means of helping children to gain knowledge about themselves and about the world seems now to be more one of space than of ideas. The implications for buildings and environments suitable for children's exploration of the material world present exciting prospects.

CONCLUSION

What is open education? Why does this term best represent the foregoing assumptions? Open education is a way of thinking about children, about learning, and about knowledge. It is characterized by openness: doors are ajar, and children come and go; classrooms are open, and children bring objects of interest in and take objects of interest out; space is fluid, not preempted by desks and chairs organized in rows or in any permanent way; a variety of spaces are filled with a variety of materials; children move openly from place to place, from activity to activity. Time is open, to permit and release rather than constrain or prescribe. The curriculum is open to choices by adults and children as a function of the interests of children. The curriculum is the dependent variable, dependent on the child, rather than the independent variable upon which the child must depend.

Perhaps most importantly, open education is characterized by an openness of self on the part of children and adults. Persons are openly sensitive to and supportive of other persons, not closed off by anxiety and threat. Feelings are exposed and respected. Teachers are open to the possibilities inherent in children; children are open to the possibilities inherent in other children, in materials, and in themselves. In short, open education implies an environment in which the possibilities for exploration and learning of self and of the world are unobstructed.

Open educators assume that children learn by exploring living things, inanimate materials, and quite animate persons—in short, by exploring the real world in all its richness and variety. Learning is not distinguished from living, nor living from learning.[103]

Knowledge is a goal of open education, and the teacher and school are important means of reaching this goal; but the meaning of knowledge is radically changed. Knowledge is the child's personal capacity to confront and handle new experiences successfully, not the ability to verbalize the adult-known on demand. Knowledge is a system of strategies and processes —intellectual, personal, social—which an individual develops for handling the world.

The state of thought surrounding open education is still primitive. The foregoing assumptions are hunches, based somewhat on careful study, yet largely upon impressions, gut feelings, emotional responses, and informal observations in classrooms. Collectively the assumptions do not constitute a coherent system or structure. There are inconsistencies and voids; there is little supporting research. Indeed, some of these assumptions (such as No. 7: "Children have both the competence and the right to make significant decisions concerning

their own learning") are value judgments, all but impossible to
test and validate.

It is my hope that this attempt at articulating open educators' assumptions about learning and knowledge will lead to a
more critical and complete explication. However, one cannot
lightly push aside the possibility that an effort such as this can
prove dangerous. Any attempt to clarify a phenomenon as important, as fundamental and as complex as open education in-
troduces a disturbing dilemma: at best such an attempt can be
only tentative, incomplete, and subjective; at worst it can be
misunderstood, only partially understood, or misused. Furthermore, articulating these assumptions can have the effect of
foreclosing and restricting the development within each individual of his *own* thinking about children, learning, and knowledge. In short, there is considerable danger that by attempting
to make explicit the assumptions underlying open education,
one can do more harm than good. As William Hull has put it
(in personal correspondence of May, 1969), "I would prefer
that people be fascinated and puzzled than that they think
they understand something which they don't."

Yet the alternative horn of this dilemma represents in my
judgment an even less tenable and responsible position. To do
nothing is to perpetuate the mystique, romanticism, and confusion which so envelop open education today. To make no attempt at clarification is to sanction the haphazard and perilous
attempts of many who are already trying to adopt the practices
and *appearances* of open education, with little or no understanding or acceptance of the beliefs about learning which ac-
company those practices.

For some, then, drawing attention to these assumptions may
terminate interest in open education. All to the good; a well-
organized, consistent, formal classroom, for example, probably
has a less harmful influence upon children than an unplanned
and chaotic, even though well-intentioned, attempt at an open

classroom in which teacher and child must live with unresolved contradiction and conflict. For others, awareness of these assumptions may stimulate confidence and competence in their attempts to change what happens to children in school. In any case, this attempt at explication will have been worthwhile if it provokes the educator to become more conscious of, to examine, and to develop his own assumptions about children, learning, and knowledge. When he is sure of that which he believes, all will profit.

2

The Teacher and
the Open Classroom

INTRODUCTION

Chapter 1 attempts to determine and describe beliefs about
learning and knowledge held by open educators. It will be the
intent of this chapter to construct a role for the teacher which
is logically and feasibly consistent with these beliefs. The role
suggested here will be as much theoretical and hypothetical as
based upon actual practices.

An attempt such as this is subject to skepticism. In particular, three reservations should be acknowledged. First, just as
the assumptions presented in Chapter 1 are not all new to educational thought, neither are the practices related to these assumptions necessarily "educational innovations." In a way,
open educators are reinventing a wheel crafted before by
Plato, Socrates, St. Augustine, Froebel, Dewey, and others. It
is the current serious and distinctive attempt by open educators to make school, educational practice, and the role of the
teacher consonant with their beliefs about children, learning,
and knowledge, which, in my judgment, justifies efforts at explication.

Secondly, one might infer from the assumptions of open education that the institution of school could be profitably eliminated. Schools may need children in order to exist, but it is by no means certain that children have an equal need for schools. Why is school necessary, when a child can explore the world in all its richness in his backyard or on the subway? Schools, even open schools, by influencing and limiting the range and depth of the child's experience, restrict learning at the same time they foster it. School, as we know it, can scarcely find justification in history. Through most of recorded time men have been educated as the need arose, on the job or through apprenticeships, but seldom in a special place and at a special time set aside for the purpose.

I am a reformer, not a revolutionary. Hopefully the explication which follows will give evidence that school, even in its necessary artificiality, is an essential social institution, one which can be justified as a place where children's learning and development is deliberately and profitably fostered. By examining the open school and what the teacher does there, in light of the foregoing assumptions, I shall attempt to show that, in addition to a "baby-sitting" function, the teacher in the open school can make a uniquely positive contribution to the personal and intellectual development of children.

Finally, it should be pointed out that many feel that teaching is an art and therefore is not subject to scrutiny and analysis through essentially nonartistic means; that the teacher is an artist whose creative idiosyncrasies neither should nor can be carefully examined. Using an explication of the teacher's role to shed light on the complexities of the open school, this chapter will attempt to refute this position. One might also choose as an organizing principle what it is that the *child* in the open school does and is. In either case we come very soon to finding ourselves examining the nature of the important relationships which exist between adult, child, and the physical world.

Despite the absence of any powerful, centralized educational authority in the United States today, educational practice is as uniform, and as homogeneous, as if such a centralized authority existed. The predominant feature and the organizing principle characteristic of most schools and most teachers is close adherence to a fundamental concept—a "transmission-of-knowledge model." This model can be symbolized as:

$$K \longrightarrow C \longrightarrow A \longrightarrow S$$

The transmission-of-knowledge model posits the existence of an accumulated body of knowledge (K), usually encoded in written language. It is stored, from Plato to nuclear physics, in the Library of Congress. The proper business of education is to transmit as much of this knowledge as possible to students. The proper function of students is to assimilate as much of this knowledge as possible as efficiently as possible and to display its possession upon demand of school authorities. A student is judged (evaluated) according to how much K he has acquired, how fast, and how able he is to demonstrate this acquisition. This model assumes the primacy of the teaching function and the central role of language in the learning process:

. . . learning is what happens with normal children if they are properly taught. Teaching must mainly be through language (whatever supplementary aids we may also bring in), since most human knowledge is embodied in this and can only, in the end, be conveyed by its means. The chief aim of education is in fact this conveyance, by methods and under conditions that will make it as effective as possible, i.e., that will successfully transfer to children the same kind of knowledge, embodied in language, as is possessed by the teacher.[1]

Because all of accumulated knowledge is too vast to be conveyed to students, educators select those parts which they consider most crucial and appropriate for children of different ages to "know": the great explorers in the fifth grade, algebra in eighth, American history in twelfth, and so on. Once this selection has been made (usually labeled the "curriculum," **C**), it is transmitted by the school board, superintendent, or principal to an agent (**A**), who in turn transmits it to the students (**S**). The agent is usually a teacher, but might also be a written program, TV set, tape recorder, movie, or computer.

The transmission-of-knowledge model is a venerable one, built upon important assumptions about knowledge, curriculum, learning, and the role of the teacher. Most schools and most teachers are wedded to this model, and it directs their actions from day to day.

Although this model dominates contemporary education, it is beset with problems. Observers[2] find that schools run according to the transmission-of-knowledge model train children to submit to adult authority (or not to); to substitute (more or less successfully) adult problems, objectives, tasks, and ideas for their own; and to resist knowledge, teachers, and school. Although current educational rhetoric flaunts phrases like "discovery," "inner motivation," "exploration," and "best interests of the child," it seems that children's natural excitement and curiosity about the world is more thwarted than nurtured by the school experience. All too often, children are eager and inventive when they arrive at school, but apathetic and unimaginative when they leave. For most teachers, as well as most students, school is adult-centered, not child-centered; suppressive, not liberating; characterized by fear and anxiety, not by enjoyment or comfort. More and more educators are coming to wonder, as Jean-Jacques Rousseau did many years ago, whether the total effect of most schools upon children may not be more negative than positive:

> With our foolish and pedantic methods we are always preventing children from learning what they could learn much better by themselves, while we neglect what we alone can teach them.[3]

The concept of open education challenges the transmission-of-knowledge model, the practices associated with it, and the fundamental assumptions upon which those practices are based.[4] Open education is not a refinement of or tinkering with the traditional model, as are programmed instruction, team teaching, nongrading, and most of today's "educational inno-vations," but rather rests on significantly different assumptions about children, learning, and knowledge. These beliefs (pre-sented in Chapter 1) give rise to significantly different kinds of educational practices and institutions. This is not surprising, for school is precisely the institutional consequence of personal beliefs about children, learning, and knowledge.

We might symbolize a "model of open education"[5] like this:

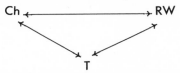

Advocates of this model believe that knowledge is unique to each individual, and that a child comes to know from direct, personal exploration of his environment. Learning is seen as a consequence of the interaction between the child (Ch) and the real world (RW)—be it an idea, a person, a gerbil, a book, or a can of paint and a brush.

The teacher's place (T) in this model is somewhere outside the learning process. The teacher's role is to provide the condi-tions which will make the child's active exploration of the real world both likely and fruitful. Thus, there is a mutual inter-change between the child, the world, and the teacher, but it is the child who is the principal agent of his *own* learning. The adult who works with the child remains important, but the na-ture of the work he does is quite different from that in the transmission-of-knowledge model—so different, in fact, that new names have been suggested for him such as "enabler," "adult in the classroom," and "facilitator of learning."[6] (For the sake of convenience, however, I shall continue to use the term "teacher.")

It is in contrast to the transmission-of-knowledge model and in terms of the open education model that we shall now examine the teacher and the open classroom.

THE TEACHER AS PERSON

Students in school, their parents, teachers, and the society of which they all are a part, hold tenaciously to a quite specific stereotype of what a teacher is: he loves and treats all his charges equally; everything he does is for his students rather than for himself; he is calm, thoughtful, impartial; he leads a moral life, untainted by cigarettes, drink, drugs, or sex; he possesses immense knowledge, which he imparts to children.

Despite a great deal of evidence that these stereotypes are neither accurate nor tenable, many teachers are subtly pressured to assume them. These expectations find expression in a number of ways in the daily life of the teacher. One teacher is not hired because she smokes during her interview. Another emerges from a liquor store on a Friday afternoon and feels uncomfortable, even guilty, when he encounters two of his students. Another feels impelled to refuse a drink offered to him at the home of one of his student's parents. During a pottery class, a teacher wants to make a coffee mug, but feels instead that he must help the children with their pots. A child spills ink on a teacher's dress, and the teacher is upset, torn between expressing anger and smiling sweetly. She chooses the latter. A teacher, when asked a question to which she doesn't know the answer, supplies one, even though she is quite sure it is not correct. Thus, in the traditional school, where he is expected to play the "paragon" role, the all-too-human teacher finds himself suppressing feelings, masking resentment and hostility behind a facade of rational and loving calm.

Open educators believe that suppression of feeling occurs at great emotional expense to the teacher. They value the teacher as a human being with all human failings and strengths. Teachers in open schools not only are permitted but are encouraged to be themselves: to be honest, angry, loving, upset, tired, happy—to be real. One does not play the role of teacher at the expense of being oneself; one *is* oneself and *thereby* a teacher.[7] Of equal importance is the fact that from the teacher's honest expression of feeling, children learn to respect, expect, and handle the wide range of behavior which they find in others, and to acknowledge and accept it in themselves. Not only is it desirable from the adult's point of view that he behave openly with children, but also it is essential from the child's point of view. Children must receive frequent and accurate responses from the personal as well as from the physical world; in order to learn, they must be provided with the interpersonal consequences of their actions as well as the physical consequences. Thus, prompt expression of annoyance and anger toward a disruptive child is essential for *both* teacher and child and for the establishment of their relationship. Withholding these feelings only results in more indirect and perhaps more insidious expression, in ways which neither teacher nor child can associate with the disruption, and therefore in ways which cannot be useful.

In stressing the importance of a rich *material* environment for children's learning, then, we must not overlook the profound effect of the personal environment. In a very real sense the learning environment of any classroom is an extension of the personality of the teacher. Consequently the teacher's personal qualities must be a central concern of anyone wishing to affect children's learning. Whatever else the teacher in the open classroom does, it is vital that he know himself and be himself, for only through encounters with real persons will children learn to know and to be themselves.

THE TEACHER AS KNOWER

The teacher in the open school is not a transmitter of knowledge, a dispenser of pearls of wisdom from the past. He does not believe there is a "right" knowledge which everyone must have. Rather, he believes that what each person knows is idiosyncratic and can never be "known" by another in exactly the same way. He does not try to impose his knowledge upon others; nor does he permit anyone to impose the "right" knowledge upon him. What each individual knows is a unique consequence of his exploration of the real world. The climate and the emphasis in the open classroom, then, is on *how* one comes to know and that one *can* come to know, rather than on *what* is to be known and knowing it. This kind of classroom is child-centered in a very basic sense.

The teacher in an informal classroom seldom distinguishes between process and content: the child comes to know *how* just as he comes to know *what*, by investigating his world. It is the teacher's job not to separate process and content or to value one more than the other but to arrange conditions for each child so that he can learn as much as he can from each experience—whether he learns that two batteries make a bulb brighter than one, or that he must observe carefully in order to determine brightness.

Currently, a shift in emphasis from a "content" to a "process" approach in teaching is taking place. Unfortunately, the means by which children are to learn process are precisely the same as the means by which they did *not* learn content, that is, by direct transmission from adult to child. A new product in the same tired old package will not affect the consumer's behavior. If process merely becomes the new content for the teacher to convey to children, they will learn it, or not, as they have done in the past. Teachers who now tell children about forming hypotheses, making inferences, and categorizing, instead of telling them about the nine planets, their moons, or the speed of light, are still tinkering with what is essentially an unsuccessful model of learning. Although the so-called "process approach" recognizes the long-range power of knowing how to learn, it has not yet squared with what we know about how children learn how to learn:

> *Process is not so much taught as it is learned.* Process implies confrontation . . . confrontation with situations that permit the practice and development of a youngster's ability to make raw experience meaningful.[8]

That the teacher's concept of knowledge is centered not on subjects but, rather, on students' interest and initiative does not mean that a teacher in an informal classroom can be an intellectual dilettante, a mere classroom administrator, ignorant of mathematics, language, science, history, and other important fields of learning and experience. It is what the teacher in the open school *does* with his knowledge, not the fact that he has more or less of it, that is different.

Since there can be no way for the teacher to predict and plan what knowledge he must have in order to respond to a child's inquiry, he must read and explore widely in areas in which his students seem to be showing a keen interest—animals, machines, cities, dinosaurs. The question "How can we find out?" becomes honest and real for both child and adult—a question which, if genuine, offers great interpersonal as well as pedagogical possibilities.

The subject-matter specialist is very important in the transmission-of-knowledge model, for if a teacher concentrates all his energies on one academic area he can dispense more sophisticated knowledge, and faster. He is a better, more efficient teacher. From the point of view of open educators, however, the practice of five adults teaching different subjects to a given child each day leads to disintegration in the temporal organization of the day, in the unity of knowledge, and, more important, in the thinking of the child. What each specialist transmits may make very good sense in terms of the structure of his discipline and its accumulated knowledge, but what is received by the children may not. Neither the subject-matter-centered curriculum nor the subject specialist teacher has a central place in the open school.

The preferred teacher for the open classroom is a "generalist," in the sense that he has facility with many domains of knowledge, has one or two areas of particular interest, experience, and competence, and is capable of growing in *any* area as the need and interest of the children dictate. The teacher who knows enough about enough and who can stimulate, assist in, and help sustain children's exploration is preferred to the specialist who may lecture with great sophistication but who can only respond to children's initiatives in a limited area, to a limited extent.

Open educators prefer to let the learner integrate knowledge of the many disciplines in his own mind, or rather, never to let him *disintegrate* knowledge; for in every experience a child has, his knowledge about it is, from the start, integrated in some way, by virtue of the fact that *he* is having the experience. Natural, experiential integration of knowledge makes far more sense to the child than contrived attempts to integrate knowledge for him.

There is in elementary education a history of attempts to create integrated curricula. The "core curriculum" is one example which has had major influence. In a core curriculum the subjects are coordinated to allow children to explore a given area in both depth and breadth, using all the resources of the school and community. The purpose is to prevent a fragmented, departmentalized approach to learning. This approach has predominated for years in many highly regarded independent schools, where children have studied such core subjects as "Indians" in the third grade, "Greeks" in the fourth, and "Colonial America" in the fifth.

A basic difference between the core curriculum and open education (which has been labeled the "integrated day" by Brown and Precious and by others) is that the former is designed by competent teachers with an eye to covering major areas of thought as well as appealing to children's interests. In an open classroom each child defines and develops his own curriculum, from minute to minute. The teacher, her scholarship and experience, is one resource for guiding the child's curriculum, but it is the learner himself who plays the intimate and creative role of directing his activities and exploration.

Teachers, curriculum designers, and children who not only hold but act upon these beliefs about knowledge enjoy frequent success, because success is no longer equated with the capacity to live up to standards and expectations posed from without, as stimulating and challenging as these may be, but rather is gauged in terms of personal involvement and private accomplishment. It makes sense to change the definition of the conditions under which people may succeed if such a change results in important learning for children.

THE TEACHER AS FACILITATOR OF LEARNING

We have seen that open educators believe that "if a child is fully engaged in an activity, learning is taking place." The key role of the teacher as facilitator of learning, then, is to *maximize the likelihood that each child will be fully engaged in an activity* for as much of the day as possible, to encourage the active exploration of his world by the child. For purposes of discussion and clarity, we shall distinguish seven important and interrelated activities of the teacher. Since these functions are simultaneous, the order in which they are presented here is of little significance. The facilitator of learning:

Respects children as individuals
Manages the environment
Provides materials
Consolidates children's experience through language
Provides direct instruction
Encourages children's activity
Encourages children's independence

The Teacher Respects Children as Individuals

Although most teachers acknowledge the importance of respecting children as individuals, the transmission-of-knowledge model prevents them from *acting as if* they respected children as individuals. There is an inherent conflict between the authority of the material to be learned and the learner. The teacher is caught in the middle, and much of his efforts go into finding a resolution, usually imperfect, to this conflict. Consequently, few teachers or children feel or have an opportunity to act respectfully. In schools where subject matter is the organizing principle which governs the relationship between teacher and student, the teacher can be assured of its conveyance to the children only by setting similar goals and expectations for the entire class, by lecturing, and by requiring the same activities of each child. Learning experiences are *group* experiences, tied to group norms. Teachers relate to students, and students relate to other students as members of a large group—but seldom as individuals. Respect for children as individuals exists only with difficulty under these conditions.

For a teacher to relate individually to many children each day, even for brief periods of time, demands an extraordinary amount of sensitivity, mobility, and energy. He must constantly scan the room, the corridor, and the space outside the room, observing children who are working with different materials and with other children. In deciding when or when not to intervene, he must constantly ask himself the question "Is there some way I can help further this child's exploration?" He must alternate group surveillance with moments spent offering a child his undivided attention, help, and support. As difficult as this is, it does not seem impossible. Within a half hour, one observer in a British primary school saw the teacher contacting all forty-one children:

> She stepped into the corridor to comment on a little boy's painting, stopping off at the woodworking bench to see how the boat was coming. Inside the room she listened to two little girls read, wrote down words in a little boy's private dictionary for the story he was writing, looked over the shoulders of the shape-manipulators and block-builders, corrected a page of sums for a little boy who had been working on arithmetic. . . .[9]

Perhaps no educational practice more vividly reveals underlying assumptions about children's learning and knowledge than the common practice of ability grouping. Ability grouping is a logical extension of the transmission-of-knowledge model of learning. If one assumes that the child learns from an agent outside himself—teacher, program, film—then, given the need to educate large numbers of students, it follows that the more closely students are matched along certain relevant dimensions (e.g., test scores, age, perhaps sex), the more efficiently knowledge can be transmitted to them. Since there is more knowledge essential for everyone to know than there is time in which to learn it, efficiency is of the utmost importance. Ability grouping would then appear to facilitate the most effective transmission of knowledge.

But the price of this kind of homogeneity and efficiency is the limitation, if not the elimination, of important individual distinctions. It becomes impossible for teachers to respect children as individuals when the more children act like individuals (i.e., differently), the more difficult it becomes to group them and instruct them; when the system, in the name of efficiency, is grouping the important individual differences out of each classroom as fast as they appear. In short, most schools pay lip service to the goal of respect for children as individuals but engage in practices which virtually exclude this kind of respect.

Open educators are universal in their condemnation[10] of ability grouping, or "streaming" as it is called in England. They believe that if a teacher is to respect children as individuals, then he cannot arrange and teach them in homogeneous groups. Objections to ability grouping rest on:

1. Inability at the present time of adults and test instruments to accurately differentiate intellectual qualities in children
2. Doubt that capacity for accumulation of knowledge is the most important quality of a human being
3. Undesirable consequences, usually in terms of children's self-confidence and self-esteem, which are associated with ability grouping
4. Close association of ability grouping with the view of teacher as transmitter and student as recipient of knowledge
5. Evidence from educational research that differences between achievement of children grouped by ability and those not so grouped, although generally favoring the former, are confined to the limited area of *measurable* attainment, and often amount to a difference of only two or three more questions right on a test of forty items

Open educators not only acknowledge but deliberately attempt to foster individual differences among children. They balance the numbers of boys and girls. They disregard apparent ability differences. They often practice "family grouping," that is, placing children of ages 5–7 or 8–11 in the same classroom, in the belief that the younger children will be constantly stimulated and extended by interaction with the older, and the older will extend their knowledge by working with the younger (a practice not unlike the old one-room schoolhouses). In these ways, open educators attempt to maximize diversity, in the belief that a child who spends each day with children who vary in age, sex, ability, interest, and background will have a richer learning experience than one who belongs to an apparently similar (i.e., homogeneous) group.

When children in open classrooms are grouped, it is usually for other purposes:

The only scheduled events that I saw during the week were an assembly period for singing and prayers, held each day; a gym period, recess, and lunch. During the rest of the day from 9 until 3, each individual child was free to follow his own choices and interests.[11]

In the course of exploring materials and posing, solving, and verifying problems for themselves, children often spontaneously form groups on the basis of *common interest:*

No, don't think that the children always work individually, because they don't. We're most of us gregarious, aren't we? The children will get into little groups. There's always a leader of a group, and the children work together. So your group is naturally formed for you.[12]

Like ability groups, these groups are functional; but rather than serving a function for the adult, they serve the child. They stimulate and assist his exploration of the human and the material world.

It is also common in open schools for teachers to select small groups of children who have a particular need and want help in meeting it, such as learning how to make papier-mâché or running an adding machine. But these groups are ad hoc, not year-long compartments as are the familiar three reading groups. They are "formed for a particular purpose, and should disappear when the purpose is achieved." [13] Thus the concept of grouping *per se* is not antithetical to learning, or to individual relationships; it is only when the adult tries to legislate the time, place, constitution, and duration of a group that the concept becomes abused, unnatural, and counterproductive.

In short, the teacher in the open school respects children as individuals by stressing the quality of the relationship between adult and child and among children, rather than the frequency or quantity, in the belief that a highly individual contact between individuals is more important for learning than continual group exposures:

> I can give all of my attention to a child for five minutes and that's worth more to him than being part of a sea of faces all day.[14]

The Teacher Manages the Environment

One obvious difference between an open classroom and the traditional classroom is the physical environment in which both child and adult live—the way the classroom *looks*. The spatial organization of the open school reflects beliefs about children's learning and about the nature of knowledge, just as a lecture hall reveals belief in a transmission-of-knowledge model of education. But physical arrangements not only *reflect* what child and adult are thinking and doing; they also *influence* thought and action.

The teacher in the open school organizes his classroom not to promote optimal conditions for transmission of knowledge but to extend the range of possibilities children can explore. Children's desks are often removed from the room, and only chairs and tables are left. In classrooms where desks remain, they may not be assigned to individual children; instead, each child may have a small cubby or drawer along one side of the room for storing sweaters, pencils, and other personal belongings. Space within the classroom is divided, often by movable screens or furniture, into "interest areas," each perhaps ten feet square.

Although subject-matter categories do not direct the organization of the open classroom, the explicitness of materials I referred to in the previous chapter, tends to suggest, at least for convenience' sake, that objects be associated with specific disciplines. Thus, "interest tables" are often devoted to math, science, reading, social studies, art, etc. Typically, a mathematics "corner" might offer Cuisenaire rods, Stern blocks, balances, geoboards, number lines, and math books; a science area, batteries and bulbs, different liquids in plastic containers, a microscope, and some bones; a nature area, gerbils, fish, rabbits, guinea pigs, leaves, twigs, stones; a social studies area, maps, globes, artifacts from various countries, books, and models of explorers' ships; a reading corner, an old stuffed easy chair or a mattress on the floor, inviting children to read from a wide variety of books displayed on shelves; an art area, usually near a source of water, paints, easels, paper, charcoal, linoleum blocks, and carving tools. These interest areas are employed more so that teachers will know where to put things and students will know where to find them, than as attempts to categorize experience and knowledge for children.[15]

When a child is given freedom to explore materials in his own way, he is likely to be oblivious to categories in which adults have placed them. If a child is building a boat for the neighboring stream, neither he nor the teacher distinguishes among his activities when he measures, studies a picture in a book, paints the sails, or notices that the current in the river changes after a rainfall, although a traditional teacher might label them "mathematics," "history," "art," and "science."

While in the traditional classroom the child learns at his desk, in the open school *the locus of learning is where something of particular interest to the child happens to be.* With this confidence, the teacher accepts and respects what each child chooses to do and where he chooses to do it. The boundaries most American children carefully draw between "school" and "home" are blurred. Children, like teachers, take things and ideas of interest home to ponder, just as they bring things and ideas of interest from home to school. The result is a more fully "integrated day" and, as Hull points out, "a sense of belonging to a much larger community than that of the individual class." [16]

There might even be an occasion when a child says, "Can I go into my friend's class? Miss Jones is going to tell a story about so and so, and I want to hear it." Or a child might say, "My friend is making a bridge, and he wants me to go and help him. Can I go and help him?" [17]

Many of the junior schools take their students for a week's trip to a lodge which the county maintains in Wales, or to other camping sites in areas of archeological interest. . . . A few schools have managed trips to Normandy or Paris, in order to supplement their studies of French language and history.[18]

The Teacher Provides Materials

A teacher cannot directly provide a child the exploratory experiences which lead to learning; he can, however, provide materials which will engage the child's innate curiosity and involve him in the learning process.

Open educators' belief in the power and importance of manipulative materials conflicts (as we shall see in Chapter 3) with the conviction of many educators, parents, and children that firsthand experiences with materials are neither appropriate nor legitimate, that secondary experiences mediated by symbols—numerals, words, pictures—are the legitimate means for learning.

For the teacher in the open school, the problem is one of selection, for through the selection of materials the teacher influences the direction of the child's exploration, and hence his learning. Rather than offering selections of appropriate materials,[19] let me suggest five criteria which can guide the teacher's selection and which may help in reaching an optimal match between child and materials.

CRITERION 1: *Whenever possible, encourage and permit children to supply their own materials.*

One way a teacher can be sure that the classroom contains materials capable of eliciting children's interest is to encourage children to bring to school items of their own. Since "given the opportunity, children will choose to engage in activities which will be of high interest to them," materials which children select from their real world are likely to encourage their exploration and learning. Furthermore, by bringing their own materials to school, children identify what they are particularly interested in and offer the teacher important clues for subsequent selection of materials. If a child with reading problems brings in model dinosaur bones to assemble, his teacher might find some easy books about dinosaurs for him to read. A child who brings in seeds might plant them, then measure and perhaps graph the plant's growth.

Children's ingenuity and imagination need not be limited to bringing materials of interest into the classroom. When they need materials or equipment *not* available either in school or at home, they can construct apparatus in the classroom: for instance, devices to measure length, time, weight, or light brightness.

Although many teachers in this country have a "show and tell" period each morning to which a child may bring things of interest, usually the goldfish, photograph, plant, or magnet provides an excuse for the child to stand up and talk before the class or to convey to the teacher and the class an interest the child has *outside school,* as if that were some other world. What the child brings in is seldom something he investigates during school time. In addition, teachers usually limit the range of acceptable materials children may bring in to books, maps, stories, newspaper clippings, etc., and in subtle ways screen out animals, bicycles, tools, comic books, sports equipment, and the like.

CRITERION 2: *Whenever possible, encourage and permit children to explore the real world outside the classroom and outside the school.*

Once the notion of the teacher as the child's only source of knowledge is dismissed, the classroom is no longer sacrosanct. It is often possible, permissible, and profitable for the teacher to release children from rigid adherence to a five-hour-a-day schedule in the classroom, so that they may explore the environment *outside* the classroom. In this way, a whole world of possibilities opens up, and the entire environment becomes the locus of the child's learning. The countryside offers a study of nature, creatures of every kind, plants, and streams; the suburbs offer opportunities to explore various forms of transportation (buses, trains, trucks, boats, cars); cities offer opportunities to view construction of roads, bridges, and skyscrapers. All give access to weather, food, buildings, movement, change, pattern, and excitement. Wherever there is a school, there is a community which is rich in potential learning experiences.

People are resources as valuable for children's learning as are objects or natural phenomena. Everyone is a potential "teacher," for all humans through their jobs, personalities, interests, and experiences hold something of interest and importance to a child. Differentiating between adults who teach children as a profession and those who don't is unfortunate— certainly not a distinction that children would make. Many British schools, for instance, view their entire staff as a resource for the children:

. . . in these schools, and others at both the infant and junior levels, the kitchen staff is not isolated. Often the women will be sought out by children for help with spelling words and other academic problems.[20]

Responsibility for the education of youngsters will probably never completely leave the schools, nor is it likely that children will be able to supply all their own materials; the teacher has major responsibility for providing materials *in the classroom* for children.

CRITERION 3: *The best materials for children are common ones, which are inexpensive, familiar, and easily available.*

Many administrators, teachers, and parents assume that *unless* materials are expensive, flashy, and manufactured, children cannot learn very much from them. This reasoning leads to a conception of educational "innovation" as moving from old buses, books, desks, and buildings to new buses, books, desks, and buildings. The question of whether a new twelve-dollar social studies textbook results in more learning than the old four-dollar copy is unasked and unanswered.

Expensive materials are not necessarily the key to children's learning. They often better serve teachers' and parents' needs than children's. Most manufactured items used *in* schools—microscopes, filmstrips, mathematics blocks, encyclopedias—are to be used by children *only* in school, usually under strict conditions laid down by the teacher, who fears their loss or damage. This has the effect of localizing and separating many of the child's learning activities from his out-of-school life.

Common, less expensive materials, on the other hand, have many advantages. In seeking them out, children and adults learn to be imaginative, inventive, resourceful, and instrumental. They learn to master the raw materials of the world around them. They learn to relate in-school materials and activities—animals, clay, sand, tree roots, water—and out-of-school activities. Children tend to respect and care for these inexpensive common materials with an uncharacteristic zeal, whereas they often abuse more expensive school equipment; freedom and independence surround the child's use of ordinary things, in contrast to the constraint, dependence, and resentment often associated with more "valuable" materials. This freedom makes learning more possible.

It is questionable whether American teachers can develop a sense of resourcefulness and competence in making the most of their world in a profession where their horizon is defined, on the one hand, by budget restrictions and, on the other, by the offerings of the Creative Playthings catalog. Unfortunately, most teachers are hesitant to scrounge, unsure of themselves and unsure that what *they* might select will be seen as valuable and acceptable to parents, children, and administrators. This caution, added to the availability of funds for manufactured materials (which obviates the need for creative scrounging), discourages the selection and use of common, inexpensive materials in the classroom.

In British primary schools, teachers who earn only $2,500 a year, working in schools with corresponding budgets, *must* be resourceful. They have no choice but to make the most of what they have and can dig up. In British open schools, teachers and children alike scrounge for all manner of things: old tires for swings, popsicle sticks for arithmetic, roots of trees from nearby woods for sculpture, animals caught in snares for nature study, books discarded by libraries, and the like.

You don't need a great deal of the apparatus that's on the market. You can manage quite easily with everything that's 'round you.[21]

In none of our visits to schools did we see lavish provision of equipment, books, mechanical aids, tape recorders or film projectors. . . . On the contrary, we found an attitude of making do with the materials that were to hand.[22]

The most valuable materials are the natural ones, sand, wood, clay, water and then paint, paper, materials for sewing and cooking and cleaning, and then dolls, furniture, animals, etc. . . . Expensive manufactured bricks, beads, puzzles, etc., are not necessary; they have their uses and may be available in small quantities, but their educational value is much more limited.[23]

CRITERION 4: *Ambiguous, multiprogrammed materials which suggest to the child a wide number of possible paths of exploration are preferred.*

There is another important reason for preferring common, inexpensive materials over more expensive, manufactured ones: common materials tend to be more ambiguous and less directive, and thus offer each child a greater place in determining their use.

Many manufactured educational materials have been designed to exclude all but one or two possible paths for the child's exploration and thinking.[24] These materials are not only limited but limiting, for they teach the child to depend upon the structure inherent in the material (and upon the adult who constructs the materials) to pose questions, to help solve problems, and to verify the solution. The child, in short, becomes dependent upon a source outside himself to initiate, sustain, and verify his own learning.[25]

Materials structured and "programmed" by adults, which leave insufficient room for children to invent, improvise, modify, and adapt, are revealed by such phrases as "the child will be led" or "orderly stages" and by elaborate directions concerning the proper use of the materials and suggested ways to get children back on the "right" path, should their imagination cause them to depart from it. The child can assemble a plastic model in only one way; he can use the filmstrip viewer only with those filmstrips available to him. The fact that they can be exciting for the child and are legitimate from the adult's point of view makes these materials no less limiting.

Open educators' emphasis on flexibly structured materials rests on the belief that a child should be instrumental in posing for himself both the problem and the path that he will take in pursuing that problem. Materials are to assist him in these choices, not to direct or restrict him. But one must not condemn all materials which have structure, only those whose structure strictly directs and limits the child's thinking. Many common materials exist which have not been designed by anyone for anyone, for any particular purpose, and yet which have definite structure. A magnet, sand, or a set of wooden blocks has definite structure and the capacity to influence and organize children's thought. But they are ambiguous and multiprogrammed; they do not confine the child but, rather, offer him a major part in determining their use, depending upon the questions they suggest to him. With the magnet he can make a motor, a test to see which materials are attracted to it, or a study of polarity with iron filings. With blocks, he can build a balance board, a house, a fort, a highway for his cars, or a stand for his checker game; and with the sand he can build, measure time, draw, etc.

A game that British children frequently play with "junk" provides an illustration. A child will bring to school something he has found. Regardless of the material, the teacher will encourage him to explore over a period of time all the possible uses to which the material might be put. A given object would suggest many different uses to different children. For instance, with a clothespin one child might hold a painting on an easel, make a bob for a pendulum, construct the body of a doll, make a handle for a printing stamp, project a stylized grasshopper on a screen, or hang clothes on a line. To investigate the use of a material in many contexts seems to encourage both flexibility in thinking and imaginative play.

The principle of selecting multiple-program materials, like the other principles for selection, must be employed with reference to the degree of independence of each child. For the child who is dependent upon direct adult control for his learning, structured materials and activities such as checkers or a filmstrip viewer are probably more appropriate, at least initially. The same child might be at a loss at a sand table. For the child who is more independent and self-reliant, ambiguous materials such as clay, blocks, or water—which offer a variety of entry points and paths for exploration—may be more appropriate.

The task of the teacher, then, is to select materials which will provide multiple structures and then to encourage each child to use the full range of possibilities inherent in the materials and in himself. People, like materials, can be more or less directive, rigid, and prescribing. What a teacher encourages children to do with materials has just as great an influence on the thinking and behavior of children as do the inherent properties of the materials. Hopefully, all children will, in time, develop competence, confidence, and resourcefulness when confronted with an unstructured and ambiguous situation: that is, when confronted with the real world.

CRITERION 5: *Select materials which have a high likelihood of initiating, sustaining, and extending exploration.*

Because learning is a necessary consequence of active exploration in a rich environment, it is important for the adult to select materials which will make active exploration likely. It cannot be assumed that all children will wish to explore a random collection of materials. The teacher must provide materials which will invite questions, study, examination, and activity. Although the teacher selects materials on the basis of what he *suspects* children of this age range, sex, and locality will find interesting, he should not be surprised if children use materials in unanticipated ways:

Very often the teacher will put exciting materials down which suggest something to the child. She might put some cardboard boxes and think, "That will give the children an idea. They might start making a train." Then she must be prepared to find that it's been turned into a robot.[26]

Fortunately, the necessity of selecting materials without benefit of observation of the children who will use them is short-lived. Yesterday, three children made robots out of cardboard boxes, even though the teacher may not have guessed that they would use these multiple-program materials in this way. Today he can provide paint, tin cans, and buttons for these same children, should they want to embellish their robot. He might also have on hand robot books, robot models, and robot pictures.

After the first days, then, the teacher selects materials which will sustain and extend each child's exploration, although he may continue to introduce new materials on the hunch that children will find use for them. His job gradually becomes less speculative and based more on careful observation of what the children are saying and doing.

The timing of the introduction of materials is as important as the nature of the materials to child and adult. Lesson plans, curriculum guides, and literature on child development are of little relevance in making time discriminations. Only keen, firsthand observation can guide the teacher. Thus, one cannot separate the role of the teacher in selecting and supplying materials from the role of the teacher in observing and diagnosing children's behavior. In order to prescribe and select materials to make available to children tomorrow, we must take advantage of what they are telling us today.

The Teacher Consolidates Children's Experience Through Language

Given personal encouragement from the teacher and an environment rich in manipulative materials, a child is likely to engage in a variety of rewarding activities. He learns from essentially private experiences between himself and objects in his real world. His learning, however, does not end with the experiences themselves; when he has learned something, he will feel a need to make explicit the implicit.

Because learning can be refined and extended through the conversion of experience into language, the teacher can exercise a delicate, yet powerful, function: he can encourage the child to verbalize his discoveries, provide the child with a word for a concept or an idea, and help the child to associate a useful symbol with a concrete experience. In these ways the teacher can help the child to translate his experience, which is private, into language, which is public.

The teacher's intervention in the child's encounters with other children and with materials must be subtle. It is as possible for the teacher to interfere with children's learning by labeling and abstracting as by directing and prescribing. As a child investigates a pendulum, for instance, he will invent and use his own words for what he sees and does: "swing," "round trip," "tick-tock." The teacher can help him to develop, establish, and enrich these concepts by talking with the child in the child's words. After the child has worked with the pendulum, the teacher may even introduce the technical words for the child's experience: "period," "amplitude," etc. In any case, learning is labeled by child and adult alike during the time and after it has taken place, not before. Words come out of experiences, not out of predetermined lesson plans and curriculum guides.

For the teacher to help the child in this way demands careful observation and diagnosis of children's behavior. In one way, observing in a classroom full of materials is easy, because of the abundance of *overt* behavior. But in another way, observing children and making sense out of their behavior is never easy. At best, it is risky to infer what children are thinking—particularly for the beginning teacher. When children are given materials and encouraged to explore, they tend not to behave in adultlike ways, nor do they always talk in adult language or think in adult concepts. But when a child does or says something, he sends off signals, even though he may be unable or unwilling to give an account of what he is thinking in a way which would make sense to the adult. The teacher must be very careful that the words he supplies to the child are related to what the child is thinking. He must try to decipher the child's own language; he must also pay careful attention to the child's nonverbal behavior, which often conveys as much information as does his language. Rather than trying to force the child to convey his ideas in adult terms, as most teachers are inclined to do, the teacher must be ready to adapt to the child's thinking, language, and behavior.

The effect of the teacher's consolidating children's experience with appropriate language is to help relate the thinking of the child to the thinking of the adult; to anticipate a more detailed investigation of the phenomenon; to develop the child's vocabulary; to develop a commonly used abstraction, a shorthand that helps the child better recall what he has done and learned; and to enable the child to communicate with others if he wants to. In the final analysis, however, the important question is not whether the child recognizes, understands, or uses the "right" word for his experiences but whether he has developed a working concept of his own. His personal and idiosyncratic concept is more important than the correct word for it, as convenient and as impressive as that word might be. Vocabulary is more important as an aid in the development and extension of concepts than as a medium for displaying them.

The Teacher Provides Direct Instruction

Open educators believe that there *are* times when it is appropriate and essential for the teacher to be directive, times when he might even be a transmitter of knowledge. Rather than reacting emotionally against the directive role, or assuming it with unquestioning comfort, it is important for the teacher to understand when and why didactic behavior is appropriate.

There are two circumstances when the teacher must be didactic: when children are unlikely to discover for themselves skills or information needed to pursue activities which are important to them; and when it is likely that a child's exploration will result in significant danger to himself or others or to the equipment he is using. Take, for instance, use of a simple camera. Most children, although fascinated by cameras, initially have little idea of what the different dials mean or how and when to use them. If they use the camera *without* such knowledge, their photos are unlikely to be successful. This will result in frustration and probably put an end to the activity and to that opportunity for learning.

A child interested in a microscope may be strongly absorbed in studying a frog's egg. But in the process of focusing, he may move the lens down into the glass slide or onto the specimen, thereby damaging the lens and perhaps breaking the slide or the instrument in the process. Similarly, the child without sufficient instruction in the use of the camera can damage it or can waste quantities of film. The child trying to light a 110-volt light bulb with forty flashlight batteries may experience pain or be harmed unless he is instructed in the ideas of insulation, voltage, amperage, etc.

There are cases, like these, when the teacher must explain in careful detail to children how to use equipment and what each part does. To be sure, sensitive teachers can help children to learn the skill by drawing them out in a discussion with such questions as "What do you think this is for?" and "How do you think this works?" The teacher may also make good use of one or two children in the classroom who have already mastered the skill and can convey it to others. But the teacher's objective is the same: to make sure that every child arrives at a piece of information or a skill specified and judged by the teacher to be essential to the child's further exploration.

Usually the teacher is given important clues by the children which help him to decide when to be directive and didactic: "How do I get the film in the camera?" is a legitimate question and deserves a legitimate answer. But the teacher cannot rely entirely upon the child's verbalized need in determining his action. Even if the child *thinks* he knows what he's doing, even if the child does not ask if it is all right to cut the concrete block with a crosscut saw, the teacher has a responsibility for the safety and success of the child and the safeguarding of the tool. The fact that the child may discover in time, by trial and error, that cinder blocks make saws dull is not sufficient justification for the teacher to withhold instruction at the proper moment. Summerhill's A. S. Neil found himself locking up all his fine tools in a tight closet rather than allowing children to abuse them. The third alternative, instruction and perhaps supervision in the use of the tools, did not seem appropriate.

In summary, conditions which require direct, didactic instruction are those in which there is likelihood that the child's failure will curtail exploration and those in which there is danger to self, others, or equipment. As in all adult-child relations, the line between helping the child by staying out of his way and helping by intervening is difficult to draw. It is very easy to err on either side, as Hawkins has suggested:

[A] teacher can kill a subject by his own eagerness—egoness—to show himself its master.[27]

The Teacher Encourages Children's Activity

In his role as facilitator of learning, the teacher must consciously and actively *encourage* children's activity and exploration. Given a classroom full of interesting materials, the teacher can establish certain conditions which will make children's exploration of these materials more likely and fruitful.

Two are especially important: developing a mutual, personal trust between teacher and child; and permitting and encouraging the child to make important choices.

Characteristic of most teachers is a chronic, uneasy sense of distrust: distrust of what the children might do that the teacher doesn't want them to do, and of what they might not do that the teacher wants them to do. A good deal of a teacher's daily energy output and behavior is a response to this pervasive distrust and fear of children: teachers are taught not to turn their backs on the class but, instead, to write at the blackboard at an awkward angle which permits them constant surveillance of the classroom; children often are not permitted to leave the room, let alone the building, without a special "pass"; they are given tests to see if they have done the required work and are placed at a maximum distance apart so that they will not cheat during the tests. This sense of uneasiness, fear, and distrust is reciprocal. Most children fear and distrust their teachers. They expect a test to be sprung on them without warning; they worry when parents and the teacher confer, lest the teacher betray their shortcomings; they come to school armed with multiple excuses to fend off unreasonable or unexpected demands made by the teacher; they recoil on report card day, less because they are unaware of the quality of the work they have done over the term than because they see little connection between the work they have done— which is theirs—and the grades which they will receive— which are the teacher's. Just as much of the teacher's daily energy is expended in response to a distrust of children, so a large part of a student's energy is dissipated in anxiety and anticipation stemming from his distrust of the teacher. Thus the conventional relationship between teacher and child is essentially one of adversaries in a constant struggle.

A sense of mutual trust and confidence between child and teacher is essential for the child's learning and the teacher's effectiveness. Where teacher and child are threatened, teaching and learning are difficult at best. Only in a situation of trust will children feel free to explore comfortably, actively, confidently, openly, and autonomously in situations not dominated by adults. The development of mutual trust is closely associated with changes taking place in many British and American open classrooms. It is becoming clear that a child outside the teacher's immediate control need not be out of all control.

As important as it is for learning, a sense of mutual trust is perhaps the most difficult attribute for teachers and children to develop. Trust is a basic personality characteristic, not something to be adopted like a principle for selecting materials. *Lack* of trust is, of course, a characteristic of most schools and pervades even many open schools. In one American open school, for instance, parents who had sent their child to a situation where he might make important choices by day tutored him in the three R's every night.

The teacher can begin to develop trust between each child and himself by attempting to arrange the child's environment so that the personal and physical inhibitions to free exploration—a troublesome peer, poor eyesight, an inability to write —are removed, thereby increasing the likelihood of the child's success. When the teacher has made frequent decisions which help remove obstacles to the children's learning,

. . . the child learns something about the adult which can be described with words like "confidence," "trust," and "respect." The teacher has done something for the child he could not do for himself and the child knows it. . . . If he thus learns that he has the competence to do something that he didn't know he could do, then the teacher has been a very crucial figure in his life. He has provided that external loop, that external feedback that the child couldn't provide for himself; he then values the one who provides the thing provided.[28]

A measure of mutual trust between teacher and child is a necessary precondition for a second major role of the teacher in encouraging children's activity. The teacher must empower the child with a significant degree of *choice* concerning the materials and the questions with which he will work.

In all schools a central question is *who* decides what the child is going to do. Does a child write a composition, for example, because he wants to or because the adult decides that he must? The question is perhaps raised more poignantly by asking, "What if the child decides *not* to engage in the activity? What if he is given a battery and a bulb, and he decides to watch the fish in the aquarium? What are the consequences?" Not behaving in an expected way reveals very clearly wherein the power and responsibility for making classroom decisions resides.

In most schools, adults are the decisionmakers. On the basis of experience, training, and status in the hierarchy, they are assumed qualified to decide what a child will learn and how he will learn it. To be sure, teachers in traditional schools give children some choice, but the concept of choice is distorted and abused. It is a usual practice to offer a child a finite number of alternatives: "Write a report on one of the explorers, Magellan, Columbus, Cortez, De Soto, etc." While this may give the child some sense of being instrumental, of involvement in the decisionmaking process, this is a situation where a child chooses from among problems *posed by the adult*. Choice is also abused when the teacher permits a child to choose from among stipulated alternatives and then rigidly forces him to adhere to his choice. The child who has chosen to write about Magellan may discover, after a few days, that Cortez is more exciting for him. The teacher's usual reply is, "You chose to write about Magellan, and you must write about Magellan." For open educators, choice implies the individual's posing questions for himself which are important to him and pursuing their solution in his own way. He may choose to write about

Magellan, or he may choose not to write about an explorer at all.

When most teachers give children a choice, they relinquish important control. Having relinquished something of value, they take something back which is important to the child—his freedom to move. Thus, when most teachers give children a choice, it is often accompanied by resentment and even hostility. It is as if the teacher permits the child to choose for pragmatic rather than educational reasons, out of expediency rather than for sound pedagogy. But there appear to be sound pedagogical reasons for permitting children to make some choices:

. . . where [children] felt really free in their choice of activities and problems, there was not only more spontaneous enthusiasm but also more genuine achievement.[29]

It seemed to me in watching that even where they were not playing things "straight" (i.e., *our* way) they were learning a great deal, and learning things that they could not learn when we were in control.[30]

Where there is no significant choice for a child to make, there is no significant observation for a teacher to make.[31]

Many contemporary critics[32] argue that *either* the adult decides *or* the student decides (and then usually end up supporting the latter). But this polarization, this "either us or them" resolution so prevalent today in higher education, must be seen as a reaction to years of authoritarian education. It is an emotional, or perhaps political solution, but not an educational one. In fact, optimal learning for children is impossible if either adults or children have all the "marbles" or if their relationship is construed in these terms. Successful learning depends upon a deliberate and conscious sharing of decisions between child and adult. Both adult and child should have certain responsibilities and exercise certain choices.

Many teachers have found a modified "contract system" a

helpful way to introduce student choice and to share decision making. In these classrooms, children (say, each Monday) are given assignments they must complete that week. These are teacher-imposed, non-negotiable tasks. However, when or where a student chooses to work on these assignments—at school or at home—is for him to determine. When he is not engaged in this teacher-assigned work he may use his time to pursue projects of his own choosing. This system, although highlighting the distinction between work and play, between teacher-set tasks and those the child poses for himself, does release a large amount of time for children to make decisions each week.

In more informal classrooms, the teacher makes choices concerning materials and the environment. The child knows the adult is doing this, but it does not seem to diminish the child's feeling that he is engaged in his own exploration and is pursuing it in his own way and toward his own ends.

Within this context children also make choices. For instance, a child in a classroom rich in manipulative materials might see a pendulum, start to swing it, and wonder how to make it swing faster. After trying a variety of methods, he might wonder *if* he had succeeded in making it swing faster. All these decisions, while perhaps not deliberate or conscious, are legitimate choices the child has made. He has selected a piece of apparatus, posed a problem with respect to it, considered various strategies for solving the problem, chosen a likely means of solving it, implemented his idea, and determined, in the face of the evidence available to him, whether his solution answers his original question. He also chooses when to terminate his investigation and with whom, if anyone, he would like to share his findings.

Because of prevalent child-rearing practices and previous school experiences, many children are not initially equipped with either the inclination or the ability to make this kind of choice. One difficulty for the teacher in the open classroom is the child who may be capable of serious exploration but who does not "get on with it." The child sitting before a pendulum aimlessly fiddling with it is quickly labeled a "time waster," particularly in efficiency-minded America. There seems to be a large amount of wasted time in open classrooms—far more than in traditional classrooms. But children of all ages spend a great deal of their time, both in and out of school, daydreaming, engrossed in their private worlds of fantasy, "wasting time." In the conventional classroom this is easy to camouflage by sitting quietly behind a book or by moving a pencil across a paper, whereas in the open classroom daydreaming means *not* being occupied with materials. In the former case, "wasting time" is all but invisible (although the child may not have anything to hand in at the end of the day); in the latter, "wasting time" is quite visible. But this is not to say that wasting time is a more common occurrence in the open classroom than in most classes.

The one important question for the teacher with a child who appears to be wasting time is, "What does it mean?" Is the child avoiding an anxiety-making situation? Is he consolidating an experience? Is he refueling? Is he watching? A second question is what to do about it—whether to intervene and how. Unless a child appears to be wasting time for an extended period, or unless he is disturbing others, it is probably best to wait and see whether he regains interest before coaxing him on. Wasting time in an environment full of interesting materials with which other children are busily engaged is not self-reinforcing for most children. It would probably help the teacher's restraint in this kind of situation to acknowledge that adults, as well as children, occasionally waste time—and that it's just as unreasonable to expect of children, as of adults, that they always work at their maximum level.

Many children have to work at assuming responsibility for their own behavior. They have to develop confidence and competence in making decisions. They learn to make judgments by making judgments. The teacher can help these children by providing intermediate levels of choice. He might, for instance, attach written questions to pieces of equipment throughout the classroom: to a scale, "How much do you weigh?"; to a pendulum, "How fast can you make it swing?"; to a battery, bulb, and wire, "Can you make it light?" The teacher might ask a child, "Can you weigh this book on that balance?" He might have available several sheets of paper with directions, accompanied by pictures, for solving different problems: for example, building a clay boat, making a leaf print, playing a math game. These intermediate aids lead successively toward the time when each child can pose problems for himself and work independently toward their solution.

Thus, the teacher's role varies from child to child. For some children, he must be very directive; for others, he merely supplies materials; for yet others, he provides only the time and space in which children may explore with their own materials. In all cases, the teacher must recognize that if a child's choice is to be genuine the teacher must accept it and must accept the condition that what is important to the child is important, that each individual is the best judge of what interests him.

The Teacher Encourages Children's Independence

The teacher as facilitator of learning in the open classroom encourages the child's independence and self-reliance. The capacity of the individual to cope with the new is more important than the ability to know and to display the old. It is more important for the child to learn to rely upon his own powers in the long run than to accept adult direction in the short run. Yet children depend upon adults to give meaning, order, control, and security to their experience. Most are still dependent in significant ways when they come to school.

Unfortunately, many adults depend upon children's depending upon them. More than a few teachers find meaning in their work from being needed and depended upon by children. They need children to ask what to do, permission to move about, the correct answer, and "Is it all right if . . . ?" For these teachers, to diminish children's dependence upon them is to threaten their own raison d'être. The child cannot become independent of the teacher until the teacher becomes less needful of the child's constant obedience and affection, until the adult learns that not being *needed* is different from being *superfluous*. The teacher must phase himself out of the dependent relationship which has dominated the learning of the child since birth. This is a particularly selfless job, for not only must the teacher resist the constant, comfortable, and powerful temptation to impart knowledge, but he must also resist the temptation to have children "do as I say." The latter task is most difficult because it often gives comfort to both adult and child.

When a child asks for help, the teacher can encourage independence by asking *himself* a series of difficult questions: "Is this child really asking for help by what he is doing?" "Does this child really need help?" "What will happen if he doesn't get help from me?" "If he needs help, is it in his best interests for *me* to provide it, or can he get it from some other source?" "What sources other than myself can he make use of?" "How *little* help can I give so that the child can sustain his exploration and yet so that I will not interfere?" If these questions are honestly asked, and if each situation is carefully assessed, the teacher will probably often exclude himself from children's experiences. His withdrawal may well have the effect of helping the child find a solution for himself.

The teacher can also encourage the child's independence by helping him to become aware of his behavior, by helping him to analyze his own experiences and to modify them on the basis of previous consequences. By encouraging the child to pose his own problems, solve them, and verify them, by providing situations in which the child can work independently and experience success, the teacher can help the child to become autonomous. Open education stresses the present, not the future; living, not preparing for life; learning now, not anticipating the future. But in the sense that development of self-reliance and independence on the part of the child will be the best assurance that he will be equipped for whatever may come, open education becomes a preparation for the future.

THE TEACHER AS MANAGER OF CHILDREN

In a sense, everything a teacher does in school in some way "facilitates children's learning," or should. We have already discussed several direct means. But the teacher in the open school has less direct, managerial functions which also ultimately enhance children's learning.[33] The phrase "managing children" may appear to contradict much of the foregoing. It need not. A certain amount of management of children by adults, a certain amount of imposed order, structure, and control, is a necessary precondition for independent exploration. Reasonable, consistent restrictions on children's behavior ultimately enable them to be more free and productive. We shall discuss two functions of the teacher as manager of children: the teacher as authority, and the teacher as evaluator.

The Teacher as Authority

Many Americans have "authority hangups." For them the word "authority" is a loaded and pejorative term. A great number of those drawn to the ideas of open education question the right of anyone to set himself above children or to consider himself different in knowledge, discipline, and power. It is useful to repeat a distinction made by Duberman:

A crucial distinction must be made between authority and authoritarianism. The former represents accumulated experience, knowledge and insight. The latter represents their counterfeits: age masquerading as maturity, information as understanding, technique as originality. Authoritarianism is forced to demand the respect that authority draws naturally to itself. The former, like all demands, is likely to meet with hostility; the latter, like all authenticity, with emulation. Our universities—our schools on every level—are rife with authoritarianism, all but devoid of authority.[34]

In Duberman's sense, it is both a legitimate and a necessary role of the adult in the open classroom to be an authority for the children[35]—a source of accumulated experience, knowledge, insight, maturity, leadership, arbitration, strength, judgment, and stability. It is vital to the successful functioning of the open classroom that the teacher be an authority, without becoming an authoritarian. Distinction in the classroom between adult and child can be blurred only up to a point. There is no escaping or hiding the fact that the adult is bigger, stronger, older, and perhaps wiser than the child. But he need not be boss; he need not be arbitrary. The teacher is not one among equals but holds a unique place in constructing and maintaining the learning environment.

The teacher as classroom authority faces the temptation of taking advantage of his special place—to establish and enhance an adult-child power relationship—to become an authoritarian. Forces at work in the school climate press for the establishment of such a superordinate-subordinate relationship, and the teacher must consciously resist these forces if he is to maintain his important place as authority in his daily relations with children and help the children learn to control their own lives. If he can restrain himself from dominating and controlling children's behavior, there is some indication, as William Hull and others have observed, that children will come to be authorities themselves and that they will control their own behavior:

The scene reminded me of an adult audience waiting for the beginning of a concert. When it was time for the assembly to begin, the children, well aware that something was about to happen, stopped talking, though we could not detect the signal to which they were responding . . . perhaps it was merely that everyone had now arrived. I had never before seen a community of young children behaving with such freedom and self-restraint. They demonstrated an awareness about the group and a sensitivity to it, together with an ability to control their own behavior.[36]

The Teacher and the "Problem Child"

A material-centered approach suggests another definition of the "problem child": In most schools the problem child is the one who behaves overtly, who makes noise, gets out of his seat, talks excitedly with other children, and the "good" child is the one who sits docilely and passively in his seat. In the open school, however, the situation may be somewhat the reverse. The "good" child is the one who responds to materials with interest, exploration, talk—the one who behaves openly and overtly. The problem child is the one who, for one reason or another, may not behave openly and overtly. He may be frightened of failure, of ridicule, or of being hurt. In most schools the problem child is "helped" by getting him to contain himself; in the open school this child needs help which will enable him to reveal himself.

What if children behave in ways which are destructive to other children and to equipment; *what if* children, given encouragement and a rich supply of manipulative materials, do not choose to explore? What can the teacher do in this kind of situation, besides shut her eyes and hope they will go away?

There are behavior problems in open classrooms, and the teacher has an important place in handling them. In a dispute between children, for instance, perhaps the most appropriate initial response of the teacher is not to interfere in any way, allowing the children to work out their own form of justice, for in the open classroom, teacher and child share responsibility for general behavior, just as they share in the choice of materi-

als. Children care just as much about disruptions which interfere with their activities as adults do, and they find many ways
of handling disturbances. Nevertheless, there are times when
the teacher must intervene. When a child is behaving in a severely destructive or disturbing way—say, destroying another
student's artwork—the teacher will be very clearly a restrain-
ing influence. In other instances, the class may be asked to
help clarify a problem, and the teacher may gather the children around and discuss the difficulty. Children are usually
willing and able to identify what is bothering them and to suggest ways of coping with it. Usually a meeting of this kind, con-
vened in response to disruptive behavior establishes the fact
that the class recognizes and objects to specific behavior on the
part of a child, thereby putting him on notice that he is disturbing others.

Open schools are not laissez-faire places where anything
goes.[37] The teacher knows and the child knows that an authority is present and that the teacher, no matter how personal and
supportive he may be, is that authority. Teachers believe that
although a child may appear to work for disorder, no child en-
joys disorder. All recognize that unless *someone* is in charge
they will not be able to move freely, explore freely, and choose
freely. In many open classes there are only two rules: (1) no
destroying equipment; and (2) no destroying or interfering
with the work of other children. These rules seem sufficient for
establishing and maintaining a climate in which learning can
flourish.

The authority, in addition to providing situations for setting
rules, has an important place in punishing their infraction. A
teacher may take away from a disruptive child the privilege of
working with materials and with other children until he comes
up with a plan for productive, constructive activity in the
classroom. This is often a very effective sanction, one which
makes more sense in terms of the goal of teaching children to
respect and value learning and human relationships than as-

signing additional math problems or requiring three composi-
tions as a disciplinary measure.

In short, when children are given guidance by the adult authority, in interpersonal relations as well as in their work with
inanimate objects, they can both identify problems and come
up with solutions. Children learn that if they persist in disturbing others or in damaging equipment *something will happen* as
a consequence. If they do not successfully handle disruptions,
by themselves or with the help of the adult, the adult authority
will intervene. Thus, in the classroom the best interests of a
group of individuals are as important as the best interests of a
single individual.

In the eyes of the deviant child, the adult authority may be
seen as an authoritarian and resented as such. Or the deviant
child may run to the authority for help in controlling his behavior. But in either case, in the eyes of the children the
teacher is the authority whose rules they respect and accept,
even if they do not always help to formulate them, for these
rules and this authority permit them the freedom to carry on
their own activities, unobstructed.

The Teacher as Evaluator

The concept of evaluation is as important for the teacher in
the open school as it is for most teachers—and no less complex
and confusing. One central idea differentiates the open educator's concept of evaluation: in the open school, evaluation is
primarily for the benefit of the learner, and only secondarily
for the convenience and benefit of parent, teacher, or administrator. The open teacher does not have a common, predetermined yardstick of academic and personal behavior against
which he compares children, rewarding those who measure up
and punishing those who do not; rather, he keeps detailed records that chronicle children's efforts. With these records he ap-
prizes the child, his parents, and himself of the child's prog-

ress. Folders of children's work may contain samples of writing, math papers, artwork, and materials he has read. The teacher may maintain an additional journal or anecdotal record of each child, containing comments and observations such as his relationship with peers, his preferences, his family . relationships, what he has brought to school, his physical demeanor, and his fears, fantasies, frustrations, joys, etc. When a parent asks "How is my child doing?" the folders are presented as the answer. "This is *what* he's doing. Let's discuss *how* he's doing."

Chronicling a child's behavior and collecting examples of his work removes the teacher from attempting to make categorical and arbitrary judgments about a child's performance. The person reading the folder can make his own judgments. Because most parents are dependent upon grades and symbols in assessing their child's work, teachers must help parents in this evaluation. In addition, the teacher himself can and does make value judgments about children's work, but these are recognized as one person's interpretation. The teacher's role as record keeper, then, is not a clerical, mechanical, and incidental one. It is vital to the child and to his parents that there is something to show for the child's many hours spent in school.

Perhaps one reason many British primary teachers find it easier than their American counterparts to maintain a relaxed approach to evaluation is that their classes often contain children whose ages span several years. Consequently, teachers look at children's development longitudinally—over a three- or even six-year period. What is not apparent today may be apparent tomorrow. What they do not see in a child's performance this year, they may see next. There is less need to worry that a child doesn't have it *now*, or even by the end of the year.[38]

In one way, evaluation is easier in a classroom full of materials. Most children in this kind of environment are behaving *overtly;* the trained eye can "see" what they are doing and can make inferences about what they are thinking. The teacher in such a situation has the unique opportunity to observe children as persons, and as investigators, in context—interacting with materials.[39] The child eagerly building robots out of cardboard, the child trying to balance the weight of a heavier friend on a balance board, the child transferring sand from one container to another—all these children, through their overt behavior, are supplying information which helps the teacher appraise their learning.

But how is the teacher to respond to mistakes by children other than noting and collecting them? How can he reduce their frequency without the red pencil, the D's, E's, and F's, the reproachful note home? Children's incorrect behavior becomes less of a problem for teachers, and to the children, if teachers can realize that for a child the end product is often only one part of the learning experience. Indeed, this is one reason why children begin so many projects but carry so few through to completion:

They enjoyed building for the sheer process of it and accepted its risks; they were not overly concerned about the product they were producing and so could afford to experiment.[40]

To the extent the adult can recognize and share the child's cognitive and emotional investment in his work, *in progress*, he will worry less about incomplete or imperfect products.

John Holt has observed that most children in a game of "20 Questions" groan with disappointment at a "no" answer and delight at a "yes" answer, despite the fact that each conveys equally important information for solving the problem. This example to some extent reflects how children are taught to avoid, hide, and abhor negative judgments by adults or errors in their performance. Schools which constantly identify mistakes and punish children for making them produce devastating effects upon learning. Children come to fear making errors and become afraid of acting at all. Afraid to act openly and spontaneously, they can learn little. The cost, as Hull has put it, is great: "A person who takes few chances will make few mistakes . . . but also few discoveries." [41]

Incorrect behavior on the part of a child may only be a temporary condition, representing a particular level of interest and competence at a particular point in the child's development. Each tentative situation is likely to be revisited by the child many times, and each time he will behave differently, and probably a little more accurately. Adults are inclined to feel that if they don't immediately "catch" every mistake a child makes and correct it, the child will somehow establish, cement, and carry the incorrect behavior with him to his grave. Hein observes that

> One difficulty for many teachers is that they set themselves up as guardians of correct science. Believing in the myth of truth they view it as their duty to enlighten the children and to keep them from error. [42]

The adult must learn to accept and live with a child's errors, with the confidence that his ideas and behavior will change as the consequences of his mistakes become evident to him. We accept children's artwork as tentative expressions of their thinking. Why can't we accept their math and reading in the same spirit? There is no evidence to suggest that a teacher's pointing out and correcting a child's *every* mistake in a written composition, for example, helps the child to write a better composition next time. To the extent that the adult can remove himself from the role of corrector of the child's work and protector of "correct behavior," the child's source of evaluation will become internalized; he will not always be looking to the teacher for rewards, punishments, approval, and corroboration.

When looking at the child's work, the adult can best help

the child to improve his performance by responding selectively to errors. His influence is greatest when he focuses on one or two "mistakes." With a few mistakes in mind, he can point out the difficulty to the child and attempt to explain ways of overcoming it—be it sloppy handwriting or confusion of "ie" and "ei" spelling. The teacher can be even more effective in helping to change behavior by arranging the circumstances so that the "world"—other children, materials, etc.—will convey to the child both the presence of the mistake and the consequences of making it.

Such a teacher will not find it difficult to learn that if a child makes a mistake it is better to suggest another task, which will make the child aware of his mistake, than to put a cross against the result.[43]

If, for instance, a child is reading a poem inaudibly, the teacher can ask him to record his reading on a tape and play it back privately, asking him how it sounds and how he might improve his delivery. If he is building a tower of blocks with a narrow base and it keeps falling over, the teacher can point this out to him and ask him how he might construct the base so it would support the tower.[44]

The teacher's intention as evaluator, then, is not to judge but to reflect back to the child the consequences of his behavior. As judge, the adult's best interests are served: he asserts his power and influence over the child. As facilitator, the child's best interests are served: he becomes aware of his difficulties, the need for improving his performance, and ways of doing so.

SUMMARY

What does the adult in the open school do? What is the role of the teacher? We found in Chapter 1 that open educators' beliefs about children, learning, and knowledge distinguish them

from most other teachers. Behaving in ways which are personally and logically consonant with these beliefs leads to a teaching role which is also distinctive from that prevalent in traditional education. Stated very simply, the role of the teacher in
an open school is to facilitate learning—to provide conditions
which will encourage children to learn for themselves and to
fulfill themselves, personally, socially, and intellectually. The
teacher is not responsible for passing on to children his own
knowledge or someone else's knowledge; instead he helps each
student to find truths inherent in his experiences and to evaluate and revise these tentative truths in the light of subsequent
experiences. The child has both the right and the competence
to make important decisions about his own learning; the
teacher has the responsibility of helping him to do so.

The distinction between facilitating learning and interfering
with learning is difficult to make. It would be comfortable if
we could neatly list the behaviors of the "facilitator of learning," on the one hand, and characteristics of one who interferes with learning, on the other. But this is impossible. What
facilitates one child's learning—a new piece of apparatus or a
suggestion from the teacher—may curtail another child's.
What stifles one child—a curt response—may be just what is
needed to encourage another. A style or behavior which is
comfortable and successful for one teacher may be awkward
for another.

We can, nevertheless, make certain generalizations: The
teacher who interferes with children's learning is one who has
not resolved a need to impart knowledge, one who sees the
child's behavior in terms of adult lenses, yardsticks, and expectations, one who has erected performance goals for a child,
with predetermined paths and time schedules leading toward
those goals. The teacher who interferes is one who lets his own
personal needs for importance, gratification, and recognition
prevail over the child's needs to explore the world and find his
own self and his own knowledge. He is one who establishes

and maintains superordinate-subordinate relationships and demands that children respond to *him.*

The facilitator of learning must be, above all, a secure person. Being secure, he has the ability to restrain himself from prematurely closing a child's exploration by "giving the answer." He doesn't need to solicit the attention, admiration, and respect of his students. He finds joy, excitement, and meaning in observing children discover ideas for themselves and takes pride in how little he needs to do to help initiate and sustain a child's exploration and learning. He sees more importance in responding helpfully to children than having them respond to him. In this sense, he is willing to be the *dependent* variable in the learning process, rather than the *independent* variable.

Implicit in all the activities of the adult in the classroom discussed in this chapter is a role as "ad hoc responder." The adult is available and accessible. He constantly scans the horizon of children's interactions, with materials and with one another, for situations when a response, an appropriate intervention, will contribute to a child's learning. As an ad hoc responder with abundant personal, intellectual, emotional, and physical resources and experience, the adult in the open classroom respects children as individuals, manages their environment, provides materials, encourages activity, provides direct instruction, expands and consolidates children's experiences through language, and encourages their independence. In the words of one open educator:

A teacher of young children is, in a sense, a *travel agent.* He helps a child go where the child wants to go. He counsels on the best way of getting there.[45]

3

Romance and Reality: A Case Study

The tasks of social change are tasks for the tough-minded and competent. Those who come to the task with the currently fashionable mixture of passion and incompetence only add to the confusion.

—John W. Gardner
Godkin Lectures
Harvard University, 1969

We have discussed some important assumptions about learning and knowledge held by open educators, and we have discussed a role of the adult in the open classroom consonant with these assumptions. But theoretical and hypothetical talk has little significance for American public education until translated into action. What happens when the words and ideas of open education enter the arena of public schools? What happens when the practices of open education confront the expectations of children, parents and administrators? In this chapter we shall describe and analyze an attempt by seven educators to set up open classrooms in an urban public school setting.

Over a thousand administrators, teachers, parents, and children participated in the first year of the Lincoln-Attucks Program. If asked, each would recall and emphasize different elements. This chapter represents my own perception of the experience. A thorough analysis of a real program like this one is extraordinarily difficult; that's why experimenters do experiments. So many variables intertwine, people act with such diverse, simultaneous motivations, that it is virtually impossible to untangle them. The best an investigator can do in such a situation is to isolate and describe the salient factors affecting a given event, even if different and contradictory variables seem to control events which precede or follow. This has been my attempt here. Thus, administrators and parents may appear to be stubborn reactionaries at one point in the narrative, and hard-thinking realists at another. Thus, the six open classroom teachers may emerge sometimes as creative, committed educators and sometimes as tactless, less-than-competent neophytes. Both were both.

BACKGROUND

In the spring of 1968 I was offered a position as instructional principal of two public elementary schools. The schools were part of a new program which sought to enlist the resources of a foundation, a university, and a large public school system with the hope of bringing both order and quality education to inner-city youngsters.

I was not the only person hired because of my interest in open education. Because several teaching positions in the program were also unfilled, an official of the public school system suggested that I ". . . encourage some teachers around Cambridge or in England to apply for positions in the subunit. . . ." Two months later, I accepted the position and recommended six others for teaching positions. All six were hired, and they shared with me (hereafter referred to as the instructional coordinator) a commitment to open education.

The new instructional coordinator and the six teachers had a great deal more in common than educational philosophy. All were young (their average age was 24), and all were white. They had little teaching experience, and that had been in suburban schools. Only one had spent a year teaching in an inner-city school. They had all graduated from outstanding liberal arts colleges: Amherst, Barnard, Chicago, Harvard, Princeton, Swarthmore, and Wesleyan. All held graduate degrees from a prominent graduate school of education (two Ed.M. in elementary education; one Ed.D. in science education) or were candidates for degrees (one Ed.D. in Curriculum and Supervision; one Ed.M. in Guidance; one M.A.T. in Reading; and one M.A.T. in Social Studies). The instructional coordinator was the "resident supervisor" for the latter three, all of whom were in their year of internship.

These seven young educators entered the project well aware that there would be great difficulties: aware of being young, white, inexperienced, liberal, and from out of town in a world of older, mostly conservative, and cautious adults. Despite these ominous conditions, the five men and two women were buoyed by the Director's support for their ideas; by the instructional coordinator's position as leader in curriculum, teacher training, and classroom supervision; and by what looked like an excellent opportunity to put their ideas into practice in an urban public school setting. As one of them put it, "All the lights lit up!" All the ingredients were there: buildings, children, money, able people, and assistance from a major university and from the educational bureaucracy. Each looked forward to participating in the development of an important educational alternative within the public schools. All were hopeful and confident, and agreed not only to sign a year's contract but to work beyond the initial year of the program as well. Although short on experience, they were long on ability, energy, confidence, and idealism. They dared believe radically different things about children, learning, and knowledge; they were now prepared to act on their beliefs.

September: the first week of school, a classroom of one of the six proponents of open education, not unlike those of the other five:

Desks arranged in clusters of four or five; no names on desks; children choose where to sit
Cardboard furniture, tables, boxes, shelves (all made by the teacher) arranged into interest areas where children are engaged in a variety of activities with a good deal of excitement and noise:
    Painting
    Leatherwork
    Looking at picture books
    Making things out of yarn
    Making things out of clay
    Watching and handling rabbits, gerbils
    Watching fish in the aquarium
Teacher's desk placed at the back of the room; teacher moving from activity to activity and from child to child, offering encouragement but also keeping children under control
Teacher is smiling, kind, soft-spoken
Children leave the room freely to go to the bathroom or to the water fountain whenever they wish
At times the teacher organizes more directed activities such as math games, blocks, puzzles, etc., or reading periods on an individualized basis, using mostly library books, few texts
Little or no homework given, unless a child chooses to bring home unfinished work or a book of interest
Variety of interesting activities available for children who are finished

December: three months later (and, by and large, for the remainder of the year), the same classroom, again not unlike those of the other five open educators:

Desks arranged in four rows with six to a row; each child assigned to and sitting at a desk with his name on it
Most of cardboard furniture gone
No animals

No evidence of leather, yarn, paints, clay

Teacher's desk dominates front of the room, from which a vast number of dittoed sheets are dispensed

Teacher does not smile in an hour's time, but directs and reprimands children, often yelling at them in what appears to be almost continuous anger

Bathroom pass required to go to the lavatory

Teacher's permission required to go to the water fountain

Children divided into ability groups for math, working silently in their seats on worksheets, workbooks, and textbooks

Children divided into three reading groups, each of which uses a different-level basal text, all well below grade level

Homework assigned each night in math and reading

What happened? The changes in these classrooms which took place over three months were major ones and, from the point of view of open educators, regressive. What caused these teachers to move so dramatically away from the open education model to which they were initially committed toward the more traditional transmission-of-knowledge model? In the answer to this question lies identification of important sources of resistance not only to open education but, more generally, to educational change itself.

Problems of educational change are often equated with problems of teacher change: "If only we could find or train teachers who care about children, who are not afraid to try something new. . . ." These six teachers and the instructional coordinator cared about children and wanted to try something new. They were not only predisposed to change but predisposed to a particular kind of change. This common goal should have made their efforts even more powerful and effective. The resistance encountered in attempting to implement open classrooms was, then, clearly not limited to teachers. The dramatic turnabout in these classrooms between September and December involved all parties to the educational enterprise: children, parents, teachers, and administrators. This chapter will follow the efforts of the seven young educators and thereby attempt to identify and analyze major sources and forms of resistance to change in the direction of open education. We shall begin by describing the Program and then consider the difficulties encountered by the open educators. Chapters 4 and 5, in turn, will speculate on possible ways of overcoming these difficulties.

THE PROGRAM

City, like many other middle-sized communities in the United States, has a population mix of white Catholics and Protestants, Jews, and Blacks. The large nearby university has attempted to help the City with some of its problems, not always successfully, and is regarded by City residents with mixed feelings. Federal funds have supported a number of urban renewal projects, some of which have been resisted by the neighborhoods affected.

Many aspects of the public schools look good. The average class size in the thirty-five elementary schools and the three middle schools is 23; in the three high schools, 21. The average annual expenditure per pupil is high in a state of many wealthy suburban communities. Beginning teachers with an A.B. earn $7,400, tenth in the state. School buildings, by and large, are new and adequate to accommodate the 20,000 students who attend them.

But here, as in other cities, the output is not commensurate with the input. Over a thousand students are suspended from school each year; in addition, as many as two hundred are "homebound" at any one time (i.e., sent home on a more or less permanent basis for emotional, disciplinary, or social reasons). Relations between the city's racial, social, educational, and economic groups are not harmonious. "Disturbances," common on the streets, spill over into the schools (particularly the middle and high schools which are deliberately integrated).

Consequently, more and more children are being removed from the public schools and enrolled in private and parochial schools or bussed to the suburbs. At the end of the previous school year, the mayor, the superintendent of schools, and the principals of the city's three high schools had all resigned.

In short, the problems of these schools and children are the problems of urban education and of so-called "deprived" children everywhere: difficulty in reading, writing, and speaking the English language; poor conceptual ability; limited capacity for social interaction; and negative self-concept. And here, too, the existing mixture of money and people does not seem to be adequate to bring order to its schools—let alone education, let alone quality education.

The Lincoln-Attucks Program was the first major attempt to combine private foundation support with the resources of a university to augment the usual offerings of the public school system:

[The Program] is designed to bring a broad range of concentrated services to its students. A high priority is being given to close alliance between parents and teachers and to developing methods of continuous cooperation of parents and teachers. . . . The focus of the program will be on basic skills, healthy self concept and student motivation.[1]

The University Center, a small prestigious group within the university, whose work in child development made staff members acutely aware of the need for change in formal education, had been involved before in the local public school system, offering

. . . indirect services to children through direct service to teachers and other school personnel. . . . Work with teachers included different approaches . . . observation in classrooms, seminars on child behavior, small group and individual teacher conferences.[2]

But university and city officials felt that

. . . participation as an integral part of the school program, with an expanded staff on an expanded time basis, could make the collaboration more beneficial.

The sponsoring foundation then "suggested that a proposal for a joint program between the University Center and a subsystem of the total school system be developed and submitted." This was done, and the foundation agreed to participate in a three-way collaboration on behalf of two inner-city elementary schools: the foundation would provide $100,000 to the city schools each year for five years and a lump sum of $500,000 to the University Center; the public school system would provide the services and funds customarily available to elementary schools, plus about $180,000 in Title I funds the first year; the university would use the $500,000 from the foundation to recruit and pay for several additions to its staff, who would work full time in the Program.

Two adjacent elementary schools were selected: Lincoln and Attucks. Underlying the remarkable concentration of resources upon these two schools, whose combined enrollment was less than 600 children, was a single major assumption, stimulated by guidelines in the U.S. Office of Education's Title I grants: because the problems of inner-city children are great, the resources necessary to solve them must be of a similar magnitude.

No good purpose is served if projects are spread so thinly over so many educationally deprived children that there is no possibility of significant and permanent advantage to any. The guidelines call for a "massive effort concentrated on fewer children," thus improving chances of achieving substantial gains.[3]

Thus when city administrators had to choose between spreading meager supplementary funds over 20,000 students or directing a heavy concentration on a few, they took the latter course. They believed that this was the only way to find a solution to the problems of urban education; when a solution was found, *then* they could apply it throughout the district.

City schools are hungry for success; indeed, they are desperate for success. On this foundation-university-city program, a great deal was riding. The foundation wanted to place its resources in a critical situation, where the likelihood of success was great and the prospect for dissemination high. University Center needed to relieve growing, often hostile pressures from within (students) and from without (community) by becoming significantly, helpfully, and quickly involved in problems of the surrounding inner city. It hoped for fuller faculty integration and wanted to make use of the problems and possibilities of the city for research, teaching, and community service. The public school system wanted to move rapidly enough to reduce the possibility of alienating the black community and to develop ideas and practices which would restore confidence in the school system. All hoped that the Lincoln-Attucks Program would ". . . be evaluated and become useful to other sectors of the university, the community, and public schools throughout the nation."

In addition to these largely unstated goals, there were publicly stated general objectives for the Program:

1. To increase our understanding of the respective roles—and their interaction—of school, home, and community in individual child development and learning
2. To permit parents, teachers, and administrators to evolve better patterns of education
3. To enrich curriculum and provide the special services necessary for quality education for all children
4. To develop instructional programs and practices flexible enough to strengthen the assets and remedy the needs of a diverse range of pupils

5. To improve the relationship between the pupils and their teachers, parents, and community

Specific objectives were:

1. To improve the students' self-respect, identity, and self-confidence
2. To improve the basic skills of the students
3. To develop patterns of shared responsibility and decisionmaking among the parents, the staff, and the students[4]

These and other goals for the Program, although providing little more than a vague echo of the ordinary rhetoric of every school in the country, were legitimate ends. The information omitted from all proposals, publicity, and rhetoric, however, was far more crucial. No one mentioned *means*, the operational specifications to be employed in achieving the goals. There was no administrative model or pedagogical theory, no talk of team teaching, nongrading, open education, programmed instruction, or new curricula because

. . . no one fully understood the problems of providing quality education in city schools. . . . Thus it was decided [at the outset] that no specific intervention or method would be introduced during an introductory period. It was felt that it would take about a year of observation and appraisal before a clear-cut indication of program direction would be apparent.[5]

This program has been initiated with no specific model to follow. It brings together a richness of resources which in interaction can generate a model.[6]

In place of clearly thought out ideas and plans for achieving the stated educational goals, a much more difficult task than their formulation, it was decided that

What has been missing as a response to the problem of providing quality education has been, in most cases, a systematic appraisal of every aspect of the school program as well as a systematic appraisal of the needs of the children. Such an appraisal is necessary to identify the critical obstacles to education in order to establish appropriate priorities and programs. The purpose of the Lincoln-Attucks Project is to be the systematic appraisal indicated and to make modifications and adjustments based on these findings.[7]

In short, unknown to most, the "game plan" for the Program was to study the problems thoroughly, for a year at least, before making any major attempts to rectify them, and before determining *how* to rectify them. Thus from its very outset, the Program was an administrative, financial, and academic shell with no philosophy and with no stated direction. The situation was not unlike setting out from England for the New World, knowing in which general direction it lay, making copious observations along the way, but waiting until reaching mid-ocean before determining the course and the nature of the vessels.

The absence of any pedagogical plan led to crippling problems. Three major factors caused most of the difficulties: selection of schools, haphazard choice of staff, and lack of administrative organization and leadership. Because each of these problems was to have a profound influence upon the efforts of the seven open educators, it is important to explore them.

THE SCHOOLS

Lincoln School was constructed in 1928, and for many years it served an Italian neighborhood with a K–6 parochial-public education. When large numbers of blacks began to migrate to the city, the Italians moved to more desirable sections and to the surrounding suburbs. The school became increasingly poor and gained the incorrect reputation of being a school for disturbed children. The neighborhood is now largely black and poor, and many individuals and families there are sustained by welfare.

With the loss of its middle-class population, the Lincoln School became a convenient dumping ground for old teachers, inexperienced teachers, misfits who could not be fired, alcoholic custodians, administrators whose productive years either had not yet come or had long since gone, and troubled, troublesome children. The year before the Program began, according to one teacher, the staff consisted of

Twelve teachers; of the twelve: eight concerned, one indifferent, three viciously cruel; nine experienced, three first-year; three intelligent and effective, nine dull and ineffectual; six believed children could learn, six did not; four in their twenties, four middle-aged, four near retirement; four Negro, eight white. . . .

Four classes held in tight restrictive discipline, six fairly democratic in spite of punishment by ruler, two chaotic. Both first-grade teachers very destructive; children (often seen standing outside classroom doors for hours rigid and weeping) were insulted and degraded.

Discipline maintained inside classes by: ruler (6); threats of beating, extra work or detention (3); reasoning (3).

Air of aimlessness, hopelessness and fear in the majority of children (large number seriously disturbed, continuously disruptive).

The little parental involvement which existed was negative. Mothers were conditioned by their own experiences in frightening, authoritarian schools and by their visits to Lincoln at the summons of the principal to chastise their children, take them home, or hear lectures on their offsprings' bad behavior.

This situation could exist in the 1940's, the 1950's, and even in the early 1960's; but in the late 1960's it was volatile. Objec-

tions of militant parents were reaching threatening proportions, and something had to be done. Because the combined
efforts of the foundation–university–public school system
seemed to offer the resources necessary for rapid, significant
change, Lincoln was immediately chosen for inclusion in the
subunit. Other factors supported the choice: it was the elementary school in the city with the highest concentration of
black students (96.7%); it was relatively small (255 pupils); its
teachers were mostly nontenured substitutes who could be dismissed easily without raising the wrath of the teacher's union.

Lincoln parents responded to incorporation of their school
in the new program with hostility, suspicion, and fear. At early
meetings they asked, "Do we have a choice to be in this program?" "Will it affect all of our children?" "Why would anyone good come to work in these schools?" "Why would anyone
want to stay more than a year?" "Will noncertified teachers
and aides be teaching our children?" "Is the University Center
going to experiment on our children?" "Why are *we* getting
this program . . . because our children are culturally deprived?" "Are we going to be able to talk with teachers?"
"Can our present principal stay on next year?" "What about a
hot lunch program?" "Who do I talk to about my child's problems?" "Will my child have to be in a split (e.g., combination
3–4 grade) class?"

The Lincoln parents were soon given further basis for their
suspicion and hostility. They were told by a representative
of the public school system that they must be included in the
Program, that the decision had already been made "downtown." Only two of the twelve teachers from the previous year
were invited to stay on in the new program. One black
woman, who had been a very successful teacher of children
with learning difficulties and who was one of the few people in
whom parents had confidence, applied for the position of instructional coordinator for the two schools and was turned
down in favor of a young, white, inexperienced (in inner city

schools) educator from out of town. The white principal of the previous year at Lincoln had applied for the position of administrative coordinator, but was rejected in favor of Attucks' principal. In short, no teachers or staff from Lincoln were placed in positions of central responsibility and decisionmaking in the Program. Thus, it was not surprising that before Lincoln School opened in September under the new program ". . . anti-program people were at work in the community preparing parents and kids to be as unreceptive as possible. . . ."

Attucks School, on the other hand, was in a working-class community, consisted of grades K–4, and had a very short history. It was selected for inclusion in the new program because it was only a mile from Lincoln; its new building appeared to offer a new start unencumbered by traditional people and practices; it was small but had the second-highest concentration of blacks in the city (96.3%); and the majority of parents were receptive to the plan.

Attucks was so new that some doubted construction would be completed by the opening of school in September, even though its completion had been promised two years earlier. During the preceding year, while the school was still being constructed, 170 children largely from black working-class families had been bussed several miles to a suburban temple, leased for the year. There, removed from the neighborhood and from normal channels of communication with parents, a group of young teachers and their principal had what parents, teachers, and children considered to be a "great" year. Teachers had a good deal of autonomy and responded with initiative and responsibility. They visited children's homes, worked hard, and enjoyed high morale. The children, in turn, also worked hard and were pleased with both the school and themselves. Parents were confident that the children were learning.

Unlike the Lincoln parents, those at Attucks jumped at the chance to participate in the new program. Good things had been happening to their children; and with a new school, more money, and more people, things could only get better. Their confidence in this decision was soon buoyed. In early May those teachers from the previous year's staff who wanted to join the new program (two blacks, three whites) were hired; in June their principal was offered the position of administrative coordinator of both schools.

When, by midsummer, it had become apparent that the rate of construction on the new building was not sufficient for its completion in September, the PTA president organized a parade (not a protest march) around the building, in which parents, children, teachers, and administrators participated, singing "We Shall Overcome" as they walked. The parade and its subsequent publicity prodded the mayor's office to prod the contractor to prod the construction unions to accelerate the work. Perhaps more important, it further unified the parents in support of what they already saw to be *their* school and *their* program. There was a common enemy—the unresponsive bureaucracy—and parent, child, teacher, and administrator allied to defeat it. On the opening day of school the building was ready (enough) for occupancy, and the parents and children were ready for the new school year.

The contrast between Attucks and Lincoln was marked, so marked that it raises the question of how these two schools could have been selected for a project which depended so completely for its success upon close cooperation. One was K–6, one K–4; one in a lower-class ghetto, one in a working-class community; one conditioned by many years of failure, one by a year of success; one was an old brick hulk surrounded by a moat of broken glass, one was a shiny new building; one was taking part in the Program under duress, one had chosen to participate.

Had the Lincoln-Attucks Program been planned with a rationale and clearly thought-out operational specifications, the choice of schools would have been more ordered and directed.

In the absence of such a rationale, the choice of schools was directed by expediency, and then a rhetoric was imposed: "The two schools, teachers, and parents will work together in every way, and cooperate fully as equal partners in the Program." But significant difficulties and incompatibilities can be neither hidden nor resolved by rhetoric.

The choice of these two schools raises an important question: when attempting to remedy a pervasive problem, when trying something new, is it better to select the *worst* possible setting, which makes the project less likely to succeed but offers greater power to transfer to other less aggravated situations, or to select a bad, but more hopeful, situation which offers a higher possibility of success, although less transferability? Whatever the answer, these schools were not well matched with each other or with the intentions of the Program. One choice was as good or as bad as the next because the Program had few apparent clear intentions.

Trying to initiate the new program by combining these two small schools made a precarious situation more precarious. One larger school might well have been better. It was doubly difficult to try and impose cooperation upon two very *different* schools, divided territorially, socially, and economically. It was triply difficult to select two small and different schools each of which was in an *unstable* condition: Lincoln, because its bad past was catching up with it; Attucks, because it was new and had *no* past. Thus, from the beginning, the selection of these two schools injected a divisive force into the Program. In this situation, the initial reception for the seven open educators was both predictable and understandable.

THE STAFF

Just as choice of appropriate schools could not intelligently be made without knowing the nature of the new program, neither could choice of appropriate personnel. With no thoughtful content for the Program, there could be no thoughtful criteria for selecting the staff for the Program.

Rather than clarifying these ambiguities, no one confronted them. If, for instance, as the foundation proposal suggested, the content of the Program was to materialize slowly, as successful ways for helping children were found, the staff should have been hired gradually as need for appropriate personnel became evident. Instead, everyone was hired at once—perhaps because of the considerable funds available, perhaps because of the excitement and expectations generated among various groups, perhaps because of the rare opportunity to do something significant in an urban community, but, more likely, because the person responsible for the hiring believed that great problems could be solved sooner by addressing great numbers of people to them sooner. Consequently, he attempted to fill the stable immediately with the best, strongest, and most able horses he could find, apparently disregarding what function they would fulfill, their ability to pull together, or their sense of direction.

Those hired had displayed competence elsewhere in a variety of endeavors and situations related to elementary education; but there, all similarity ended. Among the new staff members were a highly regarded professor of education from an urban university whose orientation was academic, analytical, and content-centered and toward the cognitive development of children; a psychologist whose primary concern was to provide children with external structure and thereby the security to learn; a child-centered psychologist whose orientation was interpersonal, supportive, and facilitative; an administrator whose orientation was providing children with materials, experiences, and the confidence which would help them become instrumental over their environment; an administrator whose orientation was to maintain a balance of power necessary to run a "smooth" school.

Staff members were selected for positions of responsibility in the new program whose perceptions of the situation were different, whose diagnoses were different, and whose prognoses for solution were different. But this was not the only problem. Somehow, in the course of being interviewed and hired, each was led to believe not only that he would have an important place in the new program but that *his* values, *his* orientation, and *his* strategies for change were uniquely valuable and appropriate for this inner-city situation. Each was led to believe that he had been singled out for inclusion in the Program *because* he believed what he did and *because* his values were consonant with the broader plans of the Program.

Thus, from the beginning, each staff member thought he was "right," each was prepared to convince doubters that he was "right," and each expected the top leadership in the Program to support him in these efforts. With this kind of loading, it was inevitable that others not similarly inclined would be viewed not as differing but as obstructing, thwarting, and defying.

Those hired by the public school system were an instructional principal and an administrative principal; two assistants to the principals; two curriculum resource teachers; two reading teachers; twenty-five classroom teachers; fifteen teacher aides; and two community relations workers. A full-time nurse and part-time pediatrician were provided for in the budget but never hired. Itinerant art and physical education teachers were also provided through the regular services of the public schools.

This Lincoln-Attucks staff was considerably larger than these schools had ever seen before. Before the Program began, thirty people worked in the two schools: twenty-five teachers, two principals, one community relations worker, and two teacher aides. Under the new program, the number of adults working full- or nearly full-time increased to 54, or almost double. In fact, 55 percent ($50,000) of the total foundation and ESEA funds was budgeted for this *additional* staff.

The University Center staff working in the Program consisted of a psychiatrist–team leader; a social worker; a psychological examiner–learning diagnostician; a curriculum consultant–evaluator; a resource person for primary grade teachers and "chronicler"; and an evaluator.

Thus, a very large staff immediately distinguished the two schools from others in the city, and this was seen as the primary method both for maintaining and observing the schools during the "introductory period":

The primary innovation in the program is the availability of support personnel to help improve the school experience for the majority of the students. . . . Sufficient staff and time would be necessary to, first, provide basic education and supporting services and, second, to evaluate, plan and study methods to improve skills necessary to diagnose learning problems, teaching and service delivery methods.[8]

But size alone does not produce an effective staff. In fact, size without coherence tends to produce an unwieldy group, likely to suffer from overlapping responsibilities and treading on toes. In this case, the whole was clearly less than the sum of its parts. Coherence was lacking, and staff polarization was assured from the outset: young/old; black/white; those from out of town/those from the city; University Center/teacher-graduates from the school of education; experienced/inexperienced; administrators/teachers; school people/university people; traditional educators/open educators; liberal/conservative; professional/paraprofessional. These tensions were aggravated even more by the absence of any clear policy on educational philosophy or methods and the lack of a clear job description for each of the twenty-five nonteaching adults.

This high-powered staff represented different, often mutually exclusive, assumptions about children, learning, and knowledge; diverse techniques for solving the problems of these particular inner-city schools; and personalities and educational values which coincided by chance, if at all. A variety of firmly held, intrinsically contradictory educational beliefs were off and running. With no overall policy or strong authority to rein them in, there was a clear field for incompatibility, dissonance, and conflict.

ADMINISTRATIVE ORGANIZATION

The third major source of difficulty within the Program was the lack of administrative organization and leadership. The decisionmaking structure of the Program put forth in the original proposal was fairly simple, even plausible: instead of having a different principal in each of the two schools who would be responsible for both administrative and instructional duties, it was decided that one principal would be responsible for all administrative duties in *both* schools. He would handle budgets, buses, schedules, meetings, etc. The other principal would be concerned with instructional matters in both schools, providing leadership in curriculum, teacher training, and classroom observation. The planners believed that separating the administrative and instructional duties in this way would make each principal more effective and efficient. Because no blacks applied who were both certified and qualified for the positions of administrative and instructional coordinators, it was decided that a black would be appointed in each school as a kind of "building leader," who, unlike the coordinators, would be permanently stationed at each of the two schools to handle the "day-to-day" decisionmaking. Each of these building leaders was given the title "assistant to the principals."

In addition to the coordinators and the building leaders, several curriculum specialists were available to help the teachers in an unspecified manner, and the University Center team was to provide supporting services to the school personnel at their request. The Director from the public schools was ". . . supposed to disappear into the woodwork once the program became operational."

This allocation of responsibilities seemed feasible, or at least feasible enough for everyone involved to sign his contract. It was not until decisions had to be made, until the Program was called upon to act, that the viability of this organizational model was tested—and broke down. "School didn't open, it exploded."

The enrollment at Lincoln the previous year had been 255; at Attucks, 170. A similar enrollment was expected at the opening of the Program in September. On the first day of school, however, 310 children appeared at Lincoln and 200 at Attucks, all looking for a place to go. Although there was no open-enrollment policy in the city, it seemed that parents from all over town had sent children to "reside" with uncles, aunts, and friends in the Program's neighborhoods. A disproportionate number of these new arrivals brought with them very unsuccessful records from other schools. Apparently word had gotten around the city that an enormous number of able people, including University Center faculty, were available at Lincoln and Attucks to help even the most disturbed children. It was also suspected, perhaps unfairly, that some of these children were being enrolled in the schools as a means of undermining the new program.

For whatever reasons the children came, many problems were caused by the unexpected influx, each requiring immediate attention. One observer recalled:

Some teachers were wild-eyed, children ran everywhere (looking happier than I'd ever seen them before). The new children lined the corridors waiting to be registered and assigned. They were delivered to teachers as fast as possible even though there often was no place for them to sit down. Supplies and equipment had not been delivered. One third-grade teacher (his first year in the classroom) had thirty-eight children, fewer desks, and almost nothing to read, write on or with.

Into which classrooms would these children be placed? What should be the class size? Where would new classrooms be set up, and who would teach them? What would the room assignments be? Who was to discipline the disruptive children and how? When would books, crayons, and other essential supplies, ordered months before, arrive? (There was evidence that administrators in other schools and downtown, not having been included in the Lincoln-Attucks windfall, moved a little more slowly than usual in helping the Program.) What would teachers and children do in the meantime? Decisions had to be made, and made quickly.

At first all those involved acted *as if* things were going the way they expected and wanted, regardless of evidence to the contrary. Everyone made decisions at once. At Lincoln, the building leader made room assignments, the instructional coordinator made room assignments, the Director made room assignments, and the teachers decided among themselves what their room assignments would be. The administrative coordinator, the instructional coordinator, the curriculum resource teacher, and the Director all assumed responsibility for getting necessary supplies from downtown. One teacher in distress with her class had eleven administrators descend on her the first day to "help." Another noted that

Organizational and administrative confusion was great; no one seemed to know who was responsible for what; teachers were patient, waiting for order. . . . The change from enthusiastic vitality to haggard confusion was instant and awesome.

Because each decision was resolved in several different ways, administrators, teachers, parents, and children quickly began to ask a reasonable, pressing question: "Who's in charge here?" Everyone was, and no one was. No one knew. The anxiety, particularly on the part of the teachers, who had twenty-five children to tend to, approached near-panic proportions. As one teacher reported, "For two days people fought, engaged in petty intrigues, and bickered until I and several others came close to losing our minds."

Battle lines formed: administrator against administrator; administrator against teacher; parents against administrators, teachers, and one another. In this state of tension, insecurity, and exhaustion (the staff was paid to work overtime five hours a week) everyone reverted to familiar alliances: University Center people met with University people at the University; blacks met with blacks; whites met with whites; and the open educators, who had been trying to dissolve themselves as a unit, regrouped. The tentative trust which for a short time had existed between individuals of diverse backgrounds gave way to intense suspicion.

Teachers, wanting inclusion in decisionmaking and respect for their ideas, were rejected and excluded. They became angry, disappointed, and disrespectful. They withdrew from the administrators, not talking, not supporting, not attending meetings. Administrators wanting and expecting respect and obedience got neither. They, in turn, were excluded from classrooms. Angry outbursts were the order of the day, and no one was immune from their crippling, demoralizing effects.

The long-awaited improvement in services for children was in jeopardy. As the situation grew worse, the likelihood of intervention from the press, the university, the foundation, the superintendent, parents, and militant black groups increased. The senior administrator of the program and the director of the University Center team, fearing a public debacle, assumed not only de facto but also public decisionmaking responsibility, announcing that henceforth they were "codirectors" of the Lincoln-Attucks Program, positions quite unheralded in the original proposals. But removing all veil of a democratic deci-sionmaking structure hardly improved matters. Because no plan existed which could provide direction and a rationale for their decisions, because they couldn't agree where they were going, the new codirectors could only attempt to minimize dis-sonance as it arose. This was a defensive and dependent orien-tation, one hardly capable of conveying confidence in leader-ship, let alone of anticipating subsequent problems.

For the remainder of the year, the codirectors tried one ad-ministrative plan, tactic, or idea after another. As each proved unworkable or prompted too-heated resistance, another was ready to take its place. But resolving conflict is never easy; and here it was virtually impossible. Teachers and parents pressed the codirectors to determine "zones of responsibility." One re-port from parents had ". . . felt it advisable to have the posi-tion of each administrator clearly defined so the teachers and parents will clearly understand the duties of each." Was the supervision of teachers, for instance, the proper domain of the building leader, the administrative coordinator, the instruc-tional coordinator, the curriculum resource people, or the Uni-versity Center team? Each of the dozen nonteaching adults in the Program had been led to believe or had come to expect that his piece of the pie was bigger than it was or, indeed, *could* be. For every important issue, the sum of the pieces far exceeded the whole.

Each plan to assign responsibilities inevitably annexed what someone felt was his rightful territory. Every important admin-istrative concern became an area for friction and open conflict. Each administrator .feared becoming superfluous and asked himself, "Am I important?" With three or four others doing the same job, the answer had to be "no." Thus, administrators increasingly saw each other not as colleagues but as competi-tors for what seemed to be a constantly shrinking turf, as threats to one another's personal and professional security.

When the establishment of "zones of responsibility" did not

work, the codirectors attempted to make the various horses tractable by harnessing them together, into committees. One committee had already been set up by the codirectors before the year began. The Program Steering Committee was an attempt to enlist constructive support of the parents and give them the promised "significant involvement" in the Program. In the hopes of unifying the two schools, members were chosen from each: two parents, two PTA chairmen, two teachers, the building leaders, plus a union representative and the codirectors. The Program Steering Committee was important because it facilitated parent-school cooperation; it was distinguished by its consistency and longevity in a situation fraught with day-to-day reversals.

The "administration committee," another creation, was to meet every few days, make decisions, and allocate responsibilities. But if "a camel is a horse designed by a committee," what is a school run this way? This committee provided little more than a regular forum for administrators to vent hostility. Paralysis continued. Parents and teachers still needed to know, as they put it, "where the buck stops." "With a committee" was not an acceptable answer. "Who's the principal principal?" became the central question. The instructional coordinator? The administrative coordinator? The building leaders? The codirectors?

Under growing pressure from all quarters, the codirectors decided to move the administrative coordinator to Lincoln to be the principal there and the instructional coordinator to be the principal at Attucks. This arrangement proved to be short-lived, however, for during the month-long power struggle, parents at Lincoln had reached some conclusions of their own:

We are . . . very concerned with the administrative policy presently being used, because we feel that it is too confusing and also unfair to require Mrs. Leader [the building leader] to serve as assistant principal to both a principal of administration and a principal of education curriculum. With her high qualifications and capabilities we feel that the present policy is totally unwarranted and feel that Mrs. Leader should be appointed immediately as principal at Lincoln School. It is our feeling that her vast understanding of our children's needs will prove a tremendous asset to the program achieving its goal, and also to the inevitable success that we know the program will be at the school. Therefore, we are asking that your immediate attention be directed to this very serious and grave problem, and would appreciate hearing from you at your earliest convenience.

Because Mrs. Leader offered at least the possibility of increasing order and productivity at Lincoln, she was appointed "acting principal," with the official appointment subject to the usual "posting" of the position and evidence of state certification. Thus, for the next few weeks, the administrative principal served as de facto assistant to the acting principal at Lincoln, and the instructional principal served as de facto assistant to the assistant principal at Attucks.

Meanwhile, the Attucks parents were learning a lesson from the Lincoln experience and began to exert pressure for a permanent principal to be appointed at their school. But their assistant to the principal was less forceful than her colleague down the street, and the parents settled for the reinstatement of the administrative coordinator, who had successfully been their principal the year before.

These appointments effectively eliminated the position of the instructional principal, who was given responsibilities for arranging trips for children, teachers, and parents for the rest of the year. He extended these duties by helping teachers in ways to be discussed in Chapter 4.

Although the new principals were responsible for decisionmaking for the remainder of the year, the codirectors never effectively left the scene, nor did they relinquish authority. Shortly before Christmas they set up four new committees: the Administrative Committee, the Evaluation Committee, the

Curriculum–Community Relations Committee, and the Administrative-Personnel Committee. These committees only provided further opportunity for administrators to vie for power, and soon the chairmen, deciding they had little authority and little taste for refereeing continuing conflict, refused to cooperate. Interest in the committees waned, and none met more than twice. Finally, in April, it was announced that "Due to teacher recruitment, planning for the summer program, and the next school year, existing committee meetings will be suspended until adequate time is available."

As a result of these many indecisive and unsuccessful administrative vacillations, parents' shaky confidence in the Program diminished over the year. They no longer believed in the educational establishment's capacity to run a school and provide a rigorous, stable education for their children. Fissures between parent groups grew deeper and sharper. All this led to a climax during the last week of school. Despite priority given to "involving parents productively and significantly in the operation of the schools," in June, the local newspaper reported:

A boycott of Lincoln School by about 300 elementary school children proved 100 per cent effective this morning, with no children arriving for classes, according to the principal. . . . The new program started at Lincoln School in September was to improve the quality of education for our children and to involve parents in all aspects of school life. Parents feel the program has not accomplished this.

The following day, the newspaper reported:

The parents of Lincoln School students today continued their boycott of the school and listed 20 criticisms of the program—

Little academic gains have been made this year by children.
Too many inexperienced teachers.
No well planned curriculum.
Lack of development of basic skills for the majority of children.
No consistent style of report cards.

Lack of use by the teachers of the reading teacher.
Late delivery of supplies, some not received until May and June.
Custodial problems . . . dirty school and grounds.
The need for renovations to provide space for classes.
Rumors about research by the University Center team.
Committees formed but never permanently active.

The parents also questioned the kinds of services being given by the University Center and the constant note-taking by someone described as a "chronicler." They objected to the two-principal system —one instructional and the other administrative—for both schools, and the lack of a permanent principal at Lincoln.

They also said they did not receive more nursing service and the part-time services of a pediatrician as promised, and scored the high rate of turnover in the staff. One parent said some children had as many as five teachers this year.

They maintain they have had no opportunity to interview the proposed new administrative coordinator and in fact question whether or not there already has been an appointment.

In all, it was a year of groping, reacting, defending, surviving. It was a period of trials and errors, during which, if dissonance was minimized, it was more because of collective exhaustion than any successful administrative strategies.

It was in this setting of disparate schools, incompatible staff, and random administrative organization and leadership that the six young teachers attempted to set up open classrooms. Let us now turn to an examination of the resistance they encountered from children, parents, and administrators.

RESISTANCE TO OPEN EDUCATION

In our society there are depths of resistance to innovation that have to be experienced to be believed.[9]

Despite their sensitivity to the perils of the Program, when the going got rough the six open-education teachers instinctively displayed well-established but inappropriate modes of operating. These behaviors, characteristic of upper-middle-class, liberal, white Americans, were strategies which the teachers had used consciously or unconsciously throughout their lives as children and students, ones which had always been valued, respected, and rewarded with success.

One of the most important of these strategies was color blindness. In the families, schools, and colleges from which they came, the open educators had been taught that skin color is only pigment and that there are no real differences between black and white people. Furthermore, to differentiate is to discriminate. Whites with this background learn to behave no differently with blacks than with whites, for to do so suggests prejudice.

If white liberal college graduates are color-blind, black children and adults are not. It is common, for instance, for black children to touch a white's face and talk about his blue eyes, blond hair, or light skin. Black children visiting a fire station ask why the chief's hat is white and the firemen's hats are black. Black adults are no less sensitive to color differences, although it often takes other forms, such as the local parent group which presented a "black paper" on the subject of community control.

The discrepancy in color sensitivity between the open educators and the blacks led to frequent difficulties. One teacher, for instance, wrote a memo inviting others to a piano sing at which a black teacher "will play by ear on the ivories." This apparently innocuous, even jocular invitation was received with rage by the blacks who read it. They saw it conjuring up the stereotype of a third-rate 1920's black barroom piano player—a condescending, insensitive, racist description. The black teacher in question replied, "I don't play by ear; I am a professional pianist."

It is doubtful that the white teacher who wrote the invitation was being condescending or racist; he was color-blind. In this instance, as in hundreds of others, it was extremely difficult for the seven whites, brainwashed by color blindness, consciously to acknowledge that black *is* different from white. They could not see that to perceive this difference and to act in terms of it is not necessarily to be prejudiced. Several blacks in the Program took it upon themselves to "sensitize" the whites, but it is hard for whites to deal with charges of racism.

As whites in a predominantly black situation—feeling the stresses of being in the minority—the young educators had a hard time. As white liberals, they wanted to care, to be friendly, to assist. When their initial attempts to help were ignored or rejected, few tried a second time or a third. Few tried to work through the hostility many blacks feel toward whites.

In addition to the color blindness of the six teachers, none of the open educators doubted that what was best for white children was also best for black children and best for all children. The nature of children, of the learning process, and of knowledge, they assumed, is the same for all. They believed that education is experience encountered, not knowledge transmitted, and that an experience curriculum is as appropriate (or more appropriate) for low-economic-status children as for high-economic-status children, for blacks as for whites. It was natural for the young teachers, then, to want to establish open classrooms in the Lincoln-Attucks Program. But they failed to consider the possibility that many of the children they would be teaching had had little previous opportunity to develop their innate capacity for self-motivated exploration.

Resistance from Children

Open educators assume that children learn by exploring a variety of materials, by making choices, and by posing and solving their own problems. They also assume that children will welcome opportunities to do these things. Children in the Program did not; the efforts of the young teachers were unsuccessful from the beginning. Following theory and intuition, they encouraged children to make decisions. But many children had limited capacity to attend to a task; the more options made available to them, the more difficult that attending became. A rich environment of manipulative materials only made it less likely that a child could focus on any one.

Children decided when to leave the room for a drink of water. They went to the lavatory without the traditional "lav pass." But with no restrictions from teachers, the children ganged up by tens and twenties outside the bathrooms and at the water fountains. A teacher would turn his back on a class, to find only three of twenty-five youngsters left in the room when he turned around again. Other teachers permitted work at the blackboard for children who did not want to work at their seats. That often ended in "offensive" drawings.

A common pattern emerged. A teacher would introduce choice into a classroom situation. The children would exercise choice, take advantage of the situation, and disrupt the classroom. The teacher would then withdraw the choice, often punishing the child as well. Everyone concerned would then feel frustrated and resentful. Repetition of this cycle taught the teachers an important lesson quite contrary to the foregoing assumptions about children: trust in children's capacity to make choices is not warranted and will be abused.

Why did this happen? The answer lies in at least two places: the needs of the children and the needs of the teachers.

As these children saw school, only two conditions could exist: firm, authoritarian order *or* chaos. This conception of school was well founded, for in their brief but intense experience it had always been one or the other. Associations with adults had been consistently stringent at best and cruelly erratic at worst, with most children preferring the former. What the open teachers were providing violated the children's expectations of school. From the children's point of view, the open classroom was a strange third alternative, closer to chaos than to order. The children were afraid of different experiences; the more different they were, the more they were afraid. School was frightening enough on familiar terms; a major change in ground rules made it doubly terrifying.

It is not surprising, therefore, that the children found opportunities to assume responsibility for their own learning and behavior neither easy nor attractive; that they were merciless in their demands for teacher-imposed order; or that they remained dependent upon adult control for productive, organized experience. The children's anger with teachers who would not or could not maintain rigid order and control had in it a large component of fear, as well as contempt.

Thus, while the open teachers' reference point was theoretical, the children's was based upon their prior experiences with strong traditional teachers and equally conventional weaklings. They could not make the subtle distinction between weakness and lack of concern, on the one hand, and creative permissiveness, on the other. They wanted stability and evidence of concern in a familiar form. The open classrooms and their teachers provided neither.

When given the opportunity, children felt helpless and incapable of controlling themselves. Discipline had to come from the outside. One teacher asked a child, "Robert, why can't you behave yourself?" He replied that he didn't know how to. "What do you want me to do to you?" the teacher asked. "Hit me," he said. A black aide advised the teacher, "You have to smack 'em hard and really let them know who's boss. You can't be afraid to hit them." But she was a middle-aged black adult, not a young white. In another instance, the instructional coordinator told a fourth-grade math class he was working with that the teacher in the adjoining class was complaining about the noise level. "How are we going to keep the noise down?" he asked. Their responses were revealing:

Tape our mouths shut.

Kick the noisy ones out of class.

Punish us.

Let's go somewhere else for math.

Send a note home to the bad people's parents.

They make noise and bother us; why can't we make noise?

What characterizes this imaginative collection of remedies is that each depends on the teacher to control the children's behavior. No one suggested that the class control itself; no one said, "We will have to try to whisper, not shout."

The children's abuse of teachers, materials, and themselves presented an overriding priority: to get the children under control. The question was no longer whether the teacher controlled the child or the child controlled himself. Either the teacher did the controlling, or no one did. It was only when the children began to feel a sense of control and stability (by their definition, imposed from without) that learning became a possibility. Indeed, one psychologist had put forth this argument earlier in the year:

A child has a certain, fixed amount of psychic energy.

For all children it takes some of this energy to control their own behavior, to restrain impulses and order their lives.

Those children who have not had the opportunity to develop internal impulse control must use a *preponderance* of their psychic energy to conform to their perceptions of adult requirements.

To the extent that such a child is called upon to use his finite energy to control himself, it is not available to him for academic learning (which also takes a great deal of energy).

Thus, these children should not be asked or expected to control themselves, but should gradually be taught how to do this in such a way that their opportunities for learning would not be diminished . . . so they would be *free* to learn.

Only in this way can the child develop both self-control and academic skills and concepts.

This argument was used by some to justify their contention that the open classroom does not work for inner-city children —a viewpoint that might not survive a more successful experience.

The teachers suffered at least as much as the children. Like the children, the six young teachers had a polarized conception of school: either authoritarian rigidity or creative freedom. Unfortunately, the dichotomies of the children and the adults were in direct conflict. Teachers' practices intended to facilitate learning were perceived as chaotic by the students, who rejected them out of hand and pushed the teachers more and more toward what the students would call order—and what the teachers themselves would call tyranny. The teachers found this acutely distressing.

Children could be equally merciless with teachers who were *unreasonably* authoritarian: for example, on May 10th, the fourth-grade teacher was absent, and a rigid and authoritarian substitute came in:

Substitute: We are now going to sing either "America the Beautiful" or "My Country 'Tis of Thee."
Children: It's not so beautiful for us, lady. It's your country; you can sing about it.
Substitute: You *will* sing one of the songs. Every class I have ever taught has begun the day singing one of these songs. Now let's sing or I'll call the police and the principal and have you arrested.

The teacher began to play the piano. At the point where the class was supposed to begin "My country 'tis . . .," they all began in unison to sing loudly and clearly, "We shall overcome . . .," and continued through one or two verses, despite the fact that the teacher had long since ceased playing the piano and was sitting open-mouthed. Later she discovered that her lunch was missing from the paper bag she had left on the windowsill. She later found it outside, lying squashed on the sand.

Children tested and abused every teacher who was attempting to run an unfamiliar classroom, until the teacher demanded conventional order or was run out and another came to take his place. Unless a traditional climate was provided, neither student nor teacher could find the classroom habitable.

Thus, to an astonishing extent children controlled, manipulated, and shaped teachers' behavior toward authoritarianism. One of the six young teachers reluctantly adopted a new criterion for selecting materials (one not mentioned in Chapter 2): What will happen when this object is thrown across the room? Therefore yarn was allowed, but a microscope wasn't; crayons were acceptable, but not paint; cardboard blocks were safe, but wooden blocks were not. Another young teacher, lamenting the fact that all his notions of facilitating, encouraging, positively reinforcing, and supporting were nowhere to be found in his daily behavior, could only mutter, "I'm only twenty-four years old and they've made me into a mean old man."

Open education was not working. One observer saw it this way:

In many cases discipline was not established, control was poor. Children were disruptive, in some cases abusive and violent toward teachers, who felt helpless to stop this since their method was reason, not the stick. Some parents, even though hostile toward the teachers, were horrified at the children's lack of respect, furious at the breakdown in discipline.

Confronted with this deteriorating situation, most of the teachers soon decided that the ideas and practices of open education and the corresponding role of the teacher were inappropriate for them in this place at this time. Some tried to revise their teaching along more traditional lines. They set up reading groups and introduced basal texts, required seats, and homework. But after each attempt, the teacher would usually hate himself and the administration, and feel hated by the children as well:

All I did was yell at the kids all day. It's a farce. I didn't do anything all day. The toughest part was planning every single minute of the day and running off the dittos. After that I just passed them out and told the kids to shut up and work.

The six open educators were firmly on the horns of a dilemma. They had come to the conclusion that it would be best to "go straight," only to discover to their dismay that they could not. With no preparation for the traditional role which was expected and being demanded of them, they were unable to assume the role of authoritarian manager of children and transmitter of knowledge. The problem could not be resolved simply by requiring a "lav pass," although this and other traditional practices had long since been adopted. One teacher observed, "What I need is a cram course in being a traditional teacher."

A major reason the six young educators had decided to become teachers was to save children from suffering the authoritarian, oppressive, and sterile experiences which they felt characterized their own education and which they were now attempting to change. One teacher expressed the futility of this conflict:

. . . all year I had worked hard at fitting into school. I regretted that I had not had more opportunity to work out my own style of teaching or to try more things that I thought might be appropriate for the children. . . . Throughout the year I sensed that the children could tell when I was doing something because I thought it was in their best interest or because I thought it was expected of me.

The difficulties these six teachers experienced in the classroom would seem to have general significance. Open education is attracting many who find the facilitator-of-learning mantle a comfortable cloak under which to hide—a place where they do not have to reveal themselves or be assertive or directive. Many advocates of open education appear not to have resolved their own authority problems and are unwilling to be, if not incapable of being, authorities themselves. Safe under the aegis of the open educator's role, they resist either becoming directive when necessary or probing into their own difficulties with authority; they identify with the children and see themselves as colleagues in the war against the oppressive administration and less-enlightened teachers.

The open educators were stunned to find that children rejected permissive facilitators of learning as much as, if not more than, they did rigid transmitters of knowledge. In the Program, and in other attempts to implement open education in this country, many teachers are beginners fresh out of college, with little experience in teacher-directed classrooms and without the confidence that accompanies such experience. Many have turned to open education through insecurity; they are permissive because they are afraid that if they are strong, the children will reject them. But children sense this insecurity and see it as weakness and insult. They exploit the teacher's conflict over assuming an authoritative role and react with anger, forcing the teacher to assume a role which he fears and detests and which he is unwilling to fill or is incapable of fulfilling.

In England, on the other hand, successful teachers in informal classrooms have often taught several years in traditional classes. They are experienced teachers who have turned to informal methods when they found the transmission-of-knowledge model inadequate. These teachers are fully capable of running a class like a Marine drill sergeant if need be. They don't want to do this, and rarely need to; but they know, parents know, and the children know that strength and confidence underlie their permissiveness and kindness. Children sense this strength and therefore feel freer to explore materials and to pose and solve their own problems. In such classrooms a child can experiment as the agent of his own learning, just as he can explore being naughty—with the confidence that a strong authority figure is there to back him up in case things go awry.

We can see that a major reason for the shift in the informal classrooms from September to December was that open education was not working. Children were angered by the apparent lack of control. They resisted opportunities to make decisions and to work with interesting materials. Given a choice, they often chose not only not to work (or play) but, rather, to disrupt and destroy. We are left with a crucial question: Are there appropriate steps or developmental stages by means of which teachers can lead children from dependence upon authoritarian adults for their control and learning toward assuming more responsibility for their own learning and behavior? Whatever else is required, it seems apparent that a sense of control and confidence on the part of the teacher is essential for setting up an open classroom. Just as in art one has to understand the basic traditional forms in order to be able to create abstractions, so teachers may need to understand and master the forms of traditional education before they can hope to establish informal classrooms. At the very least, they must have some clear notion of what these traditions entail and why they are so tenaciously adhered to.

Resistance from Parents

I want my children to get the basics in elementary school. Children can't learn the basics in an open classroom.
—Parent in the Lincoln-Attucks Program

Open educators have a definite conception of quality education. They believe the role of the teacher is to provide time, space, materials, experiences, and encouragement for children; that the relationship between teacher and student is one of partnership in the exploration of the environment; that children's legitimate activities extend outside the school and to the home; and that the teacher's respect for children's efforts will affect the children's respect for the teacher, their work, and themselves. Open educators believe that in such an environment children will explore, ask questions, answer them, and develop skills, concepts, and confidence.

The Lincoln-Attucks parents had quite a different model of quality education, one which resembled a military academy more than the open classroom. Parents expected, wanted, and demanded, clear evidence that each child was under the teacher's control at all times. The only alternative, as the parents saw it, was that the children were *out of control*. One parent, for example, expressed pleasure with the traffic patrol program: "I think it's great for them to get all neatly dressed up in uniforms, walk smartly, obey orders, have captains. If they don't behave, then they get demerits. There is a way to punish them." Most believed that the ideal relationship between teacher and student was that of superordinate to subordinate, a relation in which children obey and respect. Parents assumed that the certified teacher is qualified (and if he is not certified, he is not qualified). Being certified, he knows what and how each child should learn. In short, in the military academy model, the teacher is not merely one important agent of the child's learning, he is the *only* agent of the child's learning. If the child will but respect and obey his teacher, he will learn.

These discrepant models soon brought parents and teachers into conflict. The open classroom bears little resemblance to a military school; it tends to be characterized by a certain amount of noise, movement, and mess. A good illustration is provided by one of the six teachers:

The first day of school we were reading and came across a play which we produced on the spot. The children have since written and produced several plays of their own. The second day, the boys and I started building some bookshelves for the room. It was slow at first

. . . they had no concepts of measuring, planning, or woodworking; but we went on from that to build animal cages, furniture, and a darkroom for our photography work. We are in the process of re-building several small rooms in the school.

At one point we had ducks, gerbils, and a kitten running around the room, and had built a pond in a bath tub. These subsequently (although temporarily) have been removed. Early in the year I purchased a load of leather, and the kids started by making wallets. Twelve of them have just finished making purses for their mothers for Christmas. While their work was poor at first, these latest projects are quite good. At the point at which we lost the animals I brought in cameras, developer, and film. The kids have developed some competence at taking pictures, and three of the boys have become quite good at developing and processing the film. We also have a set of shelves filled with games which the children play in their free time, and while I can still beat them at complex games like Go or Kahla, I really have to watch it on simpler games like checkers . . . even then I lose. I've been teaching piano and recorder to a dozen kids, and we have just published the third issue of "The Basement Speaks."

A reporter from the local newspaper described his visit to the room of another of the six teachers, where he observed a dramatic production written and staged by the third-graders:

Noticeable was the lack of pressure by the adults. Particularly commendable was the support given by a young man teacher to a shy child, momentarily reduced to tears by stage fright. There was no doubt the production was the work of the children, skillfully led, not pushed. Noisy but nice.

Parents visiting the six open classrooms often saw less appealing scenes. Many were astonished and angered by what they saw: children with their backs to the teacher, playing with animals, games, and each other; teachers called by their first names; children eating candy or potato chips; children swearing at other children; spitballs being openly exchanged.

The parents considered such behavior disrespectful and a source of intense embarrassment. Like most parents, they saw their children as extensions of themselves, and anything less than model behavior reaped shame upon them.

Only one thing infuriated parents more than seeing their children behaving in these ways—namely, seeing the teacher do nothing about it. They were appalled when teachers did not acknowledge the gum chewing, cursing, or spitballs and did not severely reprimand or beat the child. As one parent put it:

I was against this program from the beginning but then I decided to wait and see . . . to give it a chance. Then I come and see this going on . . . now I'm against the whole thing.

The noise and mess of the open classrooms distressed the parents as much as the apparent disrespect:

. . . one of the parents asked me if my room was some kind of psychological experiment. . . . Did I believe that her child could not function in a neat environment?

There were at least two legitimate reasons for the teachers' tolerance of apparently disrespectful behavior. In some instances, a child's "bad" behavior was in fact a legitimate use of freedom: the child with his back to the teacher might be working on an important project of his own. In cases where the behavior was genuinely disrespectful, the teacher often chose not to reinforce it by giving it attention. Indeed, the teacher who acknowledges every child's apparently disrespectful behavior has time for little else.

One angry parent stormed into the principal's office after visiting one of the open classrooms and demanded to know, "Why can't this place *look* like a school?" A list of grievances conveyed by the parents to administrators at the end of the first week of school suggests the discrepancy between the parents' and teachers' conceptions of the conditions for learning:

The floors in the classrooms are messy—paper all over the place, sunflower seeds, pieces of yarn, leather, clay, animals' litter.

Children were running in the corridors and to the corners after school.

There was no pledge of allegiance to the flag; some rooms don't even have flags.

My child's class has a radio in it. A classroom is a place to work, not listen to the radio. My child could stay home and do that.

Gum chewing. There is no place for it in school.

I haven't received a single note telling when my child didn't do his work and when he misbehaved. Why not?

My child is scared to death of the animals. Boys chase her about with gerbils. She doesn't want to come to school in the morning. They are like mice and rats—rodents—they have no place in school.

The parents wanted quiet; they saw dancing, radios, record players, games, skits being rehearsed. They wanted order imposed by the teacher; they saw what appeared to be random behavior. They wanted to see desks in straight rows; they saw no desks, cardboard desks, or desks arranged in disorderly clusters.

Their objections were not limited to what they saw—animals, materials, talking, mess—but included what they did not see. They questioned the curriculum, or the lack of it. Where were the textbooks, reading groups, workbooks, worksheets, homework? "Show me what the children are learning," they demanded.

Where are the 3 R's? All I see is crafts, weaving, making things out of wood, leather, yarn; weighing things. Where are the *books?*

If I want my child to go to a zoo, I'll take him to a zoo. He's in school to *learn.*

Racial overtones emerged. The phrase "These teachers
don't understand black children" was heard more and more
often from parents and also from some administrators. This
meant several things: "The young white teachers are condescending to our children; they don't think they are capable of
writing, spelling, figuring, or thinking, so they let them play
with blocks and animals. What the children need is a tough
black teacher who understands them and won't let them get
away with these things."

On their part, the six open classroom teachers felt, with
some bitterness, that when they used an unorthodox and/or innovative approach with black children, this was labeled "condescending" or "prejudiced"; whereas had they employed a
similar approach with white children, this would have been
"individualized instruction."

Examined more carefully, few parents really objected to the
animals, the crafts, the woodworking, or the notion of a "rich
manipulative environment." Both the parents and the six
teachers wanted the children to "catch up" academically.
Their disagreement was over *sequence*. The teachers, by and
large, would agree that

. . . the use of manipulative physical materials holds special promise
in working with culturally deprived children, who seem more often
to require such experience in school, both because they get less of it
outside, and also because their abstract verbal communicative skills
are less fully developed . . . we *can* promote the development of abstract concepts in a very large number of children . . . especially
culturally deprived children, but not only these . . . provided we
begin by giving the child abundant opportunity to manipulate appropriate physical objects.[10]

The teachers believed a child must have many experiences
with primary materials *in order to* "catch up." They believed
that manipulative experiences are a necessary precondition for

the development of skills and abstract concepts. The parents, on the other hand, knew their children were several grade levels behind in most subjects; they saw the use of games, toys, animals, blocks, and other manipulative materials as superfluous, frivolous fun, appropriate only *after* children have "caught up" on basic skills, concepts, and disciplines through drill and workbooks. These important distinctions were not acknowledged, understood, or resolved by teachers and parents.

The parents' model stresses firm control and discipline by the teacher; it also makes suspect any display of kindness on the teacher's part. Many parents were troubled by the teachers' kindness toward their children, often for reasons which seem related to their own insecurities. Some parents seemed to find the rich environment of the open classroom, coupled with the teacher's permissive attitude, a threat to their relationships with their children. Many parents were angry and resentful. "He used to obey and respect me, and now he doesn't even *listen* to me. He only tells me that at school his teacher lets him do. . . ." "He used to run home from school glad to see me. Now he stays there until dark." "My boy was timid and quiet at home; now he comes in like a wild man, and I have no control over him. What are you doing?" "One thing I'll never be able to forgive Mr. Rice for is that Sandy sides with him and won't even talk about some of the things they do." In short, some parents appeared to depend for their children's affection on their *not* liking school, on the teacher being an ogre, in which case the parents, by comparison, came out ahead. When school becomes pleasant, when the teacher is humane, when children enjoy school, many parents feel *they* become the ogres.

The discrepancy between parents' and teachers' expectations of quality education was not limited to questions of the teacher's relationship to his students, to the appearance of the classroom and the curriculum. Perhaps provoked by what they found lacking in the teachers' professional behavior, the parents began to focus on what they expected of the teachers' personal behavior. These expectations, like others, follow a traditional model.

Parents felt, for example, that a teacher's dress should be modest and somber, supplying ample coverage. Stockings for women and coat and tie for men were an expected part of the uniform; or else, "How can children come to think of them as teachers and respect them?" The wardrobe of the six teachers included few items which met these criteria. The teachers wore bright print dresses and ties, informal slacks, miniskirts, and, for outdoor activities such as field trips or athletics, sweaters, sneakers, and jeans. The parents also had an image of a principal: he should *look* like a principal—dark suit, white shirt, polished shoes, gray hair, and a new Ford Ranchwagon. It did nothing to reduce the parents' suspicion and distrust to have these expectations violated by a young man who appeared at one of the first parent meetings wearing a blue workshirt and riding a motor scooter.

Parents were also concerned about where the school staff lived. Almost all the whites in the Program and many of the blacks lived in suburbs surrounding the city. Six of the seven open educators lived within a mile of the two schools. (The other lived on a farm complete with horse.) Parents, on the other hand, expected that anyone who could afford to should commute to the schools each day from a suitable middle-class home in the suburbs. The residence of the six young teachers, living Peace-Corps-like next door, made many parents extremely anxious. "How can my child respect a teacher who lives in that shabby house?" "I'm afraid something will happen to them if they live there." Also many of the staff members who lived in the suburbs saw the young teachers' choice of residence as a direct and uncomfortable challenge.

The quite different expectations of the open educators and the parents about what constituted quality education placed the two groups on a collision course. One teacher who had worked in the schools the previous year observed:

To the parents . . . all this was intolerable; school was becoming a zoo, children were wasting their time with animals; desks were not always arranged in rows and in some cases children's backs were even turned towards the teacher. Children were wasting time on games and moving about and talking; they were not given enough phonics or drill homework; too much time was being spent on art, music and plays, and discipline was too loose. . . . There wasn't much that the parents saw that they liked. They did not trust or understand un-traditional methods.

Some parents applied pressure to move teachers out of the neighborhood:

Not long into October, the building-leader told me that many parents were very upset about where I was living. My roommate was an aide at the other school; we had taken an apartment that was about one block from Lincoln. The leader said that parents thought that the school neighborhood was an inappropriate place for teachers to be living; she said nasty rumors were circulating about us and that it would be best for all concerned if we moved at once. We knew there was no basis for the rumors, and we were very happy living where we were, but the pressure from the school administrators became so great that we decided to move. No parent had spoken to us about this problem and no administrator had shown any interest in listening to our views about the matter.

Parents wrote petitions demanding the firing of certain teachers—not only the open educators, but always including them. Their grievances were recurrent:

She has been too free with marks on report cards. My child got all A's and B's, and I *know* my child is no A or B student.

She has problems disciplining the children.

The children aren't learning and aren't being taught to behave.

Children who are good students are falling behind because the others are taking attention away from them.[11]

She is stubborn and won't do as the principal says.

One child was swearing at her and she let him get away with it . . . she didn't do anything. She shows a semblance of weakness.

The petitions were given to administrators, the codirectors, and the superintendent but were never shown to the teachers themselves.

Nor was it uncommon for parents to march into the school and the classrooms unannounced, angry, and defiant. In this frame of mind, they could usually find sufficient evidence to support their fears, whereupon they marched abruptly out, giving the teacher no opportunity to explain what he was trying to do. Thus parent-organized opposition tended to be indirect. Seldom was a particular teacher confronted with a particular complaint by a particular parent. This caused many teachers to have doubts as well as apprehensions about parent objections.

Unfortunately, the success of any attempt at implementing open education depends upon the people involved being open, directly expressing their beliefs and objections, their likes and dislikes. Without such openness and honesty, those who would do something different are deprived of opportunities to explain, defend, and justify their actions or to display their results. The parents, encouraged by some administrators who gained power by being brokers between parent and teacher, refused to give teachers the opportunity to state their case. In effect, the teachers were muzzled. Whatever possibility existed to present their case in a satisfactory manner was thwarted.

Resistance by withholding themselves was perhaps the parent tactic that served most effectively to weaken and undermine both the personal security of the young teachers and their attempts at innovation. It was also a tactic that served generally to undermine the Program. Only a handful of parents would show up at meetings (aimed at involving them), for trips to visit other schools, or for conferences with teachers. For instance, the end-of-the-year catered dinner at one school (paid for by the Program), honoring the PTA officers and the nine room mothers, was attended by twenty-two staff members and three parents. Parents would, in effect, refuse to allow administrators and teachers to include them in decisions and then would refuse to go along with decisions which had been made because they had no part in the deliberations. Although always a threat and a possibility, parental resistance rarely came out in the open. The most dramatic instance of it was the picketing of the Lincoln School.

More than a concern for appearances, traditions, and morality led parents to a military academy concept of quality education. There is a hard-nosed realism to this model. Parents care deeply about their children and want the most and the best for them. In their children are vested and invested the parents' hopes for the future, an improvement in their way of life which only their children may live to see. The parents know they have often been unsuccessful in providing order in their homes and on their streets for their children. They know that many of their children are not going to make it in a predominantly white, racist, middle-class society. Many are headed in the age-old direction of failure, hunger, and misery. As much as parents want and try to correct this almost inevitable course, they cannot alter it. In *school* they see the last hope of salvation for many children. If school does not provide the educating and socializing experiences missing at home, what will? It's no wonder these parents care about what goes on in their children's schools. When you depend, you *must* care. At stake are children's lives.

The reasoning which causes parents to adopt and hold tenaciously to the military academy model has a powerful, legitimate logic to it:[12]

We want our children to go to high school, to college, to get a good, white-collar job, to have a home, a car, and raise a family. In short, we want them to do what *you* (whites) have done.

You have had a certain kind of educational experience . . . teacher as source of knowledge and control, child as respectful and obedient responder, and you made it. If our children have the same kind of educational experience, *they too* will make it.

But, since our children are starting with many strikes against them, since many are already behind in reading, writing, and arithmetic, and self-control, they will have to have your educational experience, only *more so*. More respect, more obedience, more authority, more homework, more books, more discipline.

Thus the conventional transmission-of-knowledge model, pushed to its extreme, becomes the military academy model. Parents see this model as the way to save their children; any departure from it is an experiment and a risk.

Parents had originally feared that the program was an "experiment" and that their children might be exploited. They did not distinguish between experiment defined as moving away from existing archaic school patterns and experiment as conducting research into the unknown by trying out new ideas at the expense of their children. The lack of an apparent plan drove the parents even more toward their faith in traditional ways and made them even less open to change.

Paradoxically, then, although parents did not like what had been happening to their children in school, they were reluctant to risk anything different. Their implicit mandate to members of the Program staff was to improve dramatically their children's education—without significantly changing anything. Under such a mandate, the greater the deviation from traditional educational methods, the more resistance could be expected from parents. Looked at in this way, educational innovation becomes more real and less romance; more sober and less exciting; more an opportunity to help parents fulfill *their* hopes for their children than a chance for teachers to fulfill theirs. In a very disturbing way, the parents are right.

Resistance from Administrators

The six open education teachers believed that the faculty should have a major part in formulating important school decisions, particularly those which directly concerned them. They believed that the only decisions appropriate for administrators to make without teachers' participation were those dealing with routines, schedules, budgets, etc. All decisions concerning substantive issues, such as curriculum, report cards, discipline, homework, or rules, should be group decisions. In short, the six open classroom teachers expected to find a *democratic* decisionmaking model in the Program, a model somehow consistent with ideas of open education. Expectations that administrators exist to facilitate faculty efforts, of a collegial relationship between administration and faculty, and the concept of academic freedom were, no doubt, brought by the six teachers from their various colleges, which professed, at least, to operate along such principles and where "participation" was an idea then coming into vogue among students.

What the teachers found in the Program was a power vacuum caused by the lack of a clear plan and strong leadership. Seeking to fill the vacuum were a dozen administrators with ill-defined spheres of power. This situation, pitting administrator against administrator, as well as administrator against teacher, hardly lent itself to open discussion and democratic decisionmaking. No administrator could afford to wait to find out what teachers thought before he acted; if he paused, another administrator would step in and corner the issue.

Each member of the administration and of the University Center team had a great deal—personally and professionally—riding on the Program. The director may have felt that he needed a winner after a prior record of involvement with unsuccessful programs. Members of the University Center team felt that their appointment to positions in a major university entitled them to direct and influence others as they had for so long been directed and influenced. All expected the Program to have a national impact and wanted to be favorably associated with this widespread recognition.

The school administrators had also worked long and hard to get where they were. For most, this was their first position of significant responsibility; and, like all first experiences, it carried with it unreasonably high expectations and a good deal of insecurity. These administrators had come up through the ranks for fifteen or twenty years, as teachers, as assistant principals, and in other subordinate positions. Like the University Center team, they felt that these long years of personal experience, superior knowledge of their own race (for the blacks), and their positions of responsibility in the Program entitled them to make important judgments and to have those judgments respected and carried out, unquestioned by the rest of the staff, particularly by teachers. In short, the University Center and school administrative personnel expected the same respect and obedience they had accorded their superiors for many years. For every administrator, control of teachers was the most sought-after prize.

The administrators' decisionmaking model was not only authoritarian—with themselves in the position of authority—but also consonant with the parents' military academy model. The military academy model appealed to the parents for pedagogical reasons; it appealed to the administrators for expedient reasons. For example, an assistant to the principal issued *Rules and Policies Concerning the Children of Lincoln School*:

Teachers are *RESPONSIBLE* for conduct of children.

Teachers will *TAKE* children to and from lavatory and will *SUPERVISE* them while there.

As of March 3, *no* food or drinks of any kind will be allowed in the school. A snack will be provided. Any food or drinks brought into the school will be confiscated. There is to be *no* gum chewing at *any* time.

Children are not to run in the halls at any time. They should walk quietly and talk quietly.

At *DISMISSAL* time, children are to walk in a group behind their teacher to the corner.

Older brothers and sisters who escort younger children to their classes should leave them at their doors and then go directly to their own classes. *Any* child found where he or she does not belong will be reported at once.

No child is to go into *another* classroom unless he has a note from his teacher.

Both *LESSON PLANS* and *SUBSTITUTE FOLDER* should be readily available at all times.

Confronted with demands for traditional practices by authoritarian administrators, many of whom were black, the six open classroom teachers found themselves in a situation they neither had anticipated nor were ready to handle. On the one hand, they had been taught to respect blacks as people; on the other, they had developed a pronounced hostility toward and distrust of authority figures—parents, professors, or school administrators. Black authority figures defied their categorization system and produced acute conflict. What teachers saw to be incompetent behavior could not be called "incompetent" without either the black or white fearing that such accusations were based upon color of skin, not on performance.

The six teachers reacted against the *Rules and Policies* and other regulations which they had no part in defining. They also objected to the authoritarian manner in which the rules were handed down. Their first, and perhaps easiest response, was to make concessions of form, while keeping the substance of their efforts intact. The teachers soon became aware of administrators' (and parents') desires for familiar appearances and were often quite successful in providing a traditional cloak for important elements such as choice, materials, and play. When traditional lesson plans were demanded, teachers learned to write (although seldom use) them. When "orderly" rooms were demanded, they arranged children's desks in straight rows but changed them once or twice a day for skits, dances, or games. Miniskirts and loud ties were replaced by more conservative garb.

Similarly, teachers modified nomenclature to fit administrators' demands. When opportunities for children to explore materials in "play periods" or "free time" met with objection, the names (but not the function) were changed to "activity period" or to "work period." [13] When being an advocate of "open education" became more of a liability than an asset, these words disappeared from the vocabulary.

The Lincoln-Attucks experience suggests that, both literally and figuratively, the radical *without* the beard can be a far less threatening, and more effective agent of change than the radical *with* the beard. If the teacher's ego and educational principles permit him to give up on the little more apparent things— the beard, the sideburns, the motor scooter, the arrangement of desks—and if he has his class walk quietly in the halls, keeps his room neat, and demands a bit of homework, then he is likely to encounter far less resistance on the larger, more important issues.

But altering appearances as a means of coping with resistance did not ensure success in this program. In many schools, particularly large ones, teachers can shut their doors and do as they please. If the place doesn't fall apart or if the children aren't physically injured, administrators and parents aren't likely to know what goes on. Not knowing, they are unlikely to object. In the Lincoln-Attucks Program visibility was unlimited; consequently, all deviation from rules had to be surreptitious. As a result, the open classroom teachers further coalesced as a kind of underground, apart from the administration, the blacks, the University Center team, and the parents. They were surprised and disappointed that their surface concessions were not sufficient, and reverted to characteristic (although usually inappropriate) strategies which, like color blindness, had enabled them to resolve difficult problems in the past: verbal facility, honesty, efficiency, and emotional and physical withdrawal.

Color blindness of the white teachers had another meaning in this context. Because being black was rightly seen by blacks as being endowed with special wisdom about the experience of black children, many blacks needed recognition of their color to lend credence to their decisions. In a situation where credentials came to mean power, *not* to acknowledge a black's color was an aggressive act, intended to deprive the black of his credentials.

When an offensive decision was made by an administrator, the six young teachers responded by preparing and delivering a well-reasoned, careful, persuasive, and logical argument against it.[14] Administrators recognized that the counterargument was well reasoned, careful, persuasive, logical, and often compelling. But threatened by what seemed to be an attack, they become even more rigidly entrenched in their decision. Unable to verbally outmaneuver the teachers, administrators had to pull rank in order to emerge from the confrontation without loss of face or control. In this way, the teachers time and again won the arguments (in a way that would make their college seminar professors proud), but lost the battle. In this way, issues such as homework, lesson plans, discipline, and use of texts were resolved verbally, pedagogically, and theoretically by the teachers, and practically by the administrators.

Thus, one teacher responded to the announcement of an assembly for the purpose of promulgating school rules by saying,

[the] announcement was too much for me, and in my usual polite and conservative manner, I explained that first of all you do not discipline kids or change their behavior by lecturing to them in an assembly, and then went on to say that I resented decisions about school policy being made by a small group and then presented to the staff.

A seemingly petty policy concerning gum chewing became the focus of another battle. The building leader (no doubt speaking for the majority of parents) felt that there should be *no* gum chewing in the school at any time. The young teachers argued heatedly that each teacher should decide the policy with his own class. It was clear that about half of the teachers, if given the choice, would permit the children to chew gum discreetly. Like so many other cases, this was not only a pedagogical conflict (Is gum chewing in the best interests of children?) but also a political confrontation over who was to decide. In this instance, teachers made their own rules about gum chewing and the building leader had her rule: no gum chewing allowed in the building.

In addition to the color blindness and verbal facility, the six open classroom teachers were almost compulsively honest. Asked what was bothering them, they told frankly—lack of equipment, lack of clear leadership, lack of money, promises broken, no books. When they didn't respect an administrator, they told him so. When they didn't believe an administrator, they told him so. When one administrator asked a teacher, "What *would* you like to have me do around here?" he was told, "Supply paper, pencils, books, and paper clips when I need them."

Statements such as "I don't respect you" or "I don't think you're doing a very good job" undoubtedly have a certain shock value, and may command respect in colleges and graduate schools. But such interpersonal confrontations were not appreciated by parents and administrators in the Program or, indeed, elsewhere in the real world.

In most schools, teachers and administrators have very different ideas about efficiency. The Lincoln-Attucks schools were no exception. When the six teachers saw ways of making things operate more efficiently, they suggested them: one line for boys and girls rather than one line for each; teacher aides assigned to filling out forms; children helping to clean up the school.

But many administrators use *in*efficiency as an indirect, even unconscious, means of getting teachers to do what they want or of preventing teachers from doing what they don't want them to do. To the extent that these teachers became more and more efficient and self-sufficient, they escaped this indirect administrative control. Teachers who wanted to buy animals for their classrooms and were told that money was slow in coming from downtown went out on their lunch hour and opened an account in the school's name at a nearby pet shop. When told that school carpenters were too busy to build shelves in their classrooms, they opened an account at a hardware store, bought their own materials and tools, and made the furniture over the weekend. When told that an individualized reading program was ordered but wouldn't be in for "awhile" and that texts would have to be used, the teachers went that afternoon to a nearby public library and checked out whole shelves of children's literature. When told there wasn't enough time to organize parent meetings before Thanksgiving, teachers wrote individual letters to parents of all their children explaining their plans for the year. These initiatives were taken by administrators as indications that the teachers were outside their control—which they were.

As conflicts between administrators and the young teachers

became more frequent and more intense, each group made a judgment about the other which was to persist throughout the year:

Teachers decided administrators just didn't give a damn about classrooms or teachers' problems. Administrators determined that teachers were basically anarchical, resisting all authority.

Administrators were threatened, offended, and alienated. Their response was prompted by two quite different factors: first, these teachers gave no sign of the respect and obedience which the administrators had expected; second, their unorthodox teaching practices violated parents' expectations and wishes, placing the administrators (who wanted to minimize dissonance) in jeopardy. Faced with threats from two sides, the administrators resisted, first by excluding the open educators from decisionmaking, then by thwarting the attempts of the six teachers in several other ways. One method was to prevent the teachers from gaining direct access to the parents. To succeed in their aims, these teachers had to have frequent and open interaction with parents. But all they were allowed to know about the parents' feelings was what the administrators told them: the parents wanted them out—unless. . . .

The complaints never came to us directly, but rather were delivered by the administrators. The University Center people also informed us on several occasions that matters were close to blowing up and that various teachers were to be asked to leave by petitions being circulated among the parents. Obviously, this created a tremendous amount of anxiety and frustration among the teachers, and the frustration was only compounded when the administrators used the situation with the parents to threaten various teachers during faculty meetings.

Another means of administrative control was to cut off funds and make materials difficult to secure. In an attempt to give teachers some measure of choice over classroom materials, the instructional coordinator had allocated each teacher $300 out of the substantial materials budget to spend as he saw fit over the year. The teacher needed only to submit a receipt to be immediately reimbursed. Although initially approved by the administration, this system was immediately curtailed (by withholding the $300) on the grounds that "teachers would spend it on popcorn and games."

School systems, like other bureaucracies, assume that everyone is out to fleece them, and therefore no one is to be trusted. Consequently, numerous safeguards and forms of red tape surround and protect the system against assumed dishonest behavior of teachers. But these protective devices—countless slips to fill out for reimbursement, each to be signed by countless officials, a waiting period of two to ten weeks for reimbursement—all frustrate and infuriate employees of the system. Red tape provokes anger and hostility and makes dishonest behavior more likely, thereby reinforcing administrators' suspicion and distrust and tightening even further the security precautions. This cycle was repeated many times for teachers in the Program. Thus, while parents exercised power by withholding themselves, administrators tried to curtail the "materials-centered classrooms" and gain power by withholding money.

There were other ways to get materials out of the open classrooms. During Christmas vacation, when the teachers were away, the fire marshal for some reason came to investigate "inflammable" materials in some of the classrooms. As a result, the teachers returned to find that all the cardboard furniture, animal cages, and "interest corners" had disappeared. Similarly, after the February vacation, one teacher discovered:

. . . that my classroom was one of two that had been carpeted; I was surprised, but pleased because the room seemed quieter and more cheerful. The building leader informed me, however, that the custodians had said there were to be no animals, crayons, paints or paste allowed on the newly carpeted rooms and that she thought it would be very difficult to fight the custodians' union on that issue. In addition, I noticed that nearly all the furnishings except the desks and chairs (including several things I had built for the room) had been removed.

The administration also thwarted the open educators by demanding explicit planning. A major responsibility administrators assume in schools is to ensure that teachers are working hard. If administrators do not perform this function, they assume teachers will get away with as little work as possible. The two major monitoring mechanisms are regular classroom observations and required, written lesson plans.

The lesson plan, based on the concept of predetermined learning, is a part of the transmission-of-knowledge model and is quite antithetical to open education. To be sure, if the adult is to facilitate children's learning, he must plan carefully. He must anticipate and organize. But the open educator plans much differently than the traditional teacher. In the latter case, the teacher decides what the child will learn and how he will learn it. He writes this down as his lesson plan. In the open classroom, the adult must plan very flexibly so that he can make the appropriate response, provide the right materials for the right child at the right time. This is contingency planning, no less important to the success of the open education model than are lesson plans to the transmission-of-knowledge model, and no less laborious.

The open educators refused to submit conventional, regular lesson plans, and a reasoned, intellectual, verbal defense of their position brought them intense criticism from the administration. Reluctance to make lesson plans was seen as not caring about the children, being lazy, resistant, and defiant. Administrators did not recognize the pedagogical questions involved; they would not accept the possibility of a different kind of legitimate planning. The longer and harder the teachers held out, the more certain were the administrators that the teachers were stubbornly defying them.

The degree to which administrators went to shut out the open classroom teachers is suggested by an incident which occurred late in the year. Pictures of each class and teacher were taken at school by a professional photographer. Shortly thereafter, three teachers left their positions at the school: two were suspended as a result of an argument they had had in front of their classes, and one resigned under pressure. Two weeks after the photographs were taken, the prints were distributed to the children; in none of them did there appear the teachers with whom they had been in constant contact for almost the entire year. Apparently, in the intervening two weeks, the photographer had been called back to take another picture of these three classes, *without* their teachers. This says a great deal about the opinion in which these three teachers (and the others) were held by the parents and administrators. They are not now in the school; they don't exist; nor have they ever existed.

The ultimate response of the open educators to administrators was *withdrawal*—at first emotional, then political, and finally, physical. When, despite their best effort, things didn't go their way (which was usually the case), many of the teachers considered leaving the Program. Before Christmas, one teacher explored a job in a private school. He rationalized his decision to leave the Program by saying that "blacks should staff and run and teach in their own schools. Black children will not come to value themselves and achieve a favorable self-image if they are taught by white teachers. The white teacher, by being white, is doing a disservice to black children." Another teacher planned to leave the Program to teach in a system which would both permit and encourage open education; otherwise he said he would "never know what it is like." On the surface, this willingness to leave the classroom, the Program, or even teaching was the ultimate in humility: "I am what I am. I am incapable of doing what is expected of me; therefore it is best for all concerned that I leave." But there is another side to this humility: offers or threats to pack up one's marbles and go home had always been a successful strategy for these bright, usually valuable young people. It tended to bring parents, teachers, peers, or whoever around to help them get their way.

In the Program, an offer of withdrawal was also a convenient defense which permitted the individual not to have to come to grips with a second alternative: making radical changes in his own behavior. Furthermore, in this situation, repeated offers of resignation did not elicit sympathy or influence the opposition. Such offers were met, at best, with "Why would you want to do that?" More likely, resignation was seen as weakness by those who had endured far greater hardships for far longer periods of time. To make matters worse, a teacher's offer to resign was seen by many administrators as a personal vote of no confidence. Some administrators seemed to see it as a test of allegiance: if the teacher chose to leave, he had no allegiance to the administrator; if he said, "Oh no, I couldn't leave *you*," then he passed the test.

The six young teachers were willing to work *with* most administrators as colleagues, but not *under* their control. Administrators, on the other hand, often felt threatened by the young teachers and wanted them only in subordinate and obedient roles. This conflict in role definition centered on classroom practices: each of the teachers debated whether to act according to his philosophy, saving children from perceived oppression and boredom, or to assume a more traditional role which would salvage his relationships with parents and administrators. Here was the ultimate agony and conflict of these six open classroom teachers: *Wherein lies courage?* In fighting for one's personal and professional ideals and for one's right of self-determination as a teacher, or in "going straight" by making the concessions to administrators and parents necessary for survival? Initially, most opted for the former. By the time they came around to the latter, it was too late.

Unfortunately, no one considered the third alternative—that "going straight" might ultimately be the most powerful way of fighting for one's ideals.

CONCLUSION

. . . money pours in, brains and talent are applied . . . but disagreements rage, frustrations boil over, factions struggle for power. All these concerns begin to absorb more energy than the job at hand, educating children. And the children become not the beneficiaries, but the losers.

The first year of the Lincoln-Attucks Program was a failure. Personal, pedagogical, and political conflicts all but canceled out potential benefits for administrators, teachers, parents, and children. It is difficult to sort out neatly the factors which led to the failure of open education in this public school situation from the factors which led to the failure of the Program itself. To what extent were these failures a function of a poorly planned and administered program? Of racial tensions? Of the slowness with which the public school bureaucracy responded to urgent requests? Of the unwillingness of the University Center team to work at the request of the school people, and their inability to help disturbed children as well as diagnosing their disturbances? Of the inexperience of the six open classroom teachers? Of the problems of trying to implement open education in two different communities? Of the shortcomings of the whole concept of open education?

The Lincoln-Attucks Program was firmly based on an unfortunate and a very common assumption: that the unpleasant, and unproductive, educational experience of children in school can be rectified by the infusion of *more money* and *more people*. If a bad educational system exists, saturate it with more of what it already has: new buses are better than old; new texts better than old; new buildings better than old; what one teacher can do well, three can do better; what two administrators can do adequately, twelve can do better. The Program demonstrated, if nothing else, that the principle "the more the better" is a simplistic one; that more money and more people do not necessarily lead to more learning for children.

Yet the tragedy of the Program's first year was not that there was too much money and too many people; in a sense, there can never be too much money and too many people for the problems of urban schools. The tragedy was that the climate of the Program elicited the worst far more often than the best from its participants. Few of the nonteaching adults were capable of either perceiving or acting upon the hundreds of problems which children and teachers were having each day. Instead, each searched fruitlessly for a significant sphere of influence, power, and security. A public elementary school, particularly in the inner city, is a fragile but viable social system. With one principal, fifteen teachers, and a secretary there is no question about the center of decisionmaking power—it resides with the principal who runs the ship in a more or less authoritarian way. Granted, the relationship between principal and teacher may not be harmonious, trusting, or productive, but there is little doubt in anyone's mind what the system is, how it operates, or what place each individual has in it. The traditional organization offers order.

Such a system is incapable of adapting fast enough to accommodate a sudden infusion and intrusion of many additional people. It is difficult enough for a traditional school to accommodate *one* new person. If an agent from outside the system— a private foundation or a university, for instance—intends to change a school, a critical amount of stability and continuity in terms of personnel and practices must be retained. The infusion of people and money must be carefully monitored, introduced only as evidence from the school suggests that it can accommodate and make use of these inputs. Monitoring must be done by someone from within the system who is familiar with it. There must be a person on hand under the roof who can assess needs and match appropriate people and money to them. He must be sensitive to the ways each change would threaten the system and its members and must adjust the rate at which innovations are introduced accordingly. These are judgments which require extraordinary sensitivity, work, patience, and personal security. The Program paid dearly for the absence of such a person.

There must also be a plan—a preconceived idea, an organizing principle directing the selection of people and the allocation of funds—which permits the matching of personalities and philosophies of new members. The absence of such a plan invites—indeed, demands—a frantic scramble by everyone for everything. Such a fight for power all but destroys the usefulness of those who would improve the situation. Almost any plan is better than no plan. Concerning the Lincoln-Attucks Program, the local newspaper reported that

Parents also were wary of the program's claims that there was no special new plan and wouldn't be unless parents were involved. As one parent put it, "The parents felt that there was a plan, but they weren't being told about it."

The seven advocates of open education failed, in part, because of their inexperience, stubbornness, idealism, and even arrogance. But responsibility also rests with those who hired so many educators with so many conflicting values. In a very real sense, people *are* program. Necessarily associated with the choice of personnel is choice of ideology, philosophy, and direction. With the selection of people inescapably come also the ideas they hold. The Lincoln-Attucks Program may have been conceived as an empty vessel, waiting to be filled, but people are not. You cannot hire able, bright, energetic, idealistic people who, at the same time, have no convictions and can be programmed like marionettes in some ideological or pedagogical direction at the command of an authority. Nor is it possible to have docile and obedient teachers respond to command by authorities with eagerness, imagination, intelligence, sensitivity, and commitment—as all too many school staffs attest. It is impossible to have your cake and eat it too—even though some administrators never ceased trying. An authoritarian administration elicits creative, productive behavior from neither the competent nor the incompetent.

While they may have learned a great deal, the experience of the seven open educators, like that of most of the participants in the first year of the Program, can only be called a failure. In their case, perhaps, it was a bigger and more dramatic failure because their expectations were so distinct and so completely violated. Both the ends and the means they employed were incompatible with the ends and means expected and demanded by administrators and parents.

Not only were their attempts unproductive, they were counterproductive. During the year, many got the impression that the Program was just biding its time, waiting to retool for the second year without the dissonant open educators, as attested in this excerpt from a local newspaper:

Although admitting that the Lincoln-Attucks Program hasn't gotten off the ground this year, those connected with the project believe that it can "really fly" when the coordinator now being sought is hired, and replacement teachers are found.

Perhaps the impact upon these two schools of open educators can best be seen in the reorganization of the program during its second year. The new staff was described by a continuing teacher as

. . . on the whole, older, more experienced, with more blacks, fewer men, narrower, more conservative educationally, more traditional in style and in attitudes towards change.

Thus the attempts by the six teachers to establish open classrooms had the immediate effect of eliciting a reaction which drove the schools far closer to the military academy model than they had been before the Program began.

None of the open educators was asked to stay with the Program for its second year. Of the seven who started the school year in September, three saw the last day of school in June: two teachers and the instructional coordinator. The circumstances surrounding the premature departure of the other four are not particularly significant; *any* occurrence might have served as the "reason." One teacher resigned in March when the acting principal sought to bring another, full-time "experienced" teacher into her class with primary instructional authority. One was suspended in April after a heated altercation with another teacher before an audience of several children. He soon resigned. Two teachers, a married couple, left in early May upon the death of a member of the family.

At a conference earlier in the year, the instructional coordinator was told by one of the codirectors that his participation in the Program would end in June, as would that of seven others. Of the eight so dismissed, seven were proponents of open education. Of the eighteen other teachers, all but four resigned. The administration also showed considerable turnover and turnout. The new public school superintendent decided to substantially reduce the codirectors' participation in the Program. The assistant to the principals, who had been acting principal at Lincoln, was transferred to another school as a teacher of children with learning difficulties. A black man was appointed director of the Program by the superintendent "to guide parental involvement and to assist the principals with instructional problems." He in turn appointed a black principal at Lincoln, retained the former administrative principal at Attucks, and changed the involvement of the University Center team.

As is often the case in a situation fraught with political and pedagogical conflict, children were the unfortunate pawns. Because little systematic evaluation was carried out, it is difficult to assess the impact of the Program's first year on children's skills, self-image, or ability to form concepts, except to say that their need for order, consistency, and sustained human relationships was not served by the internal dissonance and large turnover of personnel. In schools, children become priority concerns only when adult concerns have been resolved—which, unfortunately, is not very often.

The year following the Lincoln-Attucks experience, only two of the open educators were teaching: one in an independent school, and one in a university lab school—both places which encouraged an open learning environment. Thus, after the experience described here, *none* of the seven open educators was employed in the public schools. This says a great deal about hope for change in the public schools, about resistance to open education, and about those who would make the schools more open. Altruistic intentions, impeccable academic credentials, abundant vigor, and unlimited educational vision will not, in themselves, suffice. As one of the custodians in the Program put it, "That and a dime will get you a cup of coffee."

The Lincoln-Attucks experience should not be read, however, to mean that informal education is suitable only for middle-class, largely white, schools. As of this writing, the Lincoln and Attucks schools are moving, on their own terms, toward more open learning environments. The lessons to be drawn have to do with the processes of change. That is the issue to which the succeeding chapters address themselves.

4

The Principal
and Open Education

A necessary condition for teacher growth, therefore, is that the teacher be allowed to work on things which he regards as important, that he be allowed to work in ways which make sense to him, and that he have at his disposal means both abundant and convenient.[1]

An important factor contributing to the failure of the teachers advocating more informal classrooms was the absence of a person in the Lincoln-Attucks Program who both supported their efforts and had power. Someone must provide both political cover and pedagogical experience if teachers are to move toward open classrooms. Few teachers have the time, perseverance, knowledge, materials, and self-sufficiency to surmount, without help, resistance from children, parents, other teachers, and school administrators. The difficulty of the individual "going it alone" has been well stated:

Because of conspicuous gaps in communication between administrators and teachers, it is often impossible for teachers to initiate new programs, despite their logical position to do so. In order that a teacher's proposal may reach the ultimate decision-maker, it normally must move upward through several status levels. It is thus open to successive rejection in the shape of either a direct refusal or a marked lack of enthusiasm. Moreover, organizational patterns favor rejection where approval may result in additional work, transfer of responsibility, or both, to the approver. It is for this reason that educational change rarely is inspired from the bottom of the hierarchy.[2]

The principal's position of responsibility and leadership within the school is the critical and pivotal point of influence over teachers' teaching and children's learning. It is not sufficient for the administrator to permit teachers to innovate. If teachers are to move toward open classrooms, the principal must actively, deliberately, and carefully facilitate their efforts.

In most schools, teachers are told by superiors what to teach. To the extent the teacher gives children choice, children devote themselves to activities other than those prescribed, and the teacher is accountable. Consequently, teachers give children little choice. However, when the teacher is released from the necessity of following a syllabus and permitted to make instructional decisions on the basis of his observations of children, it becomes more likely that he will respect and permit children's choices, for he is no longer rigidly accountable for them. The "facilitative" principal gives teachers opportunities to make choices and to confer with others, in the belief that the teacher who consciously and deliberately decides what to do in his classroom, in light of many alternatives, will be more likely to evolve a successful, consistent philosophy and style than will the teacher who has little choice. If the school principal can become as effective in freeing and facilitating teaching and learning as he has been in constraining and directing teachers and students, the introduction of informal classrooms becomes a realistic possibility.

The function of the facilitative principal does not lend itself to theoretical construction. The principal committed to open education finds his role emerging from efforts to apply an abstract philosophy to a real situation. The role discussed here is derived primarily from my own attempt as principal to introduce the ideas and practices of open education in the particular atmosphere of the Lincoln-Attucks Program. This role evolved as a collection of practices which, moment by moment, seemed consonant with assumptions discussed earlier and which seemed to offer some possibility of positive change. Many of these practices may have relevance to other situations, especially those in which the principal is attempting to help move at least part of a school community toward open education; many can be fulfilled in schools by personnel other than the principal.

The goal of most principals is to maintain order, maximize production, and minimize dissonance. Principals attempt to achieve this goal by exercising direct, authoritarian, hierarchical leadership; by arranging schedules, writing letters, making phone calls; and by maintaining tight control over money, supplies, adults, and children. But one does not have to legislate, control, and direct behavior in order to change it:

. . . you do not need complete authority over a social organization in order to reform it. The important thing is not to control the system but to understand it. Someone who has a valid conception of the system as a whole can often introduce relatively minor changes that have extensive consequences throughout the entire organization.[3]

Indeed, it is dubious that more than superficial change can be achieved through authoritarian means. A facilitative principal attempts to lead, influence, and affect teachers' behavior by supporting and responding as well as by initiating. He attempts to determine and understand teachers' needs and provide appropriate services. If his help is valuable, teachers will recognize it, make use of it, and profit from it.

In one sense, this role, like that of a more traditional principal, entails apparently menial, insignificant, thankless responsibilities. But the principal who would encourage open education performs these clerical duties for different reasons: to broaden teachers' experiences, to expand their realm of choice, and to assist them directly in the classroom. His underlying purpose is not only to maintain a smooth-running school, but also to provide teachers with a variety of rich experiences, materials, and opportunities, on the basis of which they may make significant educational decisions. Participation in important instructional decisions helps each teacher make up his mind, take a pedagogical stand, and come to terms with major issues and with himself. In the process, the teacher is likely to become more conscious of his own ideas about children, learning, and knowledge. These beliefs, reflected in classroom practice, can be continually developed and refined on the basis of observation of children. Thus, the facilitative principal can be an advisor, as well as supervisor; a colleague, as well as superordinate; a supporter, as well as adversary; a provider, as well as requirer. The possibility of children behaving in ways suggested in Chapter 1, and of teachers behaving in ways suggested in Chapter 2, would seem to depend upon leadership by a principal who facilitates in ways which will be discussed here.

While the role of facilitative principal may appear to be a useful and nonthreatening one, it is by no means easy—in the context of the Lincoln-Attucks Program or elsewhere. The administrator who allows teachers to make important instructional decisions and helps to implement them can expect problems. His position is neither easily established nor easily maintained. No matter how carefully he defines his functions, every important issue exerts pressures to exceed those limits. One thing leads to another; and before the facilitator realizes it, he is taking over and making decisions. Few administrators can resist these temptations, particularly if it appears others will bungle a job he can do so much better and faster. What if the fourth-grade teachers wish to order $500 worth of textbooks of questionable value? In this and in countless similar situations, the principal has the responsibility both to state his ideas and opinions clearly and then to permit teachers to make their own judgment. This is difficult to do without feelings of resentment and a desire to interfere. Just as it is for the teacher in the classroom, the line between intervening and interfering is difficult to discern, and more difficult to respect.

To facilitate in one quarter is to make waves in another. There can be no "pure" role for the administrative facilitator, for principal is a political as well as a pedagogical position; he must be supportive at one point and display initiative, leadership, firmness, and authority at another. The facilitative principal can expect antagonism from teachers, many of whom want to be told what to do, even though they complain about such directives. The authoritarian principal conveniently relieves these teachers of accountability and responsibility for their actions. For this reason, many teachers, like many children, resist being confronted with "opportunities" and "alternatives" from which to choose. For them, an opportunity to make important instructional decisions is an opportunity to fail and to be blamed for failing.

The relationship between administrators and teachers in the Lincoln-Attucks Program, as in most schools, was at least initially an adversarial one. Furthermore, when the instructional principal tried to help teachers, he was considered in opposition to other administrators, who felt that anyone on the "teachers' side" had to be against them. The administrator who facilitates teachers' efforts, then, may place himself in double jeopardy: he is an administrator, and therefore assumed to be a teacher adversary; he is supportive of teachers, and therefore assumed to be antiadministrator. The continuing battle between teachers and administrators in the Program perpetuated this conflict, and the instructional principal was regularly called upon to choose sides.

Giving teachers choice over many instructional decisions raised a variety of problems with other administrators in the Program. From the beginning of the year, the principal argued that a resource person (as many of the University Center and public school administrators were often called) is one who responds to requests of teachers, not one who requires, demands, or intrudes into classrooms. Few understood, let alone accepted, this definition. On the contrary, most felt what they had to offer was so valuable that all teachers should be required to hear it or do it. They were seldom advocates of teacher choice.

At first, it was futile for one administrator to try to set up a supportive, responsive system while others functioned in more directive ways. Teachers' tentative attempts to make choices and take responsibilities were quickly discouraged. But, as the year progressed, other administrators began to accord teachers more and more choice, not so much because they believed in it but because there was little alternative. Required meetings were met with increasing resistance and decreasing attendance. Teachers were asked if they wanted to contribute to assembly programs, if they would like to confer with the University Center team, if they would be willing to attend meetings and what they would like to discuss. After Christmas, virtually every contribution of the curriculum specialists and other administrators was on an everyone-who-wishes-to-come-is-welcome basis. When one administrator gave teachers choice over important decisions, it became more and more difficult for others to withhold it.

Even though the experience of the instructional principal in the Lincoln-Attucks Program was neither sufficient nor successful enough to suggest an elegant description of the functions of a principal who would help develop informal classrooms, the experience did provide an opportunity to explore a variety of methods for working over, under, around, and through the resistance discussed in the preceding chapter. Several ideas showed promise, and at least occasional success, in broadening teachers' experiences, enriching their instructional decisions, eliciting support from the community, and making more likely the development of open classrooms. These ideas will be discussed in terms of three general categories: helping teachers develop an educational philosophy, helping teachers work with children, and supporting teachers by establishing a positive relationship with the community.

THE PRINCIPAL HELPS TEACHERS DEVELOP THEIR IDEAS ABOUT CHILDREN, LEARNING, AND KNOWLEDGE

The facilitative principal can help each teacher critically examine, develop, and refine his philosophy of education by providing instructional alternatives and the opportunity to select from among them. Some techniques found helpful in the Lincoln-Attucks Program were a newsletter, workshops to introduce new materials, showing films, and arranging professional visits.

The Newsletter. One device which seems simple but which was an important means of conveying information about workshops, films, professional visits, and other events was the calendar. In the early weeks of the Program there was no regular communication within the schools. People went places, did things, and held meetings, but usually only those directly involved in the event knew about it beforehand. Knowledge of events is a necessary precondition for choice and participation, so the instructional principal produced a regular newsletter. This entailed finding out what was going on in and around the schools and periodically distributing this information: lectures on urban education, an exhibit at the art gallery on black history, an organized walk through the neighborhood, a visit by a salesman from a textbook publisher. *This Week at the Lincoln-Attucks Program* became a regular periodical to which everyone could contribute and have access. Announcing (and implicitly recommending) events increased the involvement of parents, teachers, and administrators in a number of activities.

Workshops. The instructional principal organized many workshops during the year. In June, after most of the staff had been hired, a workshop was set up for teachers, administrators, and parents, similar to one previously attended in Loughborough, England. The school gym was divided into "interest tables" on which were placed manipulative curriculum materials: math blocks, language games, animals, crafts, etc. Curriculum specialists familiar with the materials were available to explain the materials, play games, and pose problems for participants as they wandered from table to table. This workshop introduced the staff to a wide variety of educational materials (many of which they ordered). It also served to acquaint members of the Program with one another.

After Christmas, and for most of the winter, the principal arranged workshops at one of the schools two evenings each month for parents, administrators, and teachers. A memorandum announcing each workshop told what materials and people would be on hand. Usually, a half-dozen people attended. A typical evening found a second-grade teacher making a cardboard table for her reading group; a fourth-grade teacher holding parent conferences in his room; a kindergarten and a second-grade teacher building a puppet stage and storefront of plywood; two other teachers working on large tables and bookcases; the science specialist holding a small workshop with three teachers on the use of Attribute Blocks; and two others making a balance beam.

These informal workshops, where time, space, materials, and demonstrations were available, seemed to help teachers directly influence their classroom environment, and perhaps helped many to feel secure enough working with their hands to encourage children to do likewise.

Films. Many films of open classrooms are now readily available (206–228). These provided another means of exposing the

Lincoln-Attucks staff to a range of ideas and techniques. The films were particularly useful because they allowed a large group to analyze a vicariously shared experience. On the occasion when administrators permitted the showing of a film of an open classroom, it filled this function very effectively. The film, depicting open classrooms in Washington, D.C., elicited a great deal of discussion, interest, and hostility. Anger, which had welled up within parents and administrators toward specific individuals in the Program, was directed toward the anonymous teachers in the film. Despite the strong feelings it produced, the film enabled some members of the staff to communicate for the first time. One administrator, who had been calling for more structure in classrooms, observed that the open classrooms in the film were loaded with structure of a kind he had not seen before. Similarly, a teacher interested in open education who had recoiled from the concept of structure saw its relevance and importance to children in open classrooms.

Professional Visits. Another way the principal attempted to broaden the experiences of teachers was to arrange visits and observation in other schools. The availability of ample funds for substitute teachers, baby-sitters, transportation, lodging, etc., greatly facilitated these visits. In this way, parents and teachers in the Program could see, and perhaps adopt, a variety of new practices. As with the calendar, the workshops, and the films, the principal's part was largely clerical and facilitative: seeking out interesting schools, making lists, and writing letters.

The instructional principal sent out regular notices describing workshops, conferences, demonstrations, and interesting schools and inviting anyone interested to respond. Everyone who took a trip wrote a brief account of his experience and circulated it to the rest of the staff. These periodic accounts encouraged others to make professional visits of their own, as well as to share their insights.

Staff and parents made about forty professional visits during the year: to a new reading program in White Plains; the Model Schools Program in Washington, D.C.; university seminars; a linguistics conference; and mathematics workshops. Several also visited classes elsewhere within the Program and the city.

Benefits clearly extended beyond the chance for a change from daily duties. One teacher, who visited the reading program in White Plains, commented: "What impressed me was that teachers were using no controlled vocabulary, and yet children were learning new words, some simple, one-syllable words and others far more difficult." The opportunity to see this success for herself made this teacher question the value of a controlled vocabulary in a way that no number of courses, books, or lectures could have done.

Over the year, it became clear that teachers who were provided opportunities to study alternative educational practices responded responsibly and enthusiastically. In short, the professional visits stimulated many to examine, question, and refine their own educational ideas and practices.

THE PRINCIPAL HELPS TEACHERS
WORK WITH CHILDREN

In order to encourage teachers to develop more informal classrooms, the principal must provide instructional leadership. It helps if he can run a classroom and make his expertise available to teachers. The facilitative principal must be sensitive to where each teacher is in his thinking and practice, able to make appropriate suggestions which will help extend the teacher's ideas and action. He must know what steps are comfortable for each teacher to take and at what rate, and must be able to anticipate and analyze problems so they may be avoided or resolved. In order to accomplish these goals, he must confer often with teachers and support their efforts.

The experience of the instructional principal suggests several ways for a principal to help teachers work with children: responding to teachers' requests, making classroom observations, teaching demonstration lessons, arranging class trips, and setting up learning centers.

Responding to Teachers' Requests

Teachers trying to develop open classrooms need a constant supply of materials and assistance. Therefore, a primary responsibility of the principal is to detect, acknowledge, and attempt to satisfy teachers' needs. Consequently, the instructional principal set up a simple "I want" system. A cardboard box in the outer office was labeled "I Want Box," and beside it was placed a stack of "I want" slips with spaces for a teacher to write his name, what he wanted, from whom, and when. The staff was asked to channel all requests through this system. The principal emptied the box frequently and attempted to fill each request immediately.

At first requests were for supplies: notebooks, pencils, a movable blackboard, rubber bands, staples, etc. But after a few weeks, more and more teachers began to ask for services: someone to administer a psychological test, someone to help teach an art lesson, someone to go with the class on a field trip. Ultimately, the "I want" box was used for making many kinds of requests and expressing many kinds of needs. Some teachers simply wanted easy access to materials they hadn't time to find themselves ("I want a box of straws"). Others wanted more complex resources, which they did not know exactly where to find:

I want someone to visit my class from:
    the redevelopment office
    the community school

the day-care center
the thrift shop
the fire department
the Urban League

Perhaps there are other agencies in the neighborhood we know nothing about. I would like for the person to tell my class the function of the agency he represents. How they serve the needs of seven- and eight-year-old children (if at all). Can you arrange these sessions for me during the months of February and March?

Some teachers used the system to request help from experts in other fields. ("I want someone to look at Michael Smith in afternoon kindergarten. His behavior is becoming stranger and stranger.") Others used it to reassert needs they had made clear in other ways:

I want a conference on Peter Wilk. Including myself, Nancy, Mrs. Cook, Sandy, Harriet, and Roland. I have tried to get help since the beginning of the year and will accept no answer but yes for this conference. Sorry to be such a bitch but I must get these people together. The conference must be this week due to the foul-up in the clinic appointments. I would like a time by noon tomorrow.

A few found it a handy outlet for frustration and anger. ("I want to know when I get reimbursed for the sales slips I handed in two months ago.")

This system succeeded in enabling teachers to express their needs. Meeting those needs was another matter. Many administrators resented the "I want" box and refused to respond to it. ("What am I, their servant?" "Any time they want something, I'm supposed to jump?" "They think we don't have anything to do but sit here and wait for them to tell us what to do." "They should plan ahead and get it themselves.") The hostility and impatience many teachers expressed did not help matters. Occasionally, as if in retaliation, administrators would use an "I want" slip to make a request of the teachers. ("I want your attendance figures." "I want your contribution to the United Fund.") Nevertheless, most of the "I want" requests were acknowledged and filled. Over the winter and spring several hundred requests were received, and it became a full-time job to handle them.

Too often teachers do not engage in imaginative and interesting practices in their classrooms because of the time, materials, and help such activities demand. The "I want" system was an effective mechanism for teachers to express their needs. If they were met quickly, children as well as teachers enjoyed the direct benefits. Perhaps most important, the "I want" system provided a structure for a continuing dialogue between administrator and teacher about instructional problems.

Classroom Observations

Most teachers need and want nonthreatening observation from a person who can diagnose a classroom situation and offer helpful suggestions. In the Lincoln-Attucks Program, the instructional principal helped teachers work with children by observing in classrooms on many occasions during the year at teachers' requests. Some invitations were to "Come in and see what's going on," but in most cases the teacher invited the principal to observe a class period demonstrating a particular idea he was trying out.

On these occasions, the teacher deliberately exposed his ideas and his difficulties with the confidence the principal would understand what he was trying to do and refrain from judgment. To protect this confidence, the principal observed for a long time before commenting and then limited comments to areas of the teacher's concern. Discussions with the teacher, immediately following each visit, provided an opportunity for teacher and principal to examine difficulties both had witnessed. These conferences seemed to assure teachers that what they were trying was important, that the difficulties inherent in nontraditional practices were common ones, and that someone cared about what they were trying to do and was willing to help them. Finally, the conferences frequently helped teachers find new ways and fresh energies to continue to work on the problem.

In this supportive role, the instructional principal made himself available to the twenty-five teachers during the year, although it was the six open classroom teachers who most often requested his help. The experience suggests that teachers will request help if they need it and if it is given without judgmental overtones; their requests are likely to be specific to current classroom difficulties; the teacher who requests help is likely to profit from it. In short, teacher-initiated observation seems to be beneficial.

Demonstration Lessons

Someone in the school must also be available to teach demonstration lessons involving new curriculum materials. It is one thing to provide teachers with an abundance of manipulative materials and workshops to show their use. It is quite another thing for the teacher to take the first tentative steps with these materials in his own classroom. It is not surprising, then, that a number of teachers in the Lincoln-Attucks Program asked for someone to come into their classrooms to teach a lesson—often, in an area of uncertainty.

For example, one fourth-grade teacher asked the principal for help with her math program and wanted an hour's lesson three times a week for a month, to help her class learn how to borrow and carry (skills which most had memorized but could not apply). The principal taught several lessons using paper strips and small squares of colored paper (for units, tens, and hundreds). With these, each child made his own paper abacus on which he performed arithmetical operations, physically trading one orange "10" for ten green "1's." Initially, the lessons had little influence upon the teacher, but when she discovered their positive effect on the children's arithmetic skills, she adopted the abacus as a valuable teaching technique.

In another fourth grade, the teacher asked for a demonstrated art lesson. His was a difficult group of children who, for obvious reasons, had not previously worked with art materials. The principal introduced potato printing, with knives, paints, and paper. The children responded with messy enthusiasm and some good prints, although the initial ones were closer to finger painting than to potato printing. There was mess and noise, but children were supplied with materials fast enough to sustain their interest. A teacher's aide commented that this was the first class all year in which everyone participated voluntarily. Afterward, the teacher asked for potatoes, paints, and paper to use the following week, and two other teachers requested the same lesson.

During the spring, the third- and fourth-grade teachers asked the principal to teach softball on a weekly basis. Children seldom played organized games before school, at lunch and recess, or after school, since they had difficulty cooperating long enough to sustain a game. When the instruction began, children selected their captains, who in turn chose the teams. There was a problem with two boys whom no one wanted because they always struck out. They were both very tense, cautious, and fearful (they were also having difficulty reading). The principal asked the captains if they would take them if each boy could have as many strikes as were needed to hit the ball. In other words, they could never strike out. The captains agreed to this, and the two boys were delighted. When they came up to bat, they swung with great abandon and enthusiasm for every pitch. Never again did either boy miss three pitches before he got his hit.

The first game lasted only fifteen minutes—less than an inning—before rock throwing, swearing, and fighting obliterated any semblance of softball. There was little understanding that the captain gives orders and a team member obeys them. "Rules" were whatever was made up at the time to fit the situation. A child who made a hit could expect to encounter two or hree players from the other team stationed around second base, like a hockey defense, making sure that, no matter how good the hit, the batter went no farther.

The next week, after a discussion of problems which had developed the week before, the children suggested some rules against swearing, throwing rocks, name-calling, and fighting. Their punishments were severe: an out would be called against a team at bat if one of its members broke a rule (or an out removed if the team in the field broke a rule); in addition, the offending player had to go into the school building. Everyone agreed to abide by the new rules and the game began. This time the contest lasted two innings—about a half hour. Several "almost fights" were discouraged rather than incited by teammates, although the game ultimately dissolved into name-calling, tears, and fights, and the players returned to their classrooms. Gradually, over the following two months, the children learned to obey their captains, developed some sense of supportive behavior, and sustained an hour's play. Boys began to ask if they could borrow the bases and equipment to set up their own games. Thereafter, unsupervised softball games were common events.

These and other attempts by the instructional principal seemed to have an important influence upon teachers and children. But in the Program, few administrators were willing to work with children, let alone in ways requested by teachers. It was as if they saw themselves as white-collar workers who neither needed nor wanted ever again to wear a blue collar. The person who lives under the roof of the school, the administrator who will "get his hands dirty" with children's activities, who is ready to respond to a teacher's request for help, seems most able to effect positive change.

The Learning Center

The facilitative principal can help the teacher in the class-room by assuming responsibility for children who cannot work in the regular classroom situation. In the Program, as in most inner-city schools, there were many disruptive, hyperactive children who spent the greater part of each day standing outside the office. These children were not benefiting from school, nor was the school benefiting from the adverse public relations caused by their display. This presented a dilemma: to keep these children in their classrooms would be at the expense of the class and the teacher; to send them home would be at the expense of the parents; to send them to the office was at the expense of the office and the child.

But nobody wanted to work specifically with these children. Attempting to resolve the dilemma, help the children, and introduce new curriculum materials, the instructional principal set up a "learning center." Each morning and afternoon the principal (or someone in his place) was on duty in the school library with a variety of books and learning materials. If a child became unbearably disruptive and uncontrollable in the classroom, the teacher could send him to the learning center. Those in the center then decided what the child would do (unless the teacher had given an assignment), how many children they could accommodate, and for how long.

The learning center was "open" the first week in October, staffed part time by the principal, two curriculum specialists, and a teacher's aide. Business was brisk—too brisk. Five or six children were sent the first morning, each one near hysteria. Firm rules were made: no fighting, no running inside the building, clean up after each activity, no destroying equipment. More than a single upset child was difficult for one adult to manage, but eventually most children became involved in puzzles, magnets, reading, measuring, drawing, and other activities.

One strategy for handling these children proved particularly effective: the adult would bring some of his own work to the learning center. He put the child in a corner with interesting materials, blocks, paints, sand, batteries, and bulbs and told the child not to bother him, that he had work to do. Usually the child would begin to explore the materials, apparently relieved. His initial upset had been a result of a confrontation with an adult, and he now felt free from adult demands.

Major problems emerged. More children came to the learning center than could be accommodated. Because only children whose behavior was sufficiently disruptive were sent, the center was becoming a reward for children if they were *bad* enough. The only cure was to change the ground rules: *if* a chronically difficult child behaved himself all morning and finished his work, *then* he was allowed to come. The learning center became a privilege which children earned, and many began to come to finish assignments, to select a book, to work in small groups on a project, to design and build something as part of a unit of study. In this way, the center helped to "prevent," rather than to "cure," disruptive behavior.

As time went on, the learning center expanded. Some children went outside the library and played or painted on the concrete. Others found the stove (used by the PTA) and made cookies. The principal set up a woodworking shop in a storage room, where children made birdhouses, hot rods, and doghouses. Teachers, administrators and parents came to see what the children were doing. They observed "playing" which was also clearly "learning." They talked and argued about what they saw. Thus, the learning center became a kind of open classroom laboratory for the school community.

There were other fringe benefits. One child, who had been playing with several magnets, borrowed them to take to his class. The next day, his teacher and his friends wanted to work with magnets, and a class was arranged. Then, the neighboring classes wanted magnets. In this way, the center helped to disseminate instructional ideas and materials throughout the school.

But success at anything by anyone in the Program was threatening. Many administrators, suspecting some kind of power play, refused to work with the center. One administrator commented about the instructional principal working with problem children: "We've got to get someone else to take care of them. . . . You've got more important things to do." Parents said, "I don't want my child to go to a learning center. He should be with the rest of his class." Teachers said, "Don't make it *too* good or we won't have any kids left." Thus it came as no surprise when shortly before Christmas it was deemed that the library should be a library, not a playroom and refuge for children evading classroom work. A library aide was hired, the curriculum materials removed, and quiet and order restored. After two months, the learning center was closed.

Although in this setting the learning center was short-lived, the concept of an instructional alternative to classrooms within the school offers exciting possibilities. It provides children with an incentive to continue functioning in their classrooms or a constructive alternative for those unable to do so. It gives teachers, administrators, and parents an opportunity to observe children learning and to discuss their progress, unencumbered by sensitivity of any particular teacher. It provides a center for the dissemination of ideas and materials within the school, and it stimulates teachers to examine and refine classroom practices on the basis of what they see children doing in a different setting. Perhaps most important, it is an example of the educational system learning to adapt itself to children who will not or cannot adapt themselves to it.

Class Trips

The principal can help teachers extend the children's learning environment beyond the classroom by facilitating the planning of trips. When a class studied a subject appropriate for a field trip—for example, a trip to a zoo for a first-grade class studying animals—the teacher was encouraged to contact the principal, who made the necessary arrangements: money for admission, lunches, a bus, and whatever information was available or necessary.

At first there were few trips. But as word of exciting ventures spread from child to child, parent to parent, and teacher to teacher, and as spring and longer, warmer days arrived, requests became more frequent. Teachers made full use of trips as motivation: "When we have read about life in colonial New England, we can visit Sturbridge Village." After trips, children wrote about, talked about, and drew pictures of what they had seen.

Teachers, given choice and administrative support, developed interests in as many directions as the children. They requested nearly two hundred trips: to local parks; to rides on different forms of transportation; to museums, zoos, and municipal buildings; and to historical sites. In this, as in other cases, a helpful idea spread of its own accord without administrative fiat.

THE PRINCIPAL ESTABLISHES A POSITIVE RELATIONSHIP WITH THE COMMUNITY

In the inner-city there is no longer a question of whether the school system wants to or will allow parents to participate in educational decisions affecting their children. Parents are participating. Liberal educators tend to favor "community control," assuming (quite incorrectly) that when parents have the choice they will opt for the humanistic, informal educational practices preferred by the liberals. As we have seen, however, many parents advocate very strict, traditional schools. An important question for the liberal is whether he cannot only accept parents' decisions but also help them toward the ends they desire.

Although school administrators are inclined to view greater parent involvement in the educational process as a threat, there is evidence that such involvement can provide strong support, pedagogically as well as politically, of programs intended to help inner-city children. The Lincoln-Attucks experience suggests that parents do not want to overthrow professional educators. On the contrary, when administrators, challenged by parents, asked, "Well, what do you think we should do?" parents often replied: "We want to have a say in policy decisions, but don't ask us what we want; tell us what you plan to do and let us respond to it." What the parents are asking for, in essence, is *veto power;* they want to know what is planned, have assurance that it is good, and be asked if they accept the plan. Parents want leadership from professional educators who will be responsive and accountable to them for professional decisions.

From the Lincoln-Attucks experience a central precept is clear: one can only move as fast and as far as parents (and children) will permit. And generally that is not very far and not very fast. Attempts to move behind parents' backs may result in small temporary gains and changes today, but by next week all that was gained may have been lost. There seems to be little hope for overcoming parental resistance either rapidly or indirectly. Slower, more direct and open means seem more promising, if more difficult.

Parents may be more likely to accept and respect open education practices if the principal includes them in the same activities as teachers: workshops, films, professional trips, demonstration lessons, classroom observations, learning centers, and frequent newsletters. Parents who are—or feel they are—kept in the dark about what is happening to their children in school will be more resistant than those who know what is going on, even if they don't fully approve of particular practices. The principal can make the acceptance of informal classrooms by some parents more likely by establishing genuine, frequent communication with them and by involving them in the professional activities of the school.

Parents are pleased to receive word from the school. They welcome a calendar of events. In addition, and perhaps more important, the principal can encourage teachers and their students to write periodic newsletters to parents, relating children's progress and activities in class and on trips. The teacher in the Program who sent out a monthly newsletter, for instance, received largely positive responses from parents, even though she employed many ideas and practices of open education. Parents came to observe their children in class, and more of them attended her conferences and parent nights than those of any other teacher in the Program. The principal can also encourage teachers to make frequent visits to parents' homes to see children in that context and to discuss a child's progress.

In addition, the principal in the open school can involve parents in professional activities of the school. Although there were few opportunities in the Lincoln-Attucks Program to offer parents workshops with curriculum materials, this appeared to be a promising idea. On Monday a mother might object to her third-grader "playing" with blocks. But if on Tuesday that parent had an opportunity to experience the educational excitement and difficulty of Attribute Blocks or Cuisenaire rods, then it might become acceptable for the child to use blocks on Wednesday.

The Washington film helped to legitimize open education practices for many parents. As long as they thought that the animals and materials in several classrooms were the perverse experiment of a few teachers, they could only resist and reject them. When they saw a film depicting children in similar classrooms in the Washington *Model* School District, the same animals and materials suddenly became more permissible and legitimate. Just as an organization comes to "exist" in an important sense as soon as it has letterhead stationery, so open education comes to exist for many when seen on film.

On some occasions, the instructional principal invited parents to observe a teacher's lesson or his demonstration lesson and to participate in the subsequent discussion with the teacher. Parents were also encouraged to take part in the many trips taken by Lincoln and Attucks classes. They not only enjoyed learning more about their community but also derived satisfaction from performing valuable services to teachers and children.

Some parents were invited to tutor children. For instance, during the spring the reading teacher, overwhelmed by the number of children needing individual attention in reading, recruited six parents, gave them a quick course in teaching reading, helped them set up schedules, and put them to work. These parents helped nearly thirty children at least three times a week.

In summary, the role of the principal in encouraging informal classrooms which has been sketched here is a difficult yet exciting, promising, and rewarding one. It carries a heavy burden of clerical, seemingly unimportant chores. But these duties can lead to important instructional options for teachers, which can, in turn, lead to teachers' increased commitment and professional growth, and thus to children's learning. But the facilitative principal is not simply a clerk. He has a crucial interpersonal function. He recruits and hires able, trustworthy teachers; he trusts them; he provides them with as many reasonable alternatives, ideas, materials, and experiences as he can; he provides opportunities for teachers to confer with other adults about the possible consequences of each alternative; he permits and encourages teachers to make significant decisions about how and what they will teach; he accepts their choices; and he brings the consequences of each to the teacher's attention so that it may enlighten future choices. He also supports teachers by interpreting classrooms to parents. In short, the facilitative principal helps teachers become agents of their own teaching, so that they in turn may help children to become agents of their own learning.

EDUCATIONAL CHANGE

In the final analysis, change comes through the efforts of individuals. Success depends on how each of us resolves the problem of imposing our values and judgments on others. The Lincoln-Attucks experience has served to make explicit for me some of the dilemmas faced by one who attempts social change. Given a desire on the part of the educator to change what is to what he would have it be, there seem to be at least four possible modes of operating:

1. One can attempt change by writing about, talking about, teaching about, dreaming about the way things should be. John Holt, Paul Goodman, and Charles Silberman are examples of this mode; so are many academicians. This role usually removes and protects the change agent from direct involvement in the process of change and from the people he is ultimately trying to change. This change agent, by providing vision, rhetoric, and reason, essentially prods others to make changes—a legitimate and frequently powerful strategy.

2. One can attempt change by establishing the structure of a system as one would have it be, explaining the ends and means of the system fully, openly, and honestly, giving individuals—say, teachers, administrators, parents, and students—the

opportunity to choose freely and consciously whether or not to participate, and informing them to the fullest extent possible of the consequences of their choices. "Free Schools," "free universities," the Philadelphia Parkway Project, neighborhood schools, and the "voucher plan" are all examples of alternative structures from which one may choose. One of the difficulties of providing systems which require choice, however, is that people may choose *not* to participate in them. If this is the case, the system may have little influence. On the other hand, this kind of competitive, capitalistic marketplace may encourage innovative, useful ideas; those systems survive which satisfy the wishes and needs of a number of members of society.

3. One can attempt change by developing a power base from which decisions can be imposed on others, even if those decisions are foreign, frightening, and unfamiliar. Neil Sullivan's integrating of the Berkeley schools and Harvey Scribner's decentralizing of the New York City schools have been essentially administrative attempts at changing the system by fiat. Although authoritarian change is rapid and often effective in the short run, effects are often more apparent than real, resulting in modifications of superficial behavior rather than changes in basic thinking. When the change agent is removed, often change disappears as well.

4. One can attempt change by gradually, informally, indirectly, even surreptitiously, intervening in the status quo. By successive approximation, the change agent can move people away from where they are toward where he would have them be. This kind of change is probably the most common among educational reformers. The principal who wants to introduce an elaborate team-teaching system may start by encouraging two teachers who want to cooperate one period each day, and then building up to a situation in which ten teachers cooperate six periods each day. Such change is slow, but may be more lasting. One of the important characteristics of this mode is

that the change agent seldom reveals his ultimate goal (which would probably be rejected). He reveals only those increments leading toward his goal which neither startle nor threaten.

What is the best tactic for the educational reformer? The answer clearly depends on the educator and the situation. But the implications of any one of the four modes are profound. Options 1 and 2 accord to members of society a large degree of control over their own destinies. These positions reject the direct imposition of an outside point of view as impractical and/or unethical. Consequently, the change agent who employs either of these modes has less need to worry about "sources of resistance" and ways of overcoming them. Those who object to *Summerhill* need not read it; those who object to "free schools" do not have to send their children to them. Position 2, for example, implies that what parents consider best for their children *is* best for their children, or at least that what parents consider best they should have a right to receive. The parent who wants to send his child to a military academy and subject him to regimentation, corporal punishment, uniform dress and behavior, and motivation by fear has every right to do so. This is easy to say, but the educational reformer, in abdicating an opportunity to influence directly the kind of education children receive, must witness and live with the choices others make. This can be painful.

On the other hand, if the reformer accepts options 3 and 4, he says in effect, "I know better than you what is best for you and your children. I have some independent, nonrelative standard of worth for my point of view which supersedes yours. Not only do I know I am right, but I will impose my ideology on you and on your children, or (more indirectly, but substantively the same), I will educate you to my way of thinking, even though you may not approve. My solution, like a penicillin inoculation, is good for you, even though it hurts." Needless to say, both of these modes assure various degrees of resistance which also may be distasteful to the liberal educator, particularly to one who values the integrity of the individual and the dignity of free choice.

Anyone who would change our educational system—or any segment of our society—must become conscious of his own position with respect to influencing others. While the authoritarian educators may have little difficulty operating in mode 3, the more subtle manipulator in mode 4, the romantic critic in mode 1, and the objective, dispassionate pluralist in mode 2, most of us will reach no such easy resolution. But without this awareness and a thoughtful, reasoned commitment to one or a combination of these modes, he who would change things shifts frantically from one tactic to another as the situation demands and permits. These erratic vacillations make the difficult impossible and render any one strategy less powerful than it would be had it been consciously and consistently adhered to.

It is one thing to know the way we would like things to be; it is another thing to have ways of changing them; it is a third—and perhaps even more essential consideration—to have examined and resolved for oneself the dilemmas inherent in attempts to change other people to be more like us.

5

Conclusions and
Some Unanswered Questions

In Chapter 1, I suggested several assumptions about children, learning, and knowledge which I believe underlie the thinking of many open educators. In Chapter 2, I outlined a role for the teacher consonant with these assumptions. Chapters 3 and 4 centered on an experience in two inner-city public elementary schools. From this experience it is clear that the assumptions and practices of open education were not suited to the first year of the Lincoln-Attucks Program. The ends and the means offered by the open educators were not only inappropriate but incompatible with the ends and means expected and demanded by parents, administrators, and children.

The case study raises, and leaves unanswered, several questions crucial for open education: To what extent are open educators' assumptions valid? Can the ideas and practices of open education be successfully introduced into a public school system? What are the personal and intellectual outcomes for children in more informal learning environments compared with those for children in more traditional situations? Are informal classrooms better able to help children learn than more traditional classrooms? Are informal classrooms appropriate for inner-city children? Can the ideas of open education—choice, freedom, materials, informality, humaneness—have meaning for children, many of whom need and demand control from adults; for teachers who transmit knowledge; for parents wed-

202

ded to a traditional pedagogy; or for administrators embedded in an authoritarian decisionmaking structure?

An examination of the first year of the Lincoln-Attucks Program has shed a good deal of light on the nature and intensity of resistance toward open education which exists in the schools. This is important. But one is tempted to go even further and make a variety of additional inferences, interpretations, and generalizations. Political: change should not be attempted without the power necessary to accomplish it. Economic: there is an optimal amount of money and resources needed for each task; too much can be as debilitating as too little. Racial: whites should not attempt to superimpose their values on blacks or attempt to direct change from superordinate positions. Academic: there is a world separating the universities and the schools; attempts to bridge these two worlds are fraught with problems.

Depending upon the preferred interpretation, one might identify the "villains" and paint a scenario of good guys vs. bad guys—a frequent pastime of those in the Program. Playing this game, *any* of the various groups can become the antagonists: the school bureaucracy, university personnel, the foundation, blacks, whites, naive youth, etc.

While a temptation in the heat of the moment, in retrospect this kind of analysis seems simplistic and unproductive. Indeed, if a label of "villain" is to be attached, it probably belongs most appropriately on the open educators who came from a white, liberal, middle-class culture and tried to impose (albeit benevolently) their educational and personal ideas and ideals upon a quite different culture. This was a misguided mission and one that should have been recognized from the beginning as doomed, for while the six young teachers believed in the importance of "free choice," "individual differences," and "each progresses according to his own rate," with respect to change and growth for *children*, they were unable and unwilling to recognize and respect these very same conditions as no less crucial to change and growth for *adults*. Whereas they had an accurate, if academic, understanding of open education, they had little intuitive or even academic understanding of this urban environment which could inform their attempts to change it.

But this, too, is a narrow and confining interpretation. If we are content to leave such a complex and valuable experience tied up in this kind of tidy bundle, we turn our back on a wealth of information and possible insight. Somehow, we must reconcile the failure of the young teachers with a predominant, unsettling fact: in the Lincoln-Attucks Program, now four years old, three dozen teachers, parents, and aides recently concluded a very successful eleven-day workshop addressed to "The Open-Structure Classroom." Interest in and successful movement toward more informal classrooms now characterizes both the Lincoln and the Attucks schools.

We need to look again at the relationship between the case study and the implementation of informal classrooms. In my judgment, the failure of the attempt by the open educators to introduce a half-dozen informal classrooms was more a consequence of their methods and of the particular conditions surrounding the first year of the Lincoln-Attucks Program than it was a rejection of the validity of open education. The case study does not constitute a fair test of either the ideas or the practices of open education. From it we can conclude neither the worth nor the worthlessness of informal classrooms in public schools.

It would be easy to go on and dismiss this experience as being out of the ordinary and therefore as irrelevant to other situations. From my subsequent work in more affluent school districts and from observations in more "ordinary" inner-city schools, I am convinced, however, that *most* public schools offer conditions which are similar to those in which the attempts of the seven open educators failed. This attempt to introduce ideas and practices of open education met with problems which might be encountered anywhere: in cities, suburbs, private schools, public schools, black schools, white schools—wherever educational change calls for significant departure from expected practice. The resistance they encountered was, no doubt, accentuated by their idealism, by the newness of the program, by racial tensions, by inner-city problems, and by the novel, "experimental" quality surrounding open education in 1968; but any educator attempting to introduce informal classrooms who believes the forms and intensities of resistance discussed in Chapter 3 do not bear upon his own situation will be no less surprised and no less devastated than were the seven of us. For, no matter *how* we define quality education or the role of the teacher or the role of the principal, efforts to change the schools will be met with resistance. The more significant the change, the more significant the resistance. Our experience was but one exaggerated instance of a more prevalent condition.

The central message of the case study (and of many other attempts as well) is plain: the forms, the intensity, and the extent of resistance to change of public schools in the direction of open education are educational constants. The fact of the matter is that *most* parents' concepts of quality education are along the lines of the traditional, rigorous, transmission-of-knowledge model. *Most* parents care deeply about their children and rely heavily upon "school" to bring them success, wealth, and satisfaction. Whereas inner-city parents might see school as providing their children a stable place in the job market, suburban parents depend equally heavily upon school to assure admission to Exeter, Harvard, and the medical or legal profession. These aspirations, although different, are held with equal tenacity. Anything which would interfere with them will be opposed with equal fierceness. When confronted with a kind of education which apparently completely violates these expectations and differs so completely from the established path toward these goals, most parents fear for the success of their children. It is not surprising then, that most parents view open classrooms as a risky, untried experiment with their children's lives—a gamble best not taken. Many inner-city parents see informal classrooms as appropriate only for middle-class children who already "have it made"; many middle-class, suburban parents see informal classrooms as appropriate only for working-class children, who aren't going to college anyway and thus have little to lose. For few parents is open education synonymous with the best education for their children.

The prevailing conception in this country of good education is education which provides and displays evidence of students' immediate, assured, measurable, cognitive achievement. This expectation is embedded in mortar no less enduring than a parent's love and concern for his progeny and for himself. Neither open education nor any alternative which would tamper with these ends, or with the commonly accepted means toward these ends, is likely to be easily accepted.

We are left with a phenomenon as immense and as discouraging as social change. The realities are apparent: American education, particularly in but by no means limited to the cities, is not working. By whatever means it tries and by whatever criteria it employs, it is failing to manage, let alone to educate, students. Open education and a host of other ideologies wait in the wings for an opportunity to take the stage. But advocates of open education are caught up in the age-old paradox limiting change: open classrooms must be established in order to learn more about their effects upon children; but in order for the necessary resources and opportunities to materialize, there must be prior evidence of effectiveness. It is difficult, at best, to determine the effects of open classrooms upon children when the prevalent climate of educational insecurity grasps frantically at the transmission-of-knowledge model and protects children from anything but a "sure bet."

What then is the future for open, more informal classrooms

in this country? It is frequently argued that the universities, by influencing the quality and the thinking of new personnel flowing into the schools, hold a powerful lever for changing public education. We saw in the Lincoln-Attucks Program that the six young teachers were inappropriately trained or inappropriately selected (or both) for teaching in these inner-city schools. But what kind of teachers *are* appropriate? What kind of teacher can best implement open education? Can teachers be trained for a model of education (open or otherwise) if they do not agree with its underlying assumptions? Can teachers be trained for open classrooms at all? Or can a staff for open classrooms be obtained only by recruiting those philosophically predisposed to this form of education? What kind of people can both retain a vision of change and manage to survive?

One thing is certain: those in the business of preparing teachers can ill afford to be either blind to or ignorant of what they are preparing teachers for; otherwise they merely fatten sheep for slaughter. Those who would prepare teachers to change public schools do an irresponsible disservice to the teachers, their students, the parents of students, and the schools unless they acknowledge certain realities: teachers must be trained to teach as they will be expected to teach. Teachers, as part of their training, must have ample opportunity to experience the problems of the real world for which they are being prepared. The training program must provide, with discrepant pedagogical *ends*, the political *means* with which to pursue those ends (i.e., a sense of timing, strategy, patience, familiarity with the culture of the community, and the skills to develop a power base necessary for both change and survival). Universities must place in schools only teachers with a strong measure of security and personal maturity; public schools are no place for liberals to resolve their identity crises.

These requisites are unpopular with teachers-in-training, drawn to work in the schools because of the cloud of romanticism which surrounds an impossibly tough, demanding, discouraging job. Yet when they find that the water really is knee-deep, muddy, hot, and often intolerably unpleasant, they are surprised, angered, and incapacitated—as if what they had been told to expect wasn't a possibility at all. How can this message be made clear to students? Is there anything short of immersion in the murky water which can convey these realities?

These requisites are equally unpopular with teacher trainers, who see them as insufficiently glamorous, radical, or academic to warrant attention; who question whether they can be provided anyway. The essential problem for the teacher-training institute which wants its graduates to reform the system can be summarized in a question: How can teachers be prepared to be both successful practitioners (as judged by those in the schools) and successful agents of educational change (as judged by educational critics within and without the institution)?

If the success of informal classrooms in America depended upon the universities, then success would indeed be unlikely. From an examination of several effective informal classroom projects it is apparent that open classrooms can be successfully implemented in this country if several crucial conditions *within the schools* are satisfied: the focus of change must be on personal philosophy rather than on classroom appearances; attention must be given to the development of children's personal qualities, not in place of but in addition to development of language and mathematical skills; supportive personnel within the schools must be provided for teachers; appropriate and abundant manipulative materials must be available for teachers and students; change must be gradual and orderly; and parents and teachers must be given the choice of whether they will participate in informal programs.

In programs such as Lincoln-Attucks, where few if any of these conditions prevailed, change has been unsuccessful. In programs with many of these characteristics, change toward informal classrooms has been and continues to be possible, positive, and enduring. Among the situations which attest to the power and possibilities of informal classrooms in urban and suburban situations are Lillian Weber's "Open Corridor Program" in a dozen New York City public schools; the Education Development Center's "Innovation Team" in Washington, D.C. (Cardoza district); Lore Rasmussen's "Learning Centers" within the Philadelphia public schools; Education Development Center's Follow Through Program in nearly a hundred classrooms in the Eastern United States; the Parmenter School in Arlington, Massachusetts; and Lincoln-Attucks II.

Let's examine more closely the conditions associated with these and other successful attempts to introduce informal classrooms in public schools. One common characteristic is that *teachers interested in moving toward more informal classrooms do so not with the intent of simulating appearances, not out of a motive to change the way their classrooms look, but out of an evolution and change in their own personal philosophy and pedagogy concerning the nature of instruction and of children's learning.*

Many teachers currently interested in open education see "opening up" their classrooms as making them more closely resemble some existing, exemplary model—a "Shady Hill" or a "Leicestershire." They see films of these classrooms and are quick to alter appearances—printing presses, tables rather than desks, classes in corridors, nature study—and vocabulary ("integrated day," "interest area," "choice," "student-initiated learning," etc.). However, few have an understanding of, let alone commitment to, the philosophical, pedagogical, and personal roots from which these practices and phrases have sprung and upon which they depend so completely for their success.

Changing appearances to more closely resemble some British classrooms, attempting to achieve a one-to-one correspondence between our classrooms and theirs, without understanding and accepting the rationale underlying these changes leads inevitably to failure and conflict among children, parents, teachers, and administrators. Open classrooms will indeed become unsuccessful experiments at children's expense if what distinguishes them from other classrooms is only their appearance. American education can withstand no more failure, even in the name of reform or revolution.

Chapters 1 and 2 notwithstanding, we must be careful not to assume that an "official" British or American type of open classroom, or a prescribed set of beliefs and practices, exists as the standard for all others. Indeed, what is exciting about British informal classrooms is the *diversity* of thinking and behavior for children and adults—from person to person, classroom to classroom, and from school to school. The essence of informal classrooms, if there is one, is not adherence to assumptions or use of stereotyped materials, but the precedent that a teacher can provide children with abundant and varied materials, carefully observe their behavior, derive a great deal of information about their thinking, and then provide subsequent materials and experiences that are capable of extending exploration, learning, and skills development. The British have demonstrated that teachers can observe children, that children can learn in school from appropriate materials and experiences, and that the roof won't fall in if they do. This is our debt to the British. These qualities, not classroom appearances, are what we should be attempting to emulate.

A second characteristic frequently associated with successful informal classrooms is the *priority given to the development of children's skills in reading, writing, and mathematics.*

I have noted earlier that many proponents of open education are using this movement as a mantle under which to escape from having to assume a position of authority with respect to children. Many are also using open education as a justification and rationalization for not helping children to develop skills. The common argument is that children's self-con-

cept, self-confidence, interest, choice, and personal development are more important than the traditional skills and should
not be sacrificed for them. Many parents reverse this argument
and state that they would rather have their children learn the
skills now and develop self-confidence at some later time. The
premise on both sides is that important personal qualities and
important cognitive skills are somehow contradictory and mutually exclusive.

Piaget's work has been hailed by many advocates of open
education, partly because his findings can be used to corrobo-
rate their intuitive feelings that children in elementary school
are expected to develop many skills which seem to require an
inordinate amount of time and effort, relative to their short-
term or eventual benefit. Evidence is mounting that we really
do not know *what* young children should be taught in elementary schools in order to ensure success in subsequent schooling,
employment, and "life." Some argue that the critical period
for skills development may be in adolescence rather than in
earlier years.[1] Further research may support the belief that the
best preparation for formal skills development is to postpone
teaching formal mental operations at the elementary level and
concentrate on the development of flexibility in thinking, self-
confidence, instrumentality, etc. But until this research materi-
alizes, I believe that open educators, for both political and
pedagogical reasons, have an obligation to carefully diagnose
each child's development in the various skills, help extend his
capabilities and be able to show evidence that these things
have taken place.

To be sure, a great deal of skills development occurs inci-
dentally in a classroom offering a variety of manipulative materials, but not all skills for all students. Teachers must be more
instrumental than laying out materials, if optimal growth in
skills is to take place. It is difficult and time-consuming to
teach mathematical and language skills such as multiplying, dividing, grammar, and punctuation in a humane, noncoercive

fashion, but it is by no means impossible, as so many British informal schools have demonstrated. A child will want to learn how to spell and punctuate a sentence if, for instance, a printing press is available at which he must correctly set the type if he is to reproduce his story. Similarly, he can learn addition facts if a balance beam with metal tags is readily available, along with a teacher to offer encouragement and assistance. A certain amount of rigor and productivity in a classroom is not for parents' benefit alone. William Hull has pointed out an important truth about children which should not be overlooked:

Children are not going to be happy for very long in schools in which they realize they are not accomplishing very much.[2]

If we expect informal classrooms to be taken seriously, then informal classrooms must become synonymous with the best possible educational experiences for children. This means that informal teachers must be able to display the "meat and potatoes" along with the cake and frosting. There can be no choice between "love of math" in an open classroom *or* skills in math in a traditional classroom; "love of reading" *or* phonics; woodworking *or* spelling, confidence *or* competence. An informal classroom is not succeeding if parents are tutoring their children at night in the 3 R's or if a parent can say (as I have frequently heard them), "you are teaching him things he could be learning at home—woodworking, weaving, photography—and I have to teach him at home what he should be learning at school."

The point is that informal classrooms do not, and need not, call for a trade-off: *either* skills *or* personal development. Teachers who abdicate responsibility for assessing and ensuring children's skills development do an irresponsible disservice not only to their students but to other teachers trying to establish successful open classrooms. If informal classrooms come to be associated with *no* diagnosis of skill levels and with random, haphazard skills development, all proponents of informal classrooms will be tarred with the same brush.

A third condition associated with successful informal classrooms in America is *the availability within the schools of supportive personnel and services for teachers.* Any teacher whose classroom deviates from what is expected will encounter resistance and problems. Anyone who attempts to help children learn in ways suggested in Chapter 2 will need continual encouragement, advice, materials, insight, and support.

The teacher in an open classroom is always learning, but someone must be on hand to help him learn, someone to encourage mature, humane, reflective, sensitive, resourceful qualities—someone who can provide at once strong political cover, pedagogical insight, and personal support. As I have suggested in Chapter 4, the natural and preferable person is the school principal, but a helpful person from outside the school is far better than no one at all.

Inexperienced teachers in many British authorities are provided with supportive services which are helping them develop effective informal classrooms. New teachers are paired with experienced teachers. Advisors who have no evaluative or administrative function whatsoever are assigned to beginning teachers and can be called upon at any time for assistance. In contrast, nonteaching roles in most American public school systems are filled by "supervisors," "directors," "coordinators," and "assistant superintendents" whose primary responsibility is to judge and direct, rather than help and support teachers. Teachers cannot and will not venture out into the uncertainty of informal classrooms unless they receive assistance—not a bop on the head—when they stick their necks out.

A fourth condition related to the success of informal classrooms is *the availability of a variety of materials for the classroom.* The abundance of materials associated with informal classrooms appears to represent a huge additional per pupil expenditure. It need not. Furthermore, if this is the cost of converting a more traditional classroom into a more informal one, an important quality of the informal classroom may have been lost. A classroom filled overnight with expensive, manufactured materials from the shelves of F.A.O. Schwarz or Creative Playthings deprives both teacher and student of the opportunity, responsibility, and excitement which comes from constructing their own materials; of scrounging materials from trash piles on the way to school; of discovering and exploring new and multiple uses for old, nonstructuring equipment such as sand, wood, water, leather, and cardboard. As I have noted, a reason why British methods may have difficulty transplanting to this country is that British teachers by necessity must be resourceful and imaginative. They *must* enlist their students' participation in constructing a rich manipulative environment in the classroom. This kind of participation may be impossible or at best contrived in the United States, where children on the whole come from more affluent homes, where teachers and schools work on more substantial (if not generous) budgets, and where the necessity for scrounging may not exist.

In short, it may be not only unnecessary but undesirable to infuse large amounts of money into schools for materials if our intention is to help move toward more humane practices. *How* the materials arrived in the classroom is every bit as important to their productive use as their presence.

In many American elementary schools there is already a great deal of exciting manipulative equipment, much of it developed during the curriculum reform movement of the 1960's. But frequently the presence of these materials in the classroom obscures the fact that the actual learning experiences of children have not significantly changed. It is not uncommon, for instance, to find a teacher giving group instruction to a class of fourth-graders, each using a math balance beam instead of a workbook or worksheet. "Everyone place one metal tag on the '9' pin on the left side and three metal tags on the '3' pin on the right side. Does $3 \times 3 = 9$?" In many cases the emphasis is still on children following teacher directives, discovering what they are supposed to discover at the same rate as others discover, in a place and at a time set aside for the purpose by the teacher. Thus materials can become a new vehicle, an appealing one perhaps, for the transmission of knowledge from teacher to student.

Nevertheless, new manipulative materials are opening the door to important changes. Children obviously get excited. Teachers see that when children are left alone they often do intriguing things, not suggested in guides. Thus the availability of materials can provide a transition for teachers who need mediating steps between traditional and more informal classrooms.

Another characteristic of successful informal classrooms is that *major changes such as materials, grouping, spatial organization, and evaluation come gradually and orderly.* Open classrooms do not have to polarize and alienate. A "revolution" is not necessary in order for the ideas behind informal methods to be understood or even accepted. To the contrary, those who would liberate the schools overnight would do well to heed Joseph Featherstone's caution:

. . . liberalizing the repressive atmosphere of our schools [will not] automatically promote intellectual development.[3]

Slow, small steps thoughtfully taken lead to small successes, and to growing confidence. Upon these small successes, additional small successes can more easily be built. Behind almost every successful informal classroom lies a sequence of these small, discrete successes, for children, teachers, parents, and administrators alike.

A decision to move gradually from existing classrooms toward more informal classrooms acknowledges and accepts what teachers and children are doing *now*, thus permitting compromises and flexibility. Characteristic of attempts at more rapid change, on the other hand, is the implicit or explicit rejection of the established manner in which teachers and children are functioning and the immediate substitution of an alien model, such as open education. This frequently results in a polarization of issues, practices, and people, forcing teachers, parents, administrators, and children to "choose up sides." The unnecessary creation of this false dichotomy, the idea of choosing between two extremes, inhibits flexibility, maximizes threat, and creates political and personal tensions which can only impede efforts to move toward more informal classrooms.

The most dramatic attempts to move from traditional to informal classrooms have led invariably to the most dramatic failures. Lincoln-Attucks is but one case in point. It is for this reason that I believe the most successful informal classroom teachers will be those who have been trained in traditional ways, who have taught several years in traditional ways, and who are beginning to question the validity and effectiveness of traditional ways. Teachers who have found traditional education wanting and who are looking for something better will move slowly, without the impatience of youth. And they will always have in reserve their competence with the traditional model and the security it provides for teacher and student alike. Therefore, they will probably make fewer mistakes. Whereas disenchanted experienced teachers have a readiness to change, enlightened by many years in the classroom and a knowledge of the system which can inform and assist that change, the idealistic beginning teacher has neither. Indeed, as we have seen, the person with a clear, single-minded conception of the "right" education, the person unable to hold his own goals in abeyance while learning to understand and accept other points of view, has little chance of having a lasting influence on the schools.

A sixth characteristic associated with successful attempts to introduce informal classrooms is that *parents and teachers are given some measure of choice.* It is becoming more and more apparent that neglecting what may appear to be a political matter of choice can have devastating educational consequences.

We live in a culture in which, rightly or wrongly, school is seen as the major avenue to personal, professional, and economic success. At the same time we provide children and their parents little choice about going to school, about which school the child will attend, who his teacher will be, and what the child will do within the classroom. In this context, as soon as a teacher, a curriculum, an administrator, or a school begins to emerge which represents a distinct, consistent, pedagogical position—one with integrity—many are necessarily offended and threatened. They resist in a variety of ways, and change is thwarted. The net consequence is a school system of *sameness*. Sameness does not imply that no one wants change in the direction of informality—or toward military academies for that matter. Our similar schools represent the least offending mean rather than the variety of positions which make up that mean. Given this situation, the introduction of informal classrooms is possible only when significant alternatives are available and when choice among them is permitted and encouraged.

To date schools have displayed little capacity to provide choice for anyone—administrators, teachers, parents, or children. It is becoming more and more apparent that neither open education nor any one pedagogical model is going to provide the acceptable panacea which will solve the problems of educating all youngsters. What is needed within our schools is the development of many, distinct pedagogical alternatives— informal schools, military academies, team-teaching schools, no schools—and the opportunity for parents and teachers to choose from among them. Choice is essential to the success and perhaps to the survival of public schools, not only for the obvious political reasons, not for idealistic reasons, but more importantly, for educational reasons. Parents who withhold their support from teacher, administrator, or school considerably reduce the influence the school can have on the child. In some situations, the negative effect of parent on school has all but nullified the positive effect of teacher on child. Parental opposition to the efforts of the school or a teacher, for whatever reason, is inevitably conveyed to children, who must then live each day in a state of conflict and anxiety between the most important adults in their lives: parent and teacher. In a situation where parents neither accept nor respect what the teacher is doing, little learning can occur.

In 1968 open education was a novelty in this country, if not an experiment. Now, because of the popular press and the development of many successful open classrooms, informal classrooms have the possibility of becoming respectable, legitimate educational alternatives. But growing interest in open education is accompanied by and is contributing to growing polarization within schools, within parent groups, and between school and parent. On one side we frequently find parents and teachers who believe that children learn best and most by having adults direct and control their learning and behavior, thereby assuring coverage of and competence in the knowledge of many subject areas. In the eyes of these parents and teachers, the adult is the best, and perhaps the only, agent of children's learning. On the other side are parents and many teachers who believe that children learn through their own direct and often untidy experience with a wide range of objects, people, and ideas of the real world. In the eyes of these parents and teachers, children are the best, perhaps the only, agents of their own learning. Labels such as "open classroom" and "traditional classroom" calcify the two positions; an implied "vs." rather than an "and" usually connect them. Although there are many comfortable and competent intermediate positions between and around these two emerging poles, and although they need not be mutually exclusive or excluding, as I have tried to suggest, because open education rests upon fundamentally different assumptions about children, learning, and knowledge, the dichotomy is creating a problem that so far has not been amenable to conventional solutions: administrative fiat, a vote of the faculty, a parents' vote, a resolution from the bottom up or from the top down. So long as parents have no choice concerning where they send their child to school or which teacher he will study with, these and other differing educational values will remain sources of major dissonance, contributing to adversarial rather than supportive relationships. A teacher, administrator, or a school system that decides to move toward more informal practices must anticipate and be prepared to deal with this situation.

This polarization is being heightened by the use of *labels*. If a classroom in a school becomes known as an "open classroom" what are the others to be called? "Closed classrooms?" "Traditional classrooms?" "Regular classrooms?" There is no term devoid of pejorative overtones. Furthermore, there is probably no teacher in the country who would admit to being a "traditional teacher." The reactions of school staffs to classrooms labeled "open" is much like the reaction to "merit pay." If one teacher receives merit pay for excellent performance, what do those not so distinguished become?

Labels and their accompanying stereotypes, in addition to introducing divisive forces within a school faculty, can also limit a teacher's flexibility of response. If I am not and do not want to become an "open classroom teacher," if the parents of children in my class do not want their children in an open classroom, it becomes difficult for me to bring in a pair of gerbils and set up a science interest corner should I decide to, for these have become motifs of the open classroom. If I am an "open classroom" teacher it is difficult for me to offer large group instruction, even if I feel this is necessary, because this somehow contradicts what a teacher in an open classroom does. It will be unfortunate indeed if labels and their accompanying constraints take the place of administrative dicta in calcifying practice and depriving teachers of the flexibility and freedom to make instructional decisions on the basis of their observations of children's needs.

How, then, can a classroom, school, or school system, characterized as ours are both by compulsory attendance and by sameness, accommodate fundamental discrepancies of philosophy and method? At the operational level the problem is: What does the principal, the superintendent, or the school committee say to the parent who demands a more teacher-directed classroom, yet whose child has been assigned to an informal classroom, or the converse? We need a thoughtful way —other than war or conversion—of handling this problem. Of war, we have already had too much; conversion is unrealistic. If open education is to have a place in the schools, means more promising than rational rhetoric must be found. There appear to be at least three possibilities:

1. Encourage the parent to transfer the child to an independent school, selected for a close compatibility of values. For financial, social, and other reasons, this is a realistic solution for very few parents.

2. Teachers could "modify" their classrooms and methods to provide at least the appearance, if not the substance, of both philosophies, thereby appeasing most parents. The teacher in the more informal classroom can superimpose workbooks, homework, tests, and grades. His counterpart in a more teacher-directed classroom can introduce gerbils, interest areas, and printing presses. This is tempting as the path of least resistance. But responding in this way results only in perpetuation of the familiar gray area of compromise and sameness at the expense of integrity, commitment, excitement, and success. Although educational research or anecdotal information is hardly compelling in support of either a more teacher-directed or a more material-child-centered classroom, each clearly has advantages for some children and for some adults. To try and *combine* the two, to try and effect a happy merger, is a little like trying to mix orange juice with milk: each taken

separately has something to offer children; when we mix them, we lose many of the advantages each has separately and create many problems neither has separately.

3. There is a third possibility being explored in several schools which may be able to retain the essential integrity and consistency of these distinctive approaches while at the same time offering compatibility of values for teachers and parents. Faculty could be selected for a school not only on the basis of general competence, but with the intent of deliberately cultivating various pedagogical positions, in proportion to parental preference. In the shorter run, diversity could be achieved by encouraging present staff members to further develop their own positions. With options of this kind available, hopefully at each grade level, parents could reflect on their own values and make preferences known each spring for the following fall. Those who valued more informal methods could place their child in more informal classrooms; those who favored a more teacher-directed classroom could have this option. Ideally, this would not be a question of a child having a "good" or a "bad" teacher, since all children would receive good examples of legitimate, but different, teaching styles; rather, it would be a question of achieving an optimal match between teacher and parent. Such an arrangement offers the advantage of letting a teacher teach in a manner closely approximating his values, while at the same time permitting parents to have their children in a learning environment approximating *their* values. Under these circumstances the teacher would be freer to devote his time to instructional rather than political questions and problems, thereby maximizing his contribution to the children. Children, removed from the anxious position between disagreeing adults, would undoubtedly value school, their teacher, and learning more.

To be sure, there are problems associated with this idea. For instance, a fine but crucial line exists between encouraging teachers to pursue their own educational values, on the one hand, and "anything they want," on the other. Secondly, matching teachers with parent preferences is difficult unless the numbers of those expressing preference coincide with the classroom space available. In addition, there is some evidence that providing parents with a variety of learning environments may not only not reduce but may rather sharpen ideological dichotomies.

Perhaps the most serious consideration is that the arrangement suggested here offers the possibility of effecting an optimal match between teacher and parent, while the more important match—educational—is between teacher and *student*. What if the parent of a child who needs a great deal of strong adult direction and controls wants him in an informal classroom? What if the parent of a child who needs to be out from under adult domination wants his child in a teacher-directed classroom? The burden rests with the school both to make its case persuasive and simultaneously to try and give the parent final say in the matter.

Aside from obtaining the most appropriate placement of a child, the availability of different kinds of classroom environments within a school raises another, related problem—the wishes of the *student* concerning the classroom into which he will be placed. It is quite possible that a placement will satisfy the school or the parents (or both) but violate the wishes of the child. For instance, a child may be placed in a teacher-directed classroom because the home (and perhaps the school) feels that this best meets his needs. But if many of his friends in a more informal setting across the hall are spending most of each day building things, exploring a nearby woods, or writing and producing plays, while his movement is limited to trips from his seat to his reading group, there will be difficulties. The fact that it is a child, not an adult, who is unhappy makes this no less of a problem. Indeed, I have seen youngsters threaten to run away from home if they were transferred from an informal classroom. Children's concerns are real.

These are all serious and complex problems, but ones which I think deserve our attention and efforts more than those which arise if we do nothing.

There is another way of providing choice for parents and teachers, as a way of helping introduce informal classrooms. Instead of developing within a particular school several alternatives, it is possible to develop within a school *system* several alternative kinds of schools: one offering all traditional classrooms, one a team-teaching school, one providing all informal classrooms, etc. This plan, recently suggested by Mario Fantini[4] and others, is currently being implemented in the Minneapolis, Berkeley, and Pierce County (Washington) public schools. It offers the possibility of reducing interfaculty and parental dissonance. Only those teachers, parents, and administrators who shared the prevailing philosophy of the school would choose to be associated with it.

This kind of organization, while perhaps easier to achieve, seems to have several limitations: in a school offering all open classrooms or all traditional classrooms or all anything classrooms, teachers see one another doing very similar things; the tendency is to be lulled into unquestioning acceptance of one's own and one another's practices. On the other hand, in a school with a great deal of diversity under its roof in terms of philosophical and pedagogical style, there will always be "the teacher across the hall" who thinks differently and who is doing something differently. This provides a very yeasty situation which constantly provokes each teacher to assess and reassess his judgments about what is best for the children.

Another disadvantage of the school whose classes and teachers are all similar along important dimensions is that it reduces the possibilities for an optimal placement of each child. If a third-grader is being placed in a fourth grade where there are apples, apples, and apples as teachers, he must be transferred to another school if the kind of teacher and environment he needs is oranges. The more diverse school, on the other hand, has the possibility of offering at each grade level apples, oranges, and pears, thereby offering a wider number of alternative learning environments and the greater possibility of suitable placement for each child each year.

A third disadvantage of the more homogeneous school is that it encourages people of similar philosophies to band together in separate buildings. Similar philosophies, however, are often little more than a disguise for similar racial, social, or economic backgrounds. Indeed, in most situations where parents have been given a choice of school (public as well as private), student bodies have tended to become all black, all white, all Jewish, all Catholic, all rich, all poor, etc.

In short, developing a school system with different kinds of schools, each of which is internally similar, as a way of helping to introduce informal classrooms into the public schools, perpetuates the high degree of sameness within each school—a major drawback of schools as they presently exist. A school with twenty informal classrooms does not seem to be so exciting and so useful an organization as a school with many different kinds of classrooms. Indeed, if there is such a thing as an "open *school*"—that is, some kind of logical extension of an open classroom—it would probably not be a school with twenty open classrooms but one with as much variety for adults and children as is apparent in an informal classroom.

An important implication for a school of diverse philosophies is that it must offer a critical number of classrooms at each grade level so that choices could be made each year and so that continuity of any one approach could be provided for children from one grade level to the next. A small K–6 elementary school, for instance, with one class at each grade level, would not lend itself to this form of organization. Schools with a minimum population of about 300 students would be essential to ensure two or three alternative classrooms at each grade level.

Choice is crucial, then, not only for the future of informal classrooms but also for the future of public schools. Only when many genuine alternative forms of education exist at the same time in the same place will teachers, parents, and administrators confront competing ideas and methods on their merits and begin to examine and question what they are doing and why. Only when each person affected by the educational process can choose the kind of learning environment most closely approximating his model of quality education will pedagogical questions replace political questions in the educational forum. Only when there are significant alternatives and opportunities to choose from them will the question "Who controls?" give way to the more important question "What kind of learning environment is best for my child." This is not a question of finding a system that works for everybody, but of finding a system that works and then determining for whom it works and under what circumstances.

Notes

CHAPTER 1

[1] Then a teacher at an independent school in Cambridge, Massachusetts, and until recently a staff member at the Education Development Center in Newton, Massachusetts.

[2] W. P. Hull, personal correspondence, May 29, 1968.

[3] In England children aged 5–7 attend "infant schools"; those aged 8–11 attend "junior schools." Taken together, the infant and junior schools comprise the "primary schools."

[4] Susan Isaacs, quoted by D. E. M. Gardner in *Experiment and Tradition in Primary Schools*, Methuen & Co., Ltd., London, 1966, p. 2.

[5] Gardner, *op. cit.*, p. 5.

[6] *Ibid.*, p. 6.

[7] *Ibid.*

[8] Much has changed, of course, in British primary education since 1963.

[9] Gardner, *op. cit.*, pp. 199–200.

[10] *Ibid.*, p. 201.

[11] *Mathematics in Primary Schools: Curriculum Bulletin No. 1*, 3d ed., Schools Council for the Curriculum and Examinations, Her Majesty's Stationery Office, London, 1969, p. 2.

[12] Lady Bridget Plowden et al., *Children and Their Primary Schools: A Report of the Central Advisory Council for Education*, Vol. 1, Her Majesty's Stationery Office, London, 1966, p. 17.

[13] Elsa H. Walters, *Activity and Experience in the Infant School*, National Froebel Foundation, London, 1951 (6th ed., 1965).

[14] David Hawkins, "On Living in Trees," *The ESS Reader*, Education Development Center, Newton, Mass., 1970, p. 62.

[15] Nathan Isaacs et al., *Some Aspects of Piaget's Work*, National Froebel Foundation, London, 1955 (reprinted 1966), p. 41.

[16] Hawkins, *op. cit.*, p. 62.

[17] Plowden, Vol. 1, p. 196.

[18] *Ibid.*, p. 462.

226

[19] *Ibid.*, p. 196.

[20] Roy A. Illsley, Talk at Elementary Science Study, Aug. 4, 1967.

[21] Beatrice F. Mann, *Learning Through Creative Work*, National Froebel Foundation, London, 1962 (rev. 1966).

[22] Merelice Kundratis, "School for Doers: Self-Starters Are Encouraged," *Christian Science Monitor*, Feb. 10, 1968.

[23] David Hawkins, "I-Thou-It," in C. H. Rathbone (ed.), *Open Education: The Informal Classroom*, Citation Press, New York, 1971, p. 96.

[24] Many at EDC and the Nuffield Foundation in England are fond of quoting this Chinese proverb.

[25] *Mathematics in Primary Schools*, xi.

[26] John Blackie, *Inside the Primary School*, Schocken Books, New York, 1971, p. 87.

[27] Philip Morrison, "The Curricular Triangle and Its Style," *ESI Quarterly Report*, Summer-Fall 1964; reprinted in *The ESS Reader*, Education Development Center, Newton, Mass., 1970.

[28] Friedrich Froebel, *The Education of Man*, 1826.

[29] Blackie, *op. cit.*, p. 30.

[30] Plowden, Vol. 1, p. 193.

[31] Blackie, *op. cit.*, pp. 32–33.

[32] Madison E. Judson, "Minimum Requirements," Elementary Science Study, Newton, Mass., 1965 (unpublished paper).

[33] Robert Levey, "Leave the Kids Alone," *Boston Sunday Globe*, Mar. 17, 1968, p. 8. This brief, largely biographical news article is about John Holt and his philosophy of education.

[34] Plowden, Vol. 1, p. 194.

[35] Joseph Featherstone, "A New Kind of Schooling," *The New Republic*, Vol. 158, No. 9 (Mar. 2, 1968), p. 12.

[36] Joy Schlesinger, "Leicestershire Report: The Classroom Environment," Publication Office, Harvard Graduate School of Education, Cambridge, Mass., 1965 (mimeo).

[37] Hawkins, "On Living in Trees."

[38] Plowden, Vol. 1, p. 273.

[39] Anthony Kallet, "Notes from Leicestershire," Elementary Science Study, Newton, Mass., 1963 (mimeo).

[40] *Mathematics in Primary Schools*, p. 1.

[41] Joseph Featherstone, *Schools Where Children Learn*, Liveright Publishing, New York, 1971, p. 26.

[42] Z. P. Dienes, *Building Up Mathematics*, Hutchinson Educational Ltd., London, 1960.

[43] David Hawkins, "Messing About in Science," *Science and Children*, Vol. 2, No. 5 (February 1965); reprinted in *The ESS Reader*, Education Development Center, Newton, Mass., 1970, p. 65.

[44] Featherstone, *op. cit.*, p. 25.

[45] Philip Morrison, "Less May Be More," *American Journal of Physics*,

Vol. 32, No. 6, June 1964. This is the edited transcript of a talk given at the Conference on Physical Science Courses for Non-Science Majors, held at Rosemont, Pennsylvania, in October 1963. (Available from the Commission on College Physics.)

[46] Featherstone, *op. cit.*, p. 9.

[47] Mann, *Learning Through Creative Work*, p. 2.

[48] Plowden, Vol. 1, p. 273.

[49] Hawkins, "On Living in Trees," p. 61.

[50] *Mathematics in Primary Schools*, p. 9.

[51] Blackie, *Inside the Primary School*, p. 86.

[52] Leonard Sealey, "Education in Leicestershire County," Elementary Science Study, Newton, Mass., 1963 (mimeo).

[53] Plowden, Vol. 1, p. 192.

[54] Sealey, *op. cit.*, p. 4.

[55] Open educators are fond of quoting A. N. Whitehead's *Science and the Modern World* (The Macmillan Company, New York, 1926).

[56] Plowden, Vol. 1, p. 196.

[57] "Introduction to the Elementary Science Study," *The ESS Reader*, Education Development Center, Newton, Mass., 1970, p. 8.

[58] *Ibid.*

[59] Hawkins, *op. cit.*, p. 66.

[60] Philip Morrison, "The Curricular Triangle and Its Style," *ESI Quarterly Report*, Summer-Fall 1964.

[61] Hawkins, *op. cit.*, p. 62.

[62] William P. Hull, "Plastic Tubes, Etc.," Elementary Science Study, Newton, Mass., 1967 (mimeo), p. 6.

[63] George E. Hein, "Science and Teaching Science: A Working Paper," Elementary Science Study, Newton, Mass., 1967 (offset).

[64] Philip Morrison, "Tensions of Purpose," *ESI Quarterly Report*, Spring-Summer 1966, Education Development Center, Newton, Mass., pp. 67–68.

[65] Hull, *op. cit.*, p. 8.

[66] William P. Hull, "A Visit to the Leicestershire Schools," Education Development Center, Newton, Mass., 1961, p. 40 (mimeo).

[67] Morrison, *op. cit.*, p. 68.

[68] Plowden, Vol. 1, p. 202.

[69] L. G. W. Sealey, "Looking Back on Leicestershire," *ESI Quarterly Report*, Spring-Summer 1966, Education Development Center, Newton, Mass.

[70] D. E. M. Gardner, *Does Progressive Primary Education Work?* Association for Childhood Education International, London, January 1967.

[71] Schlesinger, "Leicestershire Report," p. 7.

[72] Illsley, Talk at Elementary Science Study, Aug. 4, 1967.

[73] Plowden, Vol. 1, p. 196.

[74] Morrison, *op. cit.*, p. 68.

[75] Sealey, *op. cit.*, p. 41.

[76] *Ibid.*, p. 40.

[77] "Introduction to the Elementary Science Study," *The ESS Reader*, Education Development Center, Newton, Mass., 1970, p. 12.

[78] Plowden, Vol. 1, p. 202.

[79] Illsley, Talk at Elementary Science Study, Aug. 4, 1967.

[80] Evelyn Lawrence, *Froebel and English Education*, National Froebel Foundation, London, 1952, p. 10.

[81] Schlesinger, *op. cit.*, p. 8.

[82] Courtney B. Cazden, *Infant School*, Education Development Center, Newton, Mass., 1969, p. 10.

[83] Featherstone, "A New Kind of Schooling," p. 6.

[84] Morrison, *op. cit.*, p. 70.

[85] Piaget, as quoted in *Mathematics in Primary Schools*, p. 5.

[86] Benjamin Nichols, "Elementary Science Study: Two Years Later," *ESI Quarterly Report*, Summer-Fall 1965, Education Development Center, Newton, Mass., p. 10.

[87] A. P. French, "Lessons from Leicestershire," *ESI Quarterly Report*, Spring-Summer 1966, Education Development Center, Newton, Mass., p. 42.

[88] Philip Morrison, "The Curricular Triangle and Its Style," *ESI Quarterly Report*, Summer-Fall 1964.

[89] Blackie, *Inside the Primary School*, pp. 51–52.

[90] Nathan Isaacs, *Early Scientific Trends in Children*, National Froebel Foundation, London, 1958.

[91] Plowden, Vol. 1, p. 187.

[92] Hawkins (quoting Piaget), "On Living in Trees," p. 64.

[93] Philip Morrison, "Experimenters in the Classroom," *ESI Quarterly Report*, Winter-Spring 1964.

[94] Cazden, *op. cit.*, p. 20.

[95] Illsley, Talk at Elementary Science Study, Aug. 4, 1967.

[96] Cazden, *op. cit.*, p. 22.

[97] Philip Morrison, "Tensions of Purpose," *ESI Quarterly Report*, Spring-Summer 1966, Education Development Center, Newton, Mass., p. 67.

[98] Edward Yeomans, *Education for Initiative and Responsibility*, National Association of Independent Schools, Boston, Mass., 1967, p. 22.

[99] Anthony Kallet, "Unexplored Connexions . . . ," Education Development Center, Newton, Mass., April 1965 (mimeo).

[100] Sealey, "Education in Leicestershire County," p. 5.

[101] "Today science is the greatest show on earth, and if you don't know something about it you are outside the tent." (Jerrold Zacharias)

"Science is not itself the world; it is one reaction to the world. It is on this view of science, and on the view of man which underlies it, that we choose to rest the structure of our growing curriculum." (Morrison, "The Curricular Triangle and Its Style")

"Science *is* a humanity, and indeed for better or worse, that which today more distinctively stamps all our civilization, as well as shapes our material fate." (Isaacs, *op. cit.*, p. 2)

" . . . science is not only a systematized body of knowledge but also a way of learning." (*Mathematics in Primary Schools*, p. 2)

[102] "There are genuinely scientific trends present in children from the age of three to five—trends towards its methods no less than towards the knowledge that results from them." (*Ibid.*, p. 7)

"[In primary schools] the beginning of both the spirit and the attitudes of scientific inquiry can be very clearly discerned." (*Ibid.*, p. 11)

[103] Isaacs has used the term "living-learning" in trying to capture the essence of open education.

CHAPTER 2

[1] Nathan Isaacs, describing formal schooling in *Piaget: Some Answers to Teachers' Questions*, p. 13.

[2] See, for example, the writings of Ralph Mosher and Norman Sprinthall, Philip Jackson, and Robert Coles.

[3] Rousseau, *Émile*, 1762.

[4] For a development of this argument, including a statement of assumptions concerning learning and knowledge which underlie the transmission-of-knowledge model, see Roland S. Barth, "Teaching: The Way It Is; The Way It Might Be," *Grade Teacher*, Vol. 87, No. 5, January 1970.

[5] For the development of the two models here, I am indebted to Prof. Maurice Belanger of the University of Montreal.

[6] The teacher in the open school is so far removed from his historic and commanding place as transmitter of knowledge that, to many, it appears he may have no role at all:

"In one of Piaget's remarks he suggested it would be a good thing to have two rooms for each class: one where the teacher was and one where the teacher wasn't!" (David Hawkins, "On Living in Trees," *The ESS Reader*, Education Development Center, Newton, Mass., 1970, p. 65)

"It is even more surprising to speculate—as I am now beginning to do—that things [in the classroom] may go much better with much less of me, or any adult." [Anthony Kallet, "Notes from Leicestershire," Elementary Science Study, Newton, Mass., 1963 (mimeo)]

[7] When visiting an open primary school in Leicestershire, I went with three young girls looking for different kinds of plants. Each of the children carried a sharp knife and was running happily about in the wet grass. Although I was terribly worried lest they slip and fall, I said nothing, not wanting to "interfere" with their project and possibly discourage them. When this episode was related to the headmaster, he said, "For God's sake, you should have told them that what they were doing upset you, that they might get hurt, and to stop running about or to put their knives in a box or something."

[8] John McGavack, Jr., and Donald LaSalle, *Guppies, Bubbles and Vibrating Objects: A Creative Approach to the Teaching of Science to Very Young Children*, The John Day Company, New York, 1969, p. 27.

[9] Joy Schlesinger, "Leicestershire Report: The Classroom Environment," Publication Office, Harvard Graduate School of Education, Cambridge, Mass., 1965 (mimeo).

[10] "We resort to streaming, to so-called ability grouping, ignoring the uniquely important differences *within* any such group. For each group one fabricates its ladder, varying only the speed and spacing of the rungs." [Jay Hauben, "Another College Course," Elementary Science Study, Newton, Mass., 1968, p. 13 (mimeo)]

"Groups lumped as equivalent with respect to the usual measures are just as diverse in their tastes and spontaneous interests as unstratified groups." [David Hawkins, "Messing About in Science," in C. H. Rathbone (ed.), *Open Education: The Informal Classroom*, Citation Press, New York, 1971, p. 66.]

"In both [streamed and unstreamed] there will be children who are far more alike in their common human needs than they are differentiated by their background and abilities." (Plowden, Vol. 1, p. 293)

[11] Schlesinger, *op. cit.*

[12] Courtney B. Cazden, *Infant School*, Education Development Center, Newton, Mass., 1969, p. 11.

[13] Plowden, Vol. 1, p. 274.

[14] Joseph Featherstone, "The Primary School Revolution in Britain," in *Schools Where Children Learn*, Liveright, New York, 1971, p. 18.

[15] For a good description of classroom organization and the rationale behind it, see Mary Brown and Norman Precious, *The Integrated Day in the Primary School*, Agathon Press, New York, 1970.

[16] William P. Hull, "A Visit to the Leicestershire Schools," Education Development Center, Newton, Mass., 1961, p. 8 (mimeo).

[17] Cazden, *op. cit.*, p. 26.

[18] Edward Yeomans, *Education for Initiative and Responsibility*, National Association of Independent Schools, Boston, Mass., 1967, p. 15.

[19] For lists of successful materials, see: Allan Leitman and Edith H. E. Churchill, "A Classroom for Young Children: Approximation #1," in C. H. Rathbone (ed.), *Open Education: The Informal Classroom*, Citation Press, New York, 1971; Yeomans, *op. cit.*, pp. 35–40; *Equipment and Supplies*, Association for Childhood Education International, Washington, D.C., 1967; *Happenings*, periodical of the Technology for Children Project, New Jersey Department of Education, Trenton, N.J. (often contains imaginative lists of elementary classroom materials); *Instructional Aids, Materials, and Supplies*, EDC Follow Through Program, Education Development Center, Newton, Mass., 1970.

[20] William Hull, "Leicestershire Revisited," in C. H. Rathbone (ed.), *op. cit.*, p. 34.

[21] Cazden, *op. cit.*, p. 9.

[22] Plowden, Vol. 1, p. 431.

[23] Elsa H. Walters, *Activity and Experience in the Infant School*, National Froebel Foundation, London, 1951 (6th ed., 1965).

²⁴ See, for example, Tannebaum and Stillman science units and many Montessori materials.

An elaborate example of limiting materials is also offered by Friedrich Froebel, who designed a set of apparatus so the child could be led by orderly stages to deeper understanding of the world around him. "Six little boxes contained the six gifts. Gift I was a set of six little wooden balls, of the three primary colors—they symbolized the universe, the world, unity, completedness, mobility and many other things. They taught the colors, they could be rolled, swung, thrown . . . as the spirit of play impelled. They were the one great, universal, all-important plaything. Gift II was a box containing a wooden ball, a cylinder, and a cube. Where the ball symbolized mobility, the cube was stable, and the cylinder combined the properties of both; it could be rolled or stood on its end." Evelyn Lawrence, *Froebel and English Education*, National Froebel Foundation, London, 1952, p. 5.

²⁵ Two architects have recently reinforced this point: "A thing, exclusively made for one purpose, suppresses the individual because it tells him exactly how it is to be used. . . . It must be made in such a way that the implications are posed beforehand as hidden possibilities, evocative but not openly stated." (Herman Hertzberger, "Montessori Primary School in Delft, Holland," *Harvard Educational Review*, Vol. 39, No. 4, 1969)

"The more explicit an object is in the sense that it has no ambiguity, the more difficult it is to use it imaginatively in any other way." (Peter Prangnell, "The Friendly Object," *Harvard Educational Review*, Vol. 39, No. 4, 1969)

²⁶ Cazden, *op. cit.*, p. 11.

²⁷ Hawkins, "On Living in Trees," p. 66.

²⁸ David Hawkins, "I-Thou-It," in C. H. Rathbone (ed.), *Open Education: The Informal Classroom*, Citation Press, New York, 1971, p. 90.

²⁹ *Children Learning Through Scientific Interests*, Cooperative Study Scheme on "Finding Out" Activities, National Froebel Foundation, London, 1966, p. 141.

³⁰ Kallet, "Notes from Leicestershire," 1963 (mimeo).

³¹ David Hawkins, Review of *36 Children* by Herbert Kohl, in *Harvard Educational Review*, Vol. 38, No. 3, 1968, p. 619.

³² "You can't go halfway. Either the children are going to learn to be responsible for their own learning, to plan what they are going to do and carry through with it, or they are not." [Hull (quoting a British teacher), *op. cit.*, p. 39]

"The difficulty lies in the whole business of deciding what somebody else is going to learn. When you begin there you're just bound to go wrong and no amount of cleverness or trickiness is going to get away from it." (Robert Levey, "Leave the Kids Alone," *Boston Sunday Globe*, Mar. 17, 1968, p. 6)

³³ " . . . progressive teachers are aware of the need at times to exert direct influence and control." (Joan Cass and D. E. M. Gardner, *The Role of the Teacher in the Infant and Nursery School*, Pergamon Press, London, 1965)

[34] Martin Duberman, "New Directions in Education: A Radical Seminar in Radicalism—No Exams, No Papers, No Grades," *Princeton Alumni Weekly*, Vol. 68, No. 20, Mar. 5, 1968; reprinted in *Daedalus*, Vol. 97, No. 1, Winter 1968.

[35] "Although the British schools stress cooperation and children are encouraged to teach each other, there is no abdication of adult authority, and no belief that this would be desirable." (Featherstone, *op. cit.*, p. 39)

[36] Hull, *op. cit.*, p. 33.

[37] For further discussion, see Roland S. Barth, "When Children Enjoy School: Some Lessons from Britain," *Childhood Education*, Vol. 46, No. 4, January 1970.

[38] It is difficult to read Brown and Precious's [Ref. (3)] account of six children's progress over six years without playing a game of predicting from the records of the early years what direction the child's development will take him in later years. Invariably, I was premature and incorrect in my guessing. Furthermore, somehow I worried little about children with "learning problems," because their anecdotal records specified in detail what the children *had accomplished*—a great deal. This had an overwhelmingly positive and reassuring effect. I suspect that a more relaxed attitude on the part of more schools and more parents about their children's performance would have a beneficial effect both upon a child's self-image and upon the image his teachers have of him.

[39] "On the other hand, if a school is operated as those in America almost entirely are in a style in which the children rather passively sit in neat rows and columns manipulating the teacher into believing that they're being attentive because they're not making any trouble, then the teacher won't obtain very much information about them. Not gaining much information about them, he won't be a very good diagnostician, he will be a poor teacher." [Hawkins, "I-Thou-It," in C. H. Rathbone (ed.), *Open Education: The Informal Classroom*, Citation Press, New York, 1971, p. 89]

[40] Schlesinger, "Leicestershire Report," 1965.

[41] William P. Hull, "Plastic Tubes, Etc.," Elementary Science Study, Newton, Mass., 1967 (mimeo).

[42] George E. Hein, "Science and Teaching Science: A Working Paper," Elementary Science Study, Newton, Mass., 1967, p. 18 (offset).

[43] Z. P. Dienes, *Building Up Mathematics*, Hutchinson Educational Ltd., London, 1960, p. 49.

[44] For further discussion of a deliberate use of children's errors to enhance their learning, see Roland S. Barth, "Science: Learning Through Failure," *Elementary School Journal*, Vol. 66, No. 4, January 1966.

[45] Allan Leitman, "Travel Agent," *Housing for Early Childhood Education*, Bulletin No. 22-A, Association for Childhood Education International, Washington, D.C., 1968.

CHAPTER 3

[1] Excerpt from a local newspaper article.

[2] "Lincoln-Attucks Project: Statement of Background, Problem, Approach, and Goals."

[3] "City Public Schools: Report to the Board of Education on Special Projects."

[4] *Ibid.*

[5] "Lincoln-Attucks Project."

[6] "City Public Schools."

[7] "Lincoln-Attucks Project."

[8] *Ibid.*

[9] George Miller, President of the American Psychological Association, in *Psychology Today,* December 1969.

[10] Robert Davis, "In the Next Few Years," *The Arithmetic Teacher,* May 1966, p. 357.

[11] Many of the parents felt that the money should be "bet" on the best of the children, so that "some of them will make it." The strong will succeed, and the weak must suffer. Even the parents of slower, less able children expressed such a view.

[12] This position has received support from a distinguished psychology professor: "Children from advantaged family backgrounds do not have much to lose from open classrooms, even though the curriculum is not designed to provide access to college and prestige; what goes on in their homes concerning cognitive-intellective skills acquisition is likely to compensate. For low-income children, however, their chance for social mobility is more dependent on which curricular choices their schools make. . . . Without change at the upper levels of the educational sequence, an early education emphasis on the expressive arts, in line with the open classroom philosophy, could well work out to the detriment of the nation's low-income children." (Michael A. Wallach, "The Humble Things We Know—and Ignore—about Quality in Elementary Education," *Harvard Educational Review,* Vol. 41, No. 4, November 1971, pp. 548–549.

[13] In England also, "They do not call it play, because the term is not respectable enough to appear on a school timetable in some parts of the country; so they call it 'creative activity.' " (Sten Hegeler, *Choosing Toys for Children,* Tavistock Publications, London, 1963, p. ix)

[14] "Vocabulary is the opiate of radicals." (Leo Rosten, "To an Angry Young Man," *Look,* Nov. 12, 1968)

CHAPTER 4

[1] *The Nurture of Teacher Growth,* Center for Coordinated Education, University of California, Santa Barbara, Calif., 1966, p. 9.

[2] *Remaking the Educational Order: Problems of Communication and Status in the Schools,* Center for Coordinated Education, University of California, Santa Barbara, Calif., 1965, p. 7.

[3] George Miller, in *Psychology Today,* December 1969.

CHAPTER 5

[1] William D. Rohwer, Jr., "Prime Time for Education: Early Childhood or Adolescence?" *Harvard Educational Review,* Vol. 41, No. 3, August 1971.

[2] William Hull, as quoted in J. Featherstone, "Tempering the Open School Fad," *The New Republic,* September 1971, p. 19.

[3] Featherstone, *op. cit.,* p. 20.

[4] Mario Fantini, "Options for Students, Parents, and Teachers: Public Schools of Choice," *Phi Delta Kappan,* Vol. 51, No. 9, May 1971.

Bibliography*

Much of what proponents of open education are thinking has not been written; much of what has been written has not been published; and much of what has been published is not commonly known or available. Because of the vagueness surrounding the movement and because the number of available references is ever-expanding, compiling a bibliography is difficult. Items have been included here on the basis of their relevance to open education, not necessarily on the basis of excellence.

The aim has been twofold: to provide a starting place for parents, students, teachers, and administrators interested in open education; and to make available to those already familiar with these ideas and practices an extensive resource which will assist further exploration. Annotations are more descriptive than judgmental. The intent is to present as many available resources as possible to facilitate investigation of this movement; and, above all, to encourage each reader to draw his own conclusions about each of these works and, indeed, about open education itself.

To make this bibliography more useful it has been divided into five sections:

BOOKS AND PAMPHLETS (1–98)
ARTICLES (99–191)
BIBLIOGRAPHIES AND LISTS OF CURRICULUM
    MATERIALS (192–205)
FILMS (206–228)
PERIODICALS (229–249)

* An earlier version of this bibliography appeared as *A Bibliography of Open Education,* by Roland S. Barth and Charles H. Rathbone. It is available from the Advisory for Open Education, 90 Sherman St., Cambridge, Mass. 02140, or from Education Development Center, Inc., 55 Chapel St., Newton, Mass. 02160. (Price: $1.25)

Entries are numbered consecutively throughout. Listings in each category are alphabetized by author, or by title if no author is listed. Those which merit special attention have been designated with an asterisk. To assist readers, publishers' and distributors' addresses are provided in a separate list following the entries. The Name Index (page 294) will assist readers in finding all entries in the Bibliography for any author. Addresses of publishers and distributors precede the indexes.

BOOKS AND PAMPHLETS

1. Allen, Gwen et al. **Scientific Interests in the Primary School.** London: National Froebel Foundation, 1966.
   A practical guide for teachers, including extensive bibliographies and addresses of curriculum publishers.
2. Ash, Beryl and Rapaport, Barbara. **The Junior School Today.** London: National Froebel Foundation, 1958 (revised 1965).
   A Froebel Foundation pamphlet.
3. Blackie, John. **Good Enough for the Children?** London: Faber & Faber, 1963.
   A collection of lectures originally given to teachers by this Chief Inspector of Primary Schools.
°4. Blackie, John. **Inside the Primary School.** New York: Schocken Books, 1971.
   Written for laymen and parents by the former H. M. Chief Inspector of Primary Schools, this comprehensive overview of primary schools places recent developments in clear historical perspective. It includes chapters on the different subject areas.
5. Boarder, S. F. K. et al. **Aspects of Language in the Primary School.** London: National Froebel Foundation, 1960 (revised 1964).
   Hints for teachers: a pamphlet.
6. Boyce, E. R. **Play in the Infants' School.** New York: Agathon Press, Inc., 1972 (first published 1938).
   An account of an early informal school established in a

working-class district of London. New introduction by Lillian Weber.

7. Brearley, Molly. **The Teaching of Young Children.** New York: Schocken Books, 1970.

    Draws many connections between the theories of Piaget and the practices of informal education.

°8. Brown, Mary and Precious, Norman. **The Integrated Day in the Primary School.** New York: Agathon Press, Inc., 1970.

    A detailed and very practical account of open education written by two Leicestershire heads. Appendices contain a bibliography and lists of suggested equipment. Illustrated.

9. Cass, Joan and Gardner, D. E. M. **The Role of the Teacher in the Infant and Nursery School.** London: Pergamon Press, 1965.

    The authors selected 18 nursery school teachers and 30 infant school teachers each of whom was judged to represent "good" (i.e., open education) teaching practices. After each teacher had been observed for 180 minutes, their classroom behavior was separated into 80 categories and the frequency of each behavior was noted. The intent of Miss Cass and Miss Gardner was ". . . to show what constitutes good and successful teaching in informal education."

10. Cazden, Courtney B. **Infant School.** Newton, Mass.: Education Development Center, Inc., 1969. Available prepaid from the publisher @ $ .50.

    The transcription of Dr. Cazden's 1967 interview with Miss Susan M. Williams, director of Gordonbrock Infant School in London. Prepared by Adeline Naiman. Illustrated.

11. Center for Coordinated Education. **The Nurture of Teacher Growth.** Santa Barbara, Calif.: University of California, 1966.

    One of a series of pamphlets designed to promote understanding of school and teacher effectiveness. Other titles in this series include "Synergetics and the School" and "The Professional Growth of the Educator."

12. Central Advisory Council for Education (England). **Out of School.** London: Her Majesty's Stationery Office, 1948 (reprinted 1963). Available in the U.S. through Sales Section, British Information Services.

The formal report of a committee charged with investigating ways in which children's interests can be met outside the classroom. It includes a description of children's needs at various ages, an assessment of existing provisions for both outdoor and indoor activities, and recommendations for additional services which the Ministry of Education might provide. An illustrated pamphlet.

13. **Characteristics of Open Education.** Pilot Communities Program, Education Development Center, Newton, Mass., 1971.

A series of three unpublished booklets, available in small quantities:

(1) "Toward an Operational Definition" (May 1971)

(2) "A Look at the Literature for Teachers" (May 1971, condensed from #1)

(3) "Results from a Classroom Observation Rating Scale and a Teacher Questionnaire" (August 1971)

This study recognizes that "Some sort of operational definition [of open education]—albeit one that allows for flexibility and individuality in response to situational variations—is needed. An ambitious and by and large successful attempt (1) to define some of the essential pedagogical features of open education; (2) to develop explicit concrete indicators of each feature; (3) to check the validity of the indicators with the major writings on the subject and with important theorists and practitioners in the U.S. and Great Britain; and (4) to make comparisons to other relevant approaches, such as progressive and affective education.

14. Chittenden, Edward A. (project director). **Analysis of an Approach to Open Education: Interim Report.** Princeton, N.J.: Educational Testing Service.

The underlying problem confronted here is one of "developing assessment procedures which are better suited to the more humanistic but less tangible goals of education in general." More specifically, the report addresses itself to two important questions: "What does this position [open education] represent?" and "What are its implications for assessment?" Of particular interest is the classification scheme on page 23. A thoughtful and thorough attempt to accomplish a nearly impossible task.

15. Churchill, Eileen. **Piaget's Findings and the Teacher.** London: National Froebel Foundation, 1966.

A Froebel Foundation pamphlet.

16. Clegg, A. B., ed. **The Excitement of Writing.** Chatto and Windus (Educational) Ltd., 1966; Schocken Books, 1972.

A remarkable collection of writing by children from economically depressed mining communities of the West Riding of Yorkshire. Included are some suggestions by their teachers on ways of encouraging good writing—suggestions which rule out the use of drills and exercises, and substituting in their stead methods more in keeping with the approaches of open education.

17. Consultative Committee on the Primary School. **The Hadow Report: A Report of the Consultative Committee on the Primary School.** London: Her Majesty's Stationery Office, 1931 (reprinted 1962).

The precursor of the Plowden Report, a wide-ranging survey of primary school children and the way they grow, their teachers, and their schools, including reports on administrative matters, the situation of the retarded child, examinations and their effects, curriculum offerings, etc.

18. Cooper, Gertrude E. **The Place of Play in an Infant School and Junior School.** London: National Froebel Foundation, 1966.

A Froebel Foundation pamphlet describing the nature and value of play in school. Many observational reports on children of various ages.

19. Cooperative Study Scheme on 'Finding Out' Activities. **Children Learning Through Scientific Interests.** London: National Froebel Foundation, 1966.

A Froebel Foundation pamphlet including reports by thirty teachers.

20. Cox, C. B., and Dyson, A. E. **Black Paper Two.** London: Critical Quarterly Society, 1969.

A collection of essays published to stem the tide of progres-

sivism in England. The section on open education rather angrily debunks "discovery" methods, modern math, and informal approaches in the early grades. It is entitled, "Primary Schools: Moving Progressively Backwards."

21. Cox, C. B., and Dyson, A. E. **Fight for Education.** London: Critical Quarterly Society, 1969.

    Subtitled, "A Black Paper," this collection of nearly twenty essays was presented to every Member of Parliament in reaction to recent "progressive" trends in British Education.

22. Department of Education and Science. **Primary Education.** London: Her Majesty's Stationery Office, 1959. Available in the U.S. through: Sales Section, British Information Services.

    A general handbook for primary school teachers, with chapters on the different curriculum areas as well as on matters of historical and organizational importance.

23. Department of Education and Science. **Evelyn Lowe Primary School, London.** (Building Bulletin No. 36.) London: Her Majesty's Stationery Office, 1967. Available in the U.S. through: Sales Section, British Information Services.

    The thoughtful account of how a specially appointed Development Group set about planning for this new inner-London school. Though primarily concerned with architectural specifications, the group has taken great care to show how and why those specifications were determined. Illustrated and jargon-free.

24. Design Lab of Education Development Center. **Cardboard Carpentry Workshop.** Newton, Mass.: Education Development Center, Inc., 1968. Available from the Workshop for Learning Things, Inc. @ $1.50.

    A pamphlet illustrating what teachers can do with some cardboard, some time, and their own hands—a demonstration of one way of building teachers' confidence in their own manual experience.

25. Dienes, Z. P. **Building Up Mathematics.** London: Hutchinson Educational, Ltd., 1960.

    A monograph by the well-known former lecturer in mathematics at the University of Leicester, one chapter of which is devoted to how children learn—a thoughtful introduction.

26. Doncaster, Islay. **Discovering Man's Habitat.** London: National Froebel Foundation, 1963.

 This Froebel Foundation pamphlet gives a rationale as well as practical advice for environmental studies, especially at the junior school level.

27. Early Childhood Education Study. **Building with Cardboard.** Newton, Mass.: Education Development Center, Inc., 1970. @ $ .60.

 A carefully illustrated booklet showing in clear detail how to make simple but indispensable classroom furniture such as tables, storage bins, shelves, playhouses, etc. out of cardboard sheets.

28. Early Childhood Education Study. **Building with Tubes.** Newton, Mass.: Education Development Center, Inc., 1970. @ $ .60.

 An illustrated pamphlet showing how to make such common and useful classroom furniture as stools, chairs, cubbys, tables, shelves, drums, cradles, and musical instruments from easily obtained cardboard tubes.

29. Elementary Science Study. **Introduction to the Elementary Science Study.** Newton, Mass.: Education Development Center, Inc., 1966. Single copies available free from the publisher. Included also in **The ESS Reader** (no. 33).

 A brief, mostly pictorial description of ESS, its approach and its units, prepared by Adeline Naiman.

30. Elementary Science Study. **Children Printing.** Newton, Mass.: Education Development Center, Inc., 1969. Available prepaid from Elementary Science Study @ $1.00.

 Examples of children's work with simple presses, as well as some directions for teachers. This booklet, designed by Cornelia Voorhees, is included in the Elementary Science Study unit **Printing Press** *which is available from Webster Division, McGraw-Hill Book Company.*

31. Elementary Science Study. **An Interview with Bruce Whitmore.** Newton, Mass.: Education Development Center, Inc., 1969. Available prepaid from Elementary Science Study @ $1.00.

A discussion with an imaginative science teacher, from the 5th and 6th grades at the Carr School in Newton (Mass.), in which he wrestles with many of the practical problems of setting up a materials-centered classroom.

32. Elementary Science Study. **An Interview with Dorothy Welch.** Newton, Mass.: Education Development Center, Inc., 1969. Available prepaid from Elementary Science Study @ $1.00.

    In this illustrated interview, Miss Welch relates her experiences teaching in the Hollis (N.H.) Elementary School. (See also her two films, Nos. 227 and 228.)

°33. Elementary Science Study. **The ESS Reader.** Newton, Mass.: Education Development Center, Inc., 1970. Available from the publisher @ $2.00.

    A collection of working papers conveying the philosophy and general approach of the ESS staff. The introduction is written by David Hawkins, who served as Director of ESS during its formative years.

34. Elementary Science Study. **An Interview with Pat Hourihan.** Newton, Mass.: Education Development Center, Inc., 1971. Available prepaid from Elementary Science Study @ $1.00.

    The fourth grade teacher of a middle and lower income Newton school reflects on how she moved from a "traditional" teaching style towards a more open approach.

35. Engstrom, Georgianna, ed. **Open Education: The Legacy of the Progressive Movement.** Washington, D.C.: National Association for the Education of Young Children, 1970. Available from the publisher @ $2.00.

    A conference report that includes papers by David Elkind, James B. Macdonald, Roma Gans, Vincent R. Rogers, and Bernard Spodek.

°36. Featherstone, Joseph. **Schools Where Children Learn.** New York: Liveright, 1971.

    A collection of Joseph Featherstone's earlier articles, most of which have appeared in The New Republic *since 1967. Included are detailed accounts of "infant schools," "junior schools," and a description of a variety of good and bad prac-*

tices in America. For several years these pieces represented the most important and practically the only American source of information about British primary schools. Many attribute stimulation of American interest in these ideas to these articles.

37. Furth, Hans G. **Piaget for Teachers.** Englewood Cliffs, New Jersey: Prentice-Hall, 1970.

   A helpful analysis of Piaget's work with a discussion of practical applications in classroom settings.

38. Gardner, D. E. M. **Experiment and Tradition in Primary Schools.** London: Methuen & Co., Ltd., 1966.

   In three longitudinal studies spanning nearly a quarter of a century, Miss Gardner, a Reader in Child Development at the University of London's Institute of Education, compares favorably the attitudes of achievement of English children in open education schools with their counterparts in traditional primary schools. An earlier work by Miss Gardner, The Children's Play Centre (1937), has been reprinted by Agathon Press.

39. Gross, Ronald and Gross, Beatrice, eds. **Radical School Reform.** New York: Simon & Schuster, 1969.

   An anthology of articles by such writers as Paul Goodman, Edgar Friedenberg, Herbert Kohl, Jonathan Kozol, and John Holt. This book also includes a chapter entitled, "The British Infant Schools," by Joseph Featherstone.

40. Harkins, John. **Box Breaking.** Philadelphia, Pa.: Friends Committee on Education, November 1969. Available from the publisher @ $ .75.

   An informal report of a summer "Workshop in Creative Education" for teachers wishing to loosen up their classrooms. A film entitled, "Side Streets" was also produced in connection with this workshop.

41. Hawkins, Frances Pockman. **The Logic of Action: From a Teacher's Notebook.** Boulder, Colo.: Elementary Science Advisory Center, 1969. Available from the publisher @ $1.95.

   The perceptive account of work with six children in a Colorado public school. Her observations "illustrate, and perhaps help to elaborate, an essential principle of learning: that given a rich environment—with open-ended raw materials—children can be encouraged and trusted to take a large part in the design of their own learning, and that with this encouragement and trust they can learn well." Illustrated with photographs of the children at work.

42. Hegeler, Sten. **Choosing Toys for Children.** London: Tavistock Publications, 1963.

   An interesting, quick-reading little book which contains: a brief history of toys and the idea of play; a discussion of important developmental characteristics of children 0–12; an appendix listing different toys, catalogued according to price and appropriate age. Of particular interest is the thoughtful introduction by D.E.M. Gardner, in which she discusses the nature of play and the difference between play and work for the child, and a chapter by the author, "Some Problems of Play and Toys," in which he discusses children's play, why children play, the distinction between play and work, etc.

43. Hertzberg, Alvin, and Stone, Edward. **Schools Are for Children,** New York: Schocken Books, 1972.

   Two American elementary school principals share their enthusiastic observations of several informal British primary schools and offer "what you can do" sections of chapters on the arts, mathematics, language, social studies, and science. Suggestions for implementation are more helpful for teachers than administrators.

°44. Holt, John. **How Children Fail.** New York: Pitman Publishing Corporation, 1964. Also available in paperback from Dell Publishing Co.

   The earliest and most influential book by this well-known advocate of student-directed learning.

45. Holt, John. **How Children Learn.** New York: Pitman Publishing Corporation, 1967. Also available in paperback from Dell Publishing Co.

   Anecdotal accounts of children learning: much direct observation combined with thoughtful speculation about the learning processes of children as exhibited both in and out of school.

46. Holt, John. **John Holt on Testing.** Boston: Dan Pinck Associates, 1968. Available from the publisher @ $1.25.

"At best, testing does more harm than good; at worst, it hinders, distorts, and corrupts the learning process," begins Holt, as he follows with reasons and examples why this is so.

47. Holt, John. **The Underachieving School.** New York: Pitman Publishing Corporation, 1969.

    A collection of essays, book reviews, letters and talks on a variety of school topics. Most of these articles have been published previously.

°48. Hull, William P. **Leicestershire Revisited: Occasional Paper No. 1.** Newton, Mass.: Education Development Center, Inc., 1970. Available from Early Childhood Education Study @ $1.00.

    An experienced teacher's perceptive report of his 1964 visit to the schools of Leicestershire County, in which he shares his impressions and reactions, especially pointing up contrasts with American elementary schools. Also available in **Open Education: The Informal Classroom** *(no. 81).*

49. Hutchinson, Margaret M. **Practical Nature Study in Town Schools.** London: National Froebel Foundation, 1961.

    A Froebel Foundation pamphlet.

50. I/D/E/A. **The British Infant School: Report of an International Seminar.** Melbourne, Florida: I/D/E/A, 1969. Available from the publisher @ $1.00.

    A profusely illustrated occasional paper reporting a seminar held in England in 1969. This pamphlet includes position statements by Miss E. Marianne Parry, Inspector of Infant and Nursery Schools in Bristol, and by Lady Bridget Plowden, Chairman of the Central Advisory Council for Education (England).

51. **Informal Schools in Britain Today** (23 booklets). New York: Citation Press, 1971.

    This set of pamphlets, with an introduction by Joseph Featherstone, is jointly produced by the Anglo-American Primary Education Project and the Ford Foundation. Authors are British practitioners and American and British observers of informal education. Some booklets describe general aspects of British primary education: "The Government of Education,"

"Trends in School Design," "Space, Time and Grouping." Others portray various dimensions of informal practices: "The Pupil's Day," "The Teacher's Role," "The Headteacher's Role," "Evaluation of Achievement." Many are devoted to the disciplines: "Mathematics for Younger Children," "Mathematics for Older Children," "Science," "Art," "Music," etc.

52. Ironside, Margaret and Roberts, Sheila. **Mathematics in the Primary School.** London: National Froebel Foundation, 1965.
    A Froebel Foundation pamphlet.

53. Isaacs, Nathan. **A Brief Introduction to Piaget.** New York: Agathon Press, Inc., 1972.
    Two of Mr. Isaacs' essays, "The Growth of Understanding in the Young Child" and "New Light on Children's Ideas of Number," with an introductory essay on Mr. Isaacs by Evelyn Lawrence.

54. Isaacs, Nathan. **Early Scientific Trends in Children.** London: National Froebel Foundation, 1958.
    The opening lecture of a course entitled, "The Foundations of Scientific Attitudes in the Primary School," sponsored by the University of Reading Institute of Education and published by the National Froebel Foundation.

55. Isaacs, Nathan. **Piaget: Some Answers to Teachers' Questions.** London: National Froebel Foundation, 1965.
    An extended essay written in answer to a number of questions put to Mr. Isaacs of the National Froebel Foundation, by the editor of a professional mathematics journal.

56. Isaacs, Nathan. **What Is Required of the Nursery-Infant Teacher in This Country Today?** London: National Froebel Foundation, 1967.
    A Froebel Foundation pamphlet.

57. Isaacs, Susan. **The Children We Teach: Seven to Eleven Years.** London: University of London Press, Ltd., 1932 (reprinted 1967); also New York: Schocken, 1971.
    *A book about children, with chapters on individual differences, social and intellectual development—an historical antecedent of open education. Other important works by Susan Isaacs include **The Nursery Years: The Mind of the Child***

from Birth to Six Years. New York: Schocken, 1968 (first published 1929); Intellectual Growth in Young Children. New York: Schocken, 1966 (first published 1930); and Childhood and After. New York: Agathon Press, 1970 (first published 1948).

58. James, Charity. **Young Lives at Stake: The Education of Adolescents.** New York: Agathon Press, Inc., 1972.

    Mrs. James, Director of the Goldsmiths' College Curriculum Laboratory at the University of London, turns her attention to the implications of an open education approach for secondary education. Foreword by Charles Silberman.

59. Kohl, Herbert R. **The Open Classroom.** New York: Vintage Books, 1970.

    Subtitled, "A practical guide to a new way of teaching," this short book gives advice to the practitioner who wishes to "loosen up" his classroom while remaining within the public school setting.

60. Lawrence, Evelyn. **Froebel and English Education.** London: National Froebel Foundation, 1952.

    A brief pamphlet, written by the director of the National Froebel Foundation, which describes the contributions of Friedrich Froebel to both the theory and the methodology of educating young children.

61. Lawrence, Evelyn. **Friedrich Froebel and English Education.** London: Routledge & Kegan Paul, 1952 (republished, 1969); also New York: Schocken, 1969.

    A collection of essays considering Froebel's contributions to British Primary Education, with chapters on the origins of the kindergarten, his influence on primary and prep school practices, the religious roots of his philosophy and a general overview of the Froebel movement in England. Nathan Isaacs' essay, "Froebel's Educational Philosophy in 1952," relates basic Froebelian doctrine to the freedom espoused by adherents of open education.

62. Leitman, Allan. "Travel Agent." **Housing for Early Childhood Education,** Bulletin No. 22-A, 1968. Available from the publisher, Association for Childhood Education International @ $1.50.

Feeling that an individual's education should be "a subjective, non-standard, personal, human mixture," Dr. Leitman calls for a classroom which reflects a "workshop spirit" and (in a different metaphor) a teacher who acts as travel agent.

63. Leitman, Allan and Voorhees, Cornelia. **Moments in Learning.** Newton, Mass.: Education Development Center, 1968. Available from the Early Childhood Education Study @ $ .25.

"How much must a child trust himself, others, and the world in order to learn?" "Can we understand words before we have had the experience they describe?" "What and why do we teach?" These are the three questions raised in this pamphlet. Answers are implicit in the numerous photographs of children learning.

64. Mann, Beatrice F. **Learning Through Creative Work (The Under 8's in School).** London: National Froebel Foundation, 1962 (revised 1966).

The Froebel view of creative play—its description, rationale, and how teachers can best arrange for it—including a short bibliography of books for teachers and lists of suggested classroom materials.

65. Marsh, Leonard. **Alongside the Child.** New York: Praeger Publishers, 1970.

An Englishman describes English primary schools.

°66. Marshall, Sybil. **Experiment in Education.** Cambridge, England: Cambridge University Press, 1963 (paper, 1966).

A compelling, autobiographical account of Mrs. Marshall's work at the Kingston County Primary School in Cambridgeshire, during the course of which she evolved an informal, activity-oriented teaching style. Illustrated.

°67. Marshall, Sybil. **Adventure in Creative Education.** London: Pergamon Press, Ltd., 1968.

The narration of Mrs. Marshall's working with mature, experienced primary teachers in a 12-week workshop course. With the intention of placing "each teacher for a short time in the position of the thought that he should again know what it feels like to be a child faced with all kinds of demands made on him," she put her sixteen teachers through a variety of imagi-

native experiences. Throughout, she had three aims: "The first was to place the teacher as often as possible in the position of the child: the second was to ask him personally to attempt as many creative activities as possible: and the third was to give him a taste of learning as an integrated whole."

68. Mason, Edwin. **Collaborative Learning.** New York: Agathon Press, Inc, 1972.

    An analysis of the needs of students and teachers in secondary schools. Based on the author's work at the Curriculum Laboratory, Goldsmiths' College, University of London.

69. Mason, Stewart C., ed. **In Our Experience.** London: Longmans, 1970.

    A collection of essays chronicling change as it has occurred in the schools of Leicestershire County, edited by Leicestershire's long-time Director of Education.

70. Matthai, Robert A., Maw, Carlyle E. and Plummer, Davenport. **An Evaluation of Four Integrated Day Workshops.** Cambridge, Mass.: Harvard Graduate School of Education, Office of Field Activities, February 1970. Limited number of copies available from the publisher.

    An attempt to clarify objectives and begin measuring the success of four summer workshops organized by the National Association of Independent Schools to help teachers move towards open education. A further attempt is made to identify characteristics of teachers who proved successful or unsuccessful in translating their summer experience into actual teaching practices in the fall.

71. McGavack, John, Jr. and LaSalle, Donald P. **Guppies, Bubbles and Vibrating Objects.** New York: The John Day Company, 1969.

    This book is designed primarily for elementary school teachers in search of new ideas for teaching science. Of particular interest are discussions of how children learn, what science teaching has been and what it should be, the value of both success and failure for children's learning, and the process approach. The last three-quarters of the book—How To Do It— gives in considerable detail all the equipment, steps, questions,

*etc., necessary to teach 21 different science units, with a sepa-
rate bibliography for each one. Much of the philosophy and
most of the units set forth in this new book bear a close relationship to work previously done by the Elementary Science
Study.*

72. Mellor, Edna. **Education Through Experience in the Infant
School Years.** Oxford: Basil Blackwell, 1950 (reprinted 1967).

*A wide-ranging look at the life of young children both in
and out of school, replete with practical advice for teachers
and parents, quotations from educational theorists and philosophers, and photographs of children at work and play. An influential if somewhat general study.*

73. Ministry of Education and Central Office of Information.
**Moving and Growing: Physical Education in the Primary
School, Part One and Part Two.** London: Her Majesty's Stationery Office, 1952. Available in the U.S. through Sales Section, British Information Services.

*A commonsense consideration of what it means to move:
physical movement as a means and an indication of human development. Discussion of games, dances, throwing, and skip-
ping; the role of repetition, versatility, fluency, recognition of
maturity, mood, style, and character through observation of
natural movement; the stages of growth and dexterity. Thoroughly illustrated. Though not too directly concerned with recent reforms in primary education, this book does indicate one
longstanding concern of infant teachers and thus provides an
important background against which to view recent changes in
British schools.*

°74. Murrow, Casey and Liza. **Children Come First: The Inspired
Work of English Primary Schools.** New York: American Heritage Press, 1971.

*A lucid description of informal practices in the better British
primary schools. As well as describing in detail the dynamics
of various classrooms, the authors explore the history of informal methods and the psychological, philosophical, and administrative bases upon which these classrooms rest. Includes clear
statements of conditions associated with successful implemen-*

tation of informal methods and warnings to romantics and those who would make piecemeal applications. The authors' special empathy with the demands of teaching make their detailed accounts of curriculum, planning, the uses of the environment, and the enhancement of personal development particularly helpful to other teachers interested in moving in this direction. Included is an excellent description of the oft-neglected subject of movement.

75. National Froebel Foundation. **Some Aspects of Piaget's Work.** London: National Froebel Foundation, 1955 (reprinted 1966).

    A pamphlet containing three essays: "Children's Ideas of Number," by Evelyn Lawrence and T. R. Theakston, "The Wider Significance of Piaget's Work," by Nathan Isaacs, and "Piaget and Progressive Education," also by Mr. Isaacs.

76. **The Open Classroom,** Winston-Salem: The North Carolina Advancement School, November 1971 (offset).

    A compendium of several interesting pieces: a statement of "the philosophy of open education;" the log of a first-year teacher in an informal classroom; the report of a research study comparing (favorably) the learning outcomes of children in a sixth-grade open classroom with a sixth-grade control group: several reprinted articles on open education.

77. Parr, Dorothy. **Music in the Primary School.** London: National Froebel Foundation, 1966.

    A Froebel Foundation pamphlet.

78. Peters, R. S., ed. **Perspectives on Plowden.** London: Routledge and Kegan Paul, 1969.

    A selection of essays concerning the child-centered primary school education described in the Plowden Report, written by faculty of London University's Institute of Education. They are mostly critical.

°79. Plowden, Lady Bridget et al. **Children and Their Primary Schools: A Report of the Central Advisory Council for Education.** Vol. 1. London: Her Majesty's Stationery Office, 1966. Available in the U.S. through: Sales Section, British Information Services @ $4.50.

    The most comprehensive and politically significant discus-

sion to date of the rationale as well as the practices of modern British primary schools. Volume I deals with general observations and recommendations. See also Vol. II (no. 80).

80. Plowden, Lady Bridget et al. **Children and Their Primary Schools: A Report of the Central Advisory Council in Education**, Vol. II. London: Her Majesty's Stationery Office, 1966. Available in the U.S. through: Sales Section, British Information Services @ $5.85.

*Volume II of the **Plowden Report** consists in the main of statistical tables, though several of its appendices (such as those dealing with the education of gypsies, school management, and the effects of "streaming") may be of general interest. See also Vol. I (no. 79).*

°81. Rathbone, Charles H. **Open Education: The Informal Classroom**. New York: Citation Press, 1971.

A selection of articles on open education, with an introduction by John Holt.

82. Razzell, Arthur. **Juniors: A Postscript to Plowden**. Hammondsworth, England: Penguin Books, Ltd., 1968.

An historical account of recent post-Plowden developments in England's junior schools, addressed mainly to parents. Comparable to Blackie's book on the primaries, this paperback describes what the new junior schools look like inside and out, and attempts to account for recent changes.

°83. Richardson, Elwin S. **In the Early World**. Wellington: New Zealand Council of Educational Research, 1964. Also New York: Pantheon, 1969.

An exciting account of Richardson's school in Oruaiti in northern New Zealand, handsomely illustrated in color, with chapters on mathematics, nature study, techniques to establish awareness, the place of values in the development of children, etc. Although apparently developed independently of the current movement in British Primary Education, Richardson's school shows remarkable affinity to the best of these practices.

84. Ridgway, Lorna and Lawton, Irene. **Family Grouping in the Primary School**. New York: Agathon Press, Inc., 1971.

The authors discuss informal education in British primary

schools with particular reference to "family grouping," i.e., when 5's, 6's, and 7's are grouped together in one class. The authors suggest that this organization makes it mandatory for the teacher to attend to individual differences, allows children a broad range of acceptable behaviors, gives children the security of knowing the same teacher and many of the same children over a three-year period, and makes it easier to implement informal methods.

°85. Rogers, Vincent. **Teaching in the British Primary School.** New York: Macmillan, 1970.

A useful collection of essays, both on general topics and on specific curriculum areas, mostly contributed by British practitioners. This anthology includes articles on "The New Mathematics," "Teaching Reading in the Infant School," "Movement, Music, Drama and Art," and "Vertical Grouping in the Primary School."

86. Schools Council for the Curriculum and Examinations. **Mathematics in Primary Schools: Curriculum Bulletin No. 1.** London: Her Majesty's Stationery Office, 1969 (3rd edition). Available in the U.S. through Sales Section, British Information Services.

Though mostly concerned with the details of teaching mathematics, this thorough pamphlet does attempt to place current reforms in that subject area within the broad context of the changing pattern of primary school education throughout England. It attends, also, to recent research in how children learn, and provides a concise summary of the studies done by Piaget. The author is Edith E. Biggs.

87. Sargent, Betsye. **The Integrated Day in an American School.** National Association of Independent Schools, September 1970. Available from the publisher @ $2.50.

A companion study to the film of the same classroom (no. 210). An extremely thorough and thoughtful collection of the author's notes, lesson plans, spatial arrangements, lists of materials and activities related to a year's instructional program for 5, 6, and 7 year old children at the Shady Hill School in Cambridge, Mass. A marvelous resource, usefully organized, for teachers looking for creative ideas and materials.

88. Sharkey, Anthony. **Building a Playground.** Newton, Mass.: Education Development Center, 1970. Available from the Early Childhood Education Study @ $ .60.

In this illustrated pamphlet, Mr. Sharkey of the Early Childhood Education Study describes a recent playground he designed and built with the Head Start Leadership Training Program at Texas Southern University.

°89. Silberman, Charles E. **Crisis in the Classroom.** New York: Random House, 1970. Available in paperback from Vintage.

In this comprehensive review of American public education, the result of a three-and-one-half-year study commissioned by the Carnegie Corporation, Mr. Silberman takes a careful, enthusiastic look at the British infant school model.

90. University of London Institute of Education. **First Years in School: Aspects of Children's Development from the Ages of 4 to 7.** London: George G. Harrap & Co., Ltd., 1963 (reprinted 1967).

A collection of essays on various aspects of children's development from the ages of 4 to 7, including physical development, ideas about number, spiritual development, and language. Essays by Piaget, Nathan Isaacs, D.E.M. Gardner, Molly Brearley and others.

91. U.S. Dep't. of Health, Education & Welfare. **Model Programs, Philadelphia Teacher Center.** U.S. Government Printing Office, Catalog No. HE 5.220:20163 @ $ .15.

A description of how an old brick school building in downtown Philadelphia became a resource center for teachers and the profound influence the center had on their thinking.

°92. Vermont State Department of Education. **Vermont Design for Education.** Montpelier: State Department of Education, May 1968. Single copies available from the publisher. Also included in **The ESS Reader** (no. 33).

The articulation of seventeen premises which, taken in summation "constitute a goal, an ideal, a student-centered philosophy for the process of education in Vermont"; followed by a consideration of several suggested strategies for implementation of those ideals. In all, a remarkable expression of commitment by a state agency to the principles of open education.

93. Walters, Elsa H. **Activity and Experience in the Infant School.** London: National Froebel Foundation, 1951.

    An examination of the principles behind the so-called "activity method" including consideration of how children learn ("each stage of development must be lived fully if the child is to be prepared to pass on to the next"), the role of teacher in maintaining an "atmosphere of security," some ways of making the change from formal to free classroom.

94. Walters, Elsa H. **Activity and Experience in the Junior School.** London: National Froebel Foundation, 1951.

    A sequel to the author's infant school pamphlet with emphasis on the necessary differences between junior and infant schools. Freedom and respect, she warns, are also due to teachers who, given them, will continue to grow. How to help teachers change is a central concern.

°95. Weber, Lillian. **The English Infant School and Informal Education.** Englewood Cliffs, N.J.: Prentice-Hall, 1971.

    A detailed study of informal practices in an increasing number of British infant schools. Includes a discussion of the tradition of nursery education from which these practices have evolved, the history of their evolution, and the conditions which permitted this development. The author is acutely aware of the interrelatedness of the prerequisites for an informal system, so much so that the complexities frequently make it difficult for the reader to sift the more important factors from the less. Includes substantial information on curriculum, the physical plant, group structure, theoretical formulations, and teacher education.

°96. Yeomans, Edward. **Education for Initiative and Responsibility.** Boston: National Association of Independent Schools, November 1967. Available from the publisher @ $1.00.

    Thoughtful comments on a visit to the schools of Leicestershire County in April, 1967, with special attention to describing and analyzing "integrated day" and "vertical grouping." Appendix III of this pamphlet lists curriculum materials and equipment recommended for an open education classroom, including addresses of manufacturers.

97. Yeomans, Edward. **The Wellsprings of Teaching.** Boston: National Association of Independent Schools, 1969. Available from the publisher @ $1.00.

Subtitled, "A discursive report of a teachers' workshop on the philosophy and techniques of the integrated day," this pamphlet describes a one-month summer program designed to help teachers not so much to prepare directly for work in school as to explore and think about their own learning.

98. Yeomans, Edward. **Preparing Teachers for the Integrated Day.** Boston: National Association of Independent Schools, 1972.

With a thoughtful foreword by Roy Illsley, this pamphlet describes some of the ways teachers in England have been encouraged and helped to develop sensitive, responsive classrooms. There are sections on "The Advisory," "The Teacher Centers," and "The Teachers' Workshops in England." The very successful (and rapidly growing number of) workshops offered teachers in America by NAIS for the past five summers are also examined.

ARTICLES

99. Armstrong, Michael. "New Trends in Secondary Education." **Arena,** The Architectural Association, July 1967.

A relatively theoretical consideration of the implications of open education for the secondary school.

100. Barth, Roland S. "Science: Learning Through Failure." **Elementary School Journal,** Vol. 66, No. 4, January 1966.

The author describes how a fifth grade class became aware of the power of scientific techniques by trying to investigate and explore without them. The resulting failures had a profound effect upon subsequent activities. He concludes that it is possible for teachers not only to tolerate failure in children but also to take advantage of it as a powerful learning device.

101. Barth, Roland S. "The University and Urban Education." **Phi Delta Kappan,** Vol. LI, No. 1., September 1969.

A compilation of the ideas of several urban educators

(*Seeley, Sullivan, Buttenweiser, Milner, Cuban, Callendar, Sherburne, Shapiro*) *concerning ways that universities can help improve city schools.*

102. Barth, Roland S. "Open Education: Assumptions About Learning and Knowledge," **Journal of Educational Philosophy and Theory**, Vol. 1, No. 2, Cambridge (England): Pergamon Press, November 1969.

    This article identifies and classifies the assumptions held by British and American open educators concerning children's learning and the nature of knowledge.

103. Barth, Roland S. "Teaching: The Way It Is; The Way It Might Be.," **Grade Teacher**, Vol. 87, No. 5, January 1970. (Reprinted in **Follow Through Workshop**, New York State Department of Education, Albany, 1970.)

    A comparison of the assumptions about children, learning, and knowledge underlying "most schools" with those underlying open schools, and a discussion of the implications of the latter for the role of the teacher.

°104. Barth, Roland S. "When Children Enjoy School: Some Lessons From Britain." **Childhood Education,** Vol. 46, No. 4, January 1970. (Reprinted in the **Norwegian Journal of Education,** Oslo, 1971, in Wassman (ed.), **Selected Readings in Elementary Education,** Simon & Schuster, New York, 1970, and in the **Froebel Journal,** London, Autumn 1971, No. 21.

    A description of characteristics of open schools which seem to be associated with children's enjoyment of school and a discussion of some of the problems which arise when children enjoy school.

105. Barth, Roland S. "On Selecting Materials for the Classroom." **Childhood Education,** Vol. 47, No. 6, March 1971.

    The author suggests and discusses five criteria for the selection of materials in an open classroom.

°106. Barth, Roland S. "So You Want to Change to an Open Classroom," **Phi Delta Kappan,** October 1971.

    Many educators are moving toward open education with insufficient understanding of what it is, attempting to implement it by changing vocabulary and appearances in class-

rooms. The author points out the danger of this kind of educational change and suggests a number of important assumptions about children, learning, and knowledge, agreement with which, he believes, makes success more likely and fundamental change more possible.

107. Belanger, Maurice. "Description of a Psychology Course," and "Reflections, October, 1968," in **Psychology in Teacher Preparation,** Ontario Institute for Studies in Education, 1969. Available as "Monograph Series No. 5" from the publisher.

An address to the International Conference on Psychology in the Teacher Education Curriculum in which Professor Belanger describes three models of the teaching and learning process, one of which approximates open education.

108. Bernstein, Basil. "The Open School." **Where** (Supplement No. 12), 1967. Available from Advisory Centre for Education.

Viewing schools as complex social organizations à la Durkheim, Professor Bernstein posits two classifications: open (or organic) and closed (mechanical). The open school, emphasizing differences among children, educates for breadth not depth. It sees knowledge as uncompartmentalized, and teachers as problem-posers rather than solution-givers. An interesting point from which to view open education.

109. Blackie, John. "Forward from Plowden." **Froebel Journal,** No. 13, March 1969.

*A consideration of the implications of several of the **Plowden Report's** recommendations.*

110. Borton, Terry. "Reach, Touch, and Teach." **Saturday Review,** January 18, 1969.

An overview of psychological education as it is practiced in a number of schools across the country, by the former co-director of the Affective Education Research Project in the Philadelphia public schools.

111. Branan, Karen. "Ideas for Opening Up." **Scholastic Teacher** (Elementary Teacher's Edition), January 1972.

Suggestions for gradual introduction of informal techniques by the interested teacher. Includes lists of sources for materials, books, and pamphlets.

112. Bremer, John. "Curriculum, A Vigor, A Local Abstraction." **The Center Forum,** Center for Urban Education, Vol. 3, No. 5, March 1969.

On the learning of skills within a context of value, *by the director of Philadelphia's Parkway Project.*

113. Buder, Leonard. "Breaking Down Formality for Fuller Expression of the Individual." **New York Times,** July 27, 1969.

While announcing Ford Foundation grants aimed at helping American schools adapt to the British infant school model, Mr. Buder reviews a number of existing American counterparts.

114. Clegg, Alec B. "The Revolution in the English Elementary Schools." **The National Elementary Principal,** Vol. 49, No. 1, September 1969.

An address to American elementary school principals which gives background as well as the particulars of recent changes in British primary education.

115. Clemans, Martyn. "Not Just Half—All Our Future." **Trends in Education,** No. 10, April 1968.

*As an example of what the **Plowden Report** considers "best practice," **Trends'** executive editor describes the Holymead County Junior School in Bristol, England.*

116. Cohen, David K. "Children and Their Primary Schools: Volume II." **Harvard Educational Review,** Vol. 38, No. 2, Spring 1968. Single copies available from H.E.R. Editorial Offices @ $1.00.

*A critical review of the **Plowden Report's** Research component (Volume II).*

117. Collis, M. M. "Nature Study with Young Children: Exploration Beyond the Classroom." **Froebel Journal,** No. 13, March 1969.

A brief description of learning outside regular classroom boundaries.

118. Cook, Ann and Mack, Herbert. "The British Primary School." **Educational Leadership,** Vol. 27, No. 2, November 1969.

*A general overview emphasizing British commitment to the individuality of the child and the attention paid to how children learn. A summary of this article appears in **The Education Digest,** Vol. 25, No. 6, February 1970.*

119. Cornelius, E. M. "Resources in the Primary School." **Forum,** Vol. 12, No. 2, Spring 1970.

   Miss Cornelius, for 20 years head teacher of Drew Street Primary School, Brixham, Devon, England, reflects on strategies and problems involved in helping a school move toward a less formal approach to teaching and learning.

120. "Does School + Joy = Learning?" **Newsweek,** May 3, 1971.

   Quite a thorough and lengthy discussion of the theory and practice of informal education with reference to historical antecedents and contemporary examples.

121. Duberman, Martin. "New Directions in Education: A Radical Seminar in Radicalism—No Exams, No Papers, No Grades." **Princeton Alumni Weekly,** Vol. 68, No. 20, March 1968. Also in **Daedalus** (Journal of the American Academy of Arts and Sciences), Vol. 97, No. 1, Winter 1968.

   An account of how this college professor moved from a "transmission of information" model of teaching towards the objective of facilitating personal and interpersonal understanding. Though not directly concerned with open education, this narrative serves to underscore the affective dimensions of the open classroom, whatever its level.

122. Eckle, Mary. "The Spirit of Leicestershire." **Wheelock Alumnae Quarterly,** Winter 1970.

   A brief, subjective appraisal of a nine-week practice teaching experience sponsored in Leicestershire by Wheelock College.

123. Faithfull, Marjorie. "Plowden and Colleges of Education." **Froebel Journal,** No. 12, October 1968.

   *The author sees the **Plowden Report** as urging training colleges "to treat students, both in their methods of teaching and in their discipline, as responsible people who are likely to behave towards those they teach in something of the same way in which they have been treated."*

124. Farmer, Irene. "Experimental Schools." **Forum,** Vol. II, No. 3, Summer 1969.

   *A critical review of Brown and Precious, **The Integrated Day in the Primary School,** which takes the authors especially* *to task for their bland, all-inclusive conceptualization of "integrated."*

125. Featherstone, Joseph. "The Primary School Revolution in Britain." **The New Republic,** August 10, September 2, and September 9, 1967. Available from Pitman Publishing Co. @ $ .50. (2–10 copies @ $ .40 ea.)

    This collection of three 1967 articles by Mr. Featherstone has for good reason probably received the widest circulation of any printed material dealing with British primary education.

126. Featherstone, Joseph. "A New Kind of Schooling." **The New Republic,** Vol. 158, No. 9, March 1968.

    In this review of John Holt's two books, Featherstone concentrates on the terror and humiliation, dependence and duplicity fostered by those who have no basic faith in children's capacity to learn.

127. Featherstone, Joseph. "Report Analysis: Children and Their Primary Schools." **Harvard Educational Review,** Vol. 38, No. 2, Spring 1968. Single reprints available from the publisher @ $1.00.

    A review of the **Plowden Report,** *with particular emphasis on American attempts and failures to "transplant" the practices of open education. In particular, Mr. Featherstone (a contributing editor of* **The New Republic***) describes the kind of climate apparently most conducive to educational change in England, including the unique relation of theory to practice there.*

128. Featherstone, Joseph. "Experiments in Learning." **The New Republic,** Vol. 159, No. 24, December 1968.

    Describes how reading and writing are learned in the better junior schools of England. When a teacher pays serious attention to the context of the child's writing, Featherstone contends, a bond of interest unites that teacher and the child; motivated by that bond and not by grades or spelling per se, *the child will inevitably come to care about the precision with which he communicates and will attend to the mechanics of the writing in due course.*

129. Featherstone, Joseph. "Schools for Learning." **The New Republic,** Vol. 159, No. 25–26, December 1968.

On the teaching of mathematics at the junior school level, including commentary on the use of concrete materials, evaluation and procedures for recording student progress, spatial and temporal reorganization of classrooms necessitated by a changing, problem-oriented curriculum, and the special strengths and skills demanded of teachers who elect to teach this way.

130. Featherstone, Joseph. "Why So Few Good Schools." **The New Republic,** Vol. 160, No. 1, January 1969.

   An article on the teaching of the expressive arts in British junior schools.

131. Featherstone, Joseph. "The British and Us." **The New Republic,** Sept. 11, 1971.

   Summarizes the state of informal education in this country, stressing the need for a substantive evaluation of children's progress in school. Also includes a thoughtful discussion of the organization of American schools as contrasted with the British, and the priority given here to administration and management at the expense of teachers, parents, and children.

132. Featherstone, Joseph. "Tempering a Fad." **The New Republic,** Sept. 25, 1971.

   A critical examination of errant attempts, excesses, and faddism occurring in American schools in the name of "informal education." Many adults drawn to informal approaches are reacting against authority, structure, and adult responsibility. They do not serve themselves, the schools, or the children well.

133. Flurry, Ruth. "How Else?" **Young Children,** Vol. 25, No. 3, January 1970.

   Reflections on a visit to eleven primary schools in London, Nottingham, and Derbyshire by a New York State supervisor of early childhood education.

134. French, A. P. "Lessons from Leicestershire." **ESI Quarterly Report,** Spring–Summer 1966. Newton, Mass.: Education Development Center, Inc. Reprint available prepaid from the publisher @ $ .25.

   A brief description of the author's visits to the Willow Brook and Millfield Schools (both near the city of Leicester), in which this MIT physics professor comments on the "feeling of freedom with anarchy" and their "obvious overlap and continuity with real life."

135. Gardner, D. E. M. "The Plowden Report on 'Children and Their Primary Schools.'" **Froebel Journal**, No. 10, March 1968.

    *A brief and rather general review of the scope, content and recommendations of the **Plowden Report**, by Britain's renowned researcher in child development.*

°136. Grannis, Joseph C. "The School as a Model of Society." **Harvard Graduate School of Education Association Bulletin**, Vol. 12, No. 2, Fall 1967. Reprints available @ $ .55. Also included in **ESS Reader** (*no. 33*).

    Asserting that the structure of school itself instructs students, Dr. Grannis looks at three alternate models: the "factory" school, the "corporation" school, and the open education or "family" school.

137. Gross, Beatrice and Gross, Ronald. "A Little Bit of Chaos." **Saturday Review**, Vol. 53, No. 20, May 16, 1970.

    *A broad overview of the open education movement in this country, by the co-editors of **Radical School Reform**.*

138. Hapgood, Marilyn. "The Open Classroom: Protect It from Its Friends." **Saturday Review**, Sept. 18, 1971.

    Part of the "second wave" of open education literature. The first wave was enthusiastic and hopeful. Now Marilyn Hapgood and others are beginning to reveal the complexities of educational change and even the dangers inherent in the open education movement—that it will be ". . . discredited by enthusiasts who have only half-understood its principles." Caution based on experience.

139. Haskell, Henry S. "Teacher Preparation: A Dynamic, Personalized Approach." **Childhood Education**, Vol. 42, No. 7, March 1966.

    A description of an individualized teacher preparation program run at Wheelock College in cooperation with ESI (Now Education Development Center, Inc.).

140. Hastings, Jill. "The Leicestershire Group." **Wheelock Alumnae Quarterly**, Winter 1970.

A brief description of a nine-week student teaching experience in Leicestershire schools, written by one of the twelve undergraduate participants from Wheelock College in Boston.

°141. Hawkins, David. "On Living in Trees." Boulder, Colorado: University of Colorado, 1964 (unpublished speech). Also reprinted in **The ESS Reader** (no. 33).

In this Karl Muenzinger Memorial Lecture, delivered at Colorado University in December 1964, Professor Hawkins discusses the gap between how children learn (each by his own experience, discovering his own tree within the network of possibility) and how many teachers teach (forcing everyone up the same branchless ladder, à la teaching machine). He emphasizes the importance of choice, self-direction, individualization, and the exploratory motive in learning.

142. Hawkins, David. "The Informed Vision: An Essay on Science Education." **Daedalus: The Journal of the American Academy of Arts & Sciences,** Vol. 94, No. 3, Summer 1965. Reprinted in **Creativity & Learning.** Also included in **The ESS Reader** (no. 33).

Without ways of learning that are spontaneous, concretely involving, and esthetically rewarding, we are all too likely to become intellectually and esthetically alienated from new and important experiences. Confrontation with materials, first in play and later in apprenticeship, is the key (a lesson to be learned from the progressive education movement, which Professor Hawkins critiques); without this personally involved confrontation, formal instruction in method has little meaning.

°143. Hawkins, David. "Messing About in Science." **Science and Children,** Vol. 2, No. 5, February 1965; and **ESI Quarterly Report,** Vol. 3, No. 3, Summer–Fall 1965. Available as **Occasional Paper No. 2** from the Early Childhood Education Study @ $1.00. Also included in **The Ess Reader** (no. 33).

The delightful formulation of a three-phased model of learning (upon which many Elementary Science Study units rest), the initial phase of which is "messing about." The author is one of the most theoretical and thoughtful spokesmen of open education, a former director of ESS, and now professor of the philosophy of science at the University of Colorado and director of the Mountain View Center for Environmental Education.

144. Hawkins, David. "Childhood and the Education of Intellectuals." **Harvard Educational Review**, Vol. 36, No. 4, Fall 1966. Reprints available from the publisher @ $ .35.

Reviewing how several philosophers have regarded the relation of knowledge to experience, Professor Hawkins suggests that educators seek out the best of existing school practice and apprentice themselves to it, if they would understand more completely the process of education in children and in themselves.

°145. Hawkins, David. "I-Thou-It." **Mathematics Teaching**, No. 46, Spring 1969. Also included in **The ESS Reader** (no. 33).

The revised version of a talk given in April, 1967, at the Primary Teachers' Residential Course, Loughborough, Leicestershire, in which Professor Hawkins discusses the triangular relationship of teacher, child, and material. He emphasizes the importance, for the child, of having some external "it" to react to and to learn from—some non-personal, inanimate aspect of his total environment with which he can become fully and comfortably involved and into which both he and adults can project themselves. An important document, one which stresses the rationale for manipulative classroom materials.

146. Hawkins, David. "Square Two, Square Three." **Forum**, Vol. 12, No. 1, Autumn 1969.

Calling for additional theoretical work to support and strengthen recent advances in open education practice, Professor Hawkins raises difficult questions regarding such issues as the distinction between "authoritarian" and "permissive," children's selectiveness during the assimilation of culture, teachers' diagnostic problems, and the relationship of primary schools to secondary.

147. Hechinger, Fred M. " 'Open Doors' Help to Open Up the Children," **New York Times,** February 7, 1971.

A review of American involvement in British infant school methodology, including a close look at the work of Professor Lillian Weber in New York.

148. Hechinger, Fred M. "They Can Be a Bit Too Open." **New York Times,** Sept. 26, 1971.

Describes warnings from three sources (Hapgood, Featherstone, and a British report, "The Roots of Reading"), all of which point out the danger of more traditional schools moving toward more informal practices with insufficient care and thought. Discusses several conditions associated with successful implementation and the question "How much structure is optimal?" Reasonable caution.

149. Hein, George E. "Children's Science Is Another Culture." **Technology Review,** Vol. 71, No. 2, December 1968. Also included in **The ESS Reader** (no. 33).

Dr. Hein suggests that in trying to "export" the culture of science to children, curriculum developers have often failed to take into account the "culture shock" which inevitably ensues. It is much as though the adults involved are "traveling around the world on TWA flights, staying at Hilton hotels and meeting the natives in American bars"—that is, they never take into account the children's perspective, never acknowledge the children's own perception of "scientific" phenomena. He concludes with the hope that more teachers of science and curriculum designers will try "going native" in their work with children.

150. Henry, Jules. "Working Paper on Creativity." **Harvard Educational Review,** Vol. 27, Spring 1967. Single copies available from the publisher @ $ .40.

Answering the question, "How, then, does a human being learn error as a way of life?" Professor Henry observes that mistakes draw the teacher into more than routine interaction with the creative (error-making) child, thus reinforcing exceptional or "wrong" behavior. An example of how important it is for teachers to become aware of the unintended learning that goes on in classrooms.

151. Hogan, J. M. and Willcock, J. B. "In-Service Training for Teachers." **Trends in Education,** No. 8, October 1967.

A description of the facilities for in-service training available to teachers in the West Riding of Yorkshire, emphasizing the kinds of consideration which govern the establishment of teachers centers, and a permanent advisory staff.

152. Holt, John. "Letter to the Editor." **This Magazine Is About Schools,** Vol. 2, No. 2, 1968.

Critique of an article describing the behavioristic approach of Carl Bereiter and a critique of a critique of that article. Bereiter's work, according to Holt, reflects the operant conditioning view of learning, seeing people as a collection of behaviors: it neglects, he claims, the children's needs and interests, their individual capacities and concerns.

153. Holt, John. "The Values We Teach in School." **Grade Teacher,** Vol. 87, No. 1, September 1969.

An interview with John Holt, concentrating on the values which are implicitly or explicitly taught in school.

154. Howard, Leo M. **The Developmental Classroom.** Boston: Department of Title I programs, Boston Public Schools, 1968 (unpublished mimeograph). Single copies available from the author, Assistant Director, William M. Trotter School, 135 Humboldt Avenue, Roxbury, Mass.

In this speech, given at the Follow Through Conference in Washington, D.C. in the Spring of 1968, Mr. Howard forthrightly confronts the problems encountered by teachers, administrators and students as his inner-city sub-system public school attempts to move in the direction of open education.

155. Jameson, L. J. "Family Grouping and Integrated Day Programme." **Primary School Broadsheet No. 7,** Spring 1968.

A general description and defense of the British infant school today, concentrating on the importance of play and manipulation, the importance of "activity programs," and the arguments against the introduction of "subjects."

°156. Hull, William P. "Learning Strategy and the Skills of Thought." **Mathematics Teaching,** No. 39, Summer 1967. Originally appeared in **Shady Hill News,** Cambridge, Mass., 1958. Also included in **The ESS Reader** (no. 33).

Mr. Hull considers how children learn to think, particularly about mathematics. He posits a polarity between the general approaches employed by high-achieving Producers (who are

*primarily oriented toward meeting other people's requirements)
and those of more independent* Thinkers, *who, less constrained
by ambiguity, conflict, or the expectations of others, seem freer
to draw on their own past experiences). Most schools, he feels,
tend to reward the former set of strategies and neglect the latter. This inhibits the development of the mental mobility essential to coping with problem-solving situations that are in
any way novel.*

°157. Kallet, Tony. "Two Classrooms." **This Magazine Is About
Schools,** Vol. 1, No. 1, April 1966. Reprinted also in **Open Education: The Informal Classroom** (no. 81).

A *compelling, informal, descriptive comparison of two 1963
classrooms, one English and one American, by one of the first
Americans to report on visiting British Primary Schools.*

158. Kallet, Tony. "Some Thoughts on Integrity." **Primary School
Broadsheet No. 5,** 1967. Also included in **Open Education:
The Informal Classroom** (no. 81). Available in **Occasional
Paper No. 2** from Early Childhood Education Study @ $1.00.

*Mr. Kallet discusses certain characteristics of gifted chil-
dren—their inability to distinguish between questions and answers, their intuitive realization of the danger of closure and
consequent resistance to any sort of restrictive redirection by
adults, their tenacious self-reliance, which enables them to
continue to ask open-ended and uncompartmentalized questions encumbered by neither fear nor pride.*

159. Kallet, Tony. "Some Thoughts on Children and Materials."
Mathematics Teaching, No. 40, Autumn 1967 and **Primary
School Broadsheet No. 7,** Spring 1968. Included also in **Open
Education: The Informal Classroom** (no. 81).

*Viewing the relation between a child and his building blocks
as a kind of conversation, Dr. Kallet speculates about the role
of the onlooker-teacher and the requirements of a successful
intervention. When contrasting the neutrality of the material
world with the highly subjective and constantly judgmental
arena of human affairs, he touches on the same important
point raised in Hawkins' "I-Thou-It."*

160. Kallet, Tony. "Away from Stages." **Mathematics Teaching,**
No. 45, Winter 1968.

In a criticism of Piagetian models of mental development, Dr. Kallet argues against thinking in terms of discrete stages of any sort. If cycles exist, he suggests, their parts are not sequential, but rather coexistent, allowing children to hop from one to another with ease.

161. Keast, David J. "Back to School for Parents." **Forum**, Vol. II, No. 2, Spring 1969.

    The head of Otterton Primary School at Budleigh Salterton, Devon, describes his attempts to involve parents in their children's learning. In particular, he outlines a series of evening sessions in which he "tried to create the same atmosphere for parents which exists at school during the day."

162. **Kentucky School Journal**, February 1972. Louisville: The Kentucky Education Association.

    A special "Feature on Open Education" offering articles on the rationale behind informal classrooms and a description of the four-year evolution of one elementary school in the direction of open education.

163. Manas Editorial Board. "Children and Ourselves: In Behalf of Permissiveness." **Manas**, Vol. 21, No. 12, March 1968.

    According to this article, a permissive philosophy makes several assumptions about the development of children: it assumes that children are self-motivated toward becoming adults, and need not be driven and programmed through childhood; it assumes that children learn best what they themselves want to know; it respects individual differences in interests, abilities, and temperaments. From each of these assumptions, a number of testable hypotheses about learning behavior are derived.

164. McInnis, Noel. "Children and Ourselves: Lamps to Be Lighted." **Manas**, Vol. 21, No. 41, October 1968.

    A Kendall College professor examines the generation gap as reflecting a conflict between two views of education. On the one hand are those who see education as a process of enculturation: *the transfer of traditional beliefs and behaviors of the culture to its young, adjusting them in the process to its predetermined norms. In contrast are those who view education as* acculturation: *exchange and borrowing between young and old, resulting in new patterns, new norms, more dynamic and organic blending.*

165. Morrison, Philip. "Less May Be More." **American Journal of Physics,** Vol. 32, No. 6, June 1964.

Faced with the problem of inducing what he terms a "self-conscious analysis of experience," Professor Morrison proposes a new kind of physics course for prospective elementary teachers, which avoids austere overemphasis on verbal analysis and incorporates a good deal of student-directed flexibility. The final section explores several quite specific topics in physics and speculates in detail on how they might be pursued. An example of how open education might work at the college level.

°166. Morrison, Philip. "Experimenters in the Classroom." **ESI Quarterly Report,** Winter–Spring 1964. Also included in **The ESS Reader** (no. 33).

Speaking to a group concerned with curriculum design, Professor Morrison emphasizes the need in children's learning for concrete, direct experience (predisciplinary and integrated), as well as for the abstract and intellectual experiences schools normally stress. Likewise, he advocates encouraging children's interest in novelty, change, and continued experimentation.

°167. Morrison, Philip. "The Curricular Triangle and Its Style." **ESI Quarterly Report,** Summer-Fall 1964. Also included in **The ESS Reader** (no. 33).

On the relation of: curriculum to the disciplines; abstract conceptualizations to concrete material; synthesis to analysis; theory to experiment—all from the view of developing a curricular style that demands personal involvement, exploration, play, and time.

168. Morrison, Philip. "Tensions of Purpose." **ESI Quarterly Report,** Spring–Summer 1966 (Education Development Center, Inc. Reprints available from the publisher @ $ .25.

While preparing curriculum materials, Professor Morrison has discerned tensions between goals and means of evaluating those goals. After briefly describing each set of tensions, he discusses at greater length what an ideal system of evaluation might be.

169. Nyquist, Ewald B. "The British Primary School Approach to Education: Time for Reform in the Elementary Schools," December 1970 (unpublished speech). Single copies available from the Office of the Commissioner of Education, State Education Department, Albany, New York.

Remarks by New York's Commissioner of Education on opening a conference which stressed the British infant school approach to education. Dr. Nyquist emphasized the need "to make the educational system more humanistic—more humane with respect to the curriculum, administration, governance and, indeed, the whole teaching and learning process."

170. Nyquist, Ewald B., "Open Education—Its Philosophy, Historical Perspectives, and Implications." **The Science Teacher,** Vol. 38, No. 6, September 1971.

The Commissioner of Education in New York State strongly advocates more humane forms of public education, endorses open education, and briefly discusses what it is, its historical background, and implications for parents, teachers, administrators, and children.

171. Omwake, Eveline B. "From the President." **Young Children,** Vol. 24, No. 4, March 1969.

In an editorial assessing the opportunities Project Follow Through affords to reforming Early Childhood Education practices, the president of the National Association for the Education of Young Children calls for a thorough examination of British infant schools. She cautions, however, against adoption of selected practices without reference to the total program.

172. Pearce, Lucia. "Exploration-Innovation: The New Learning Environment." **The Science Teacher,** Vol. 36, No. 2, February 1969.

Searching for a structured environment which is truly an "extension of the learner" (rather than of the teacher), Mrs. Pearce sketches out the requirements of a studio-lab "free learning environment," one that very nearly fits the specifications of an open education classroom: a new teacher role (mediator, resource catalyst), mixed grouping of children, flexible spatial arrangements (including modular furniture the children themselves can assemble), considerable choice for children in what and when and how they learn—all with the goal of fostering autonomous, independent, "self-actualizing" behavior in young children.

173. Perusek, Wesley. "Open Education and Technology for Children." **Happenings,** Vol. 3, No. 3, November-December 1969.
Mr. Perusek draws a number of comparisons between the approach of open education and that of the Technology for Children Project, with which he is associated, within the Division of Vocational Education of the New Jersey Department of Education.

174. Rathbone, Charles H. "A Lesson from Loughborough." **This Magazine Is About Schools,** Vol. 3, No. 1, February 1969; reprinted in an expanded form in **Froebel Journal,** June 1969.
Recollections of an in-service, residential training course for primary teachers provided in April, 1968 by the Leicestershire Advisory Council, with special emphasis on the factors which inhibit profitable relationships between learner and materials, learner and teachers, learner and self-image as learner.

175. Rogers, Vincent R. "The Social Studies Revolution Begins in Britain." **Phi Delta Kappan,** Vol. 50, No. 3, November 1968.
While reviewing the forces influencing secondary social studies curriculum in England, Professor Rogers discusses the role of the "neo-progressive," child-centered educationists.

176. Rogers, Vincent R. "Three Lessons We Should Learn From British Education." **Phi Delta Kappan,** Vol. 50, No. 5, January 1969.
*A review of James Koerner's **Reform in Education: England and the United States,** by Professor Rogers of the University of Connecticut, in which he holds that "if there is any bastion of relatively free, child-centered, experience-based learning left in the world, it is surely the English primary school."*

°177. Rogers, Vincent. "English and American Primary Schools." **Phi Delta Kappan,** Vol. LI, No. 2, October 1969.
In this well-organized, perceptive article, Professor Rogers of the University of Connecticut grapples with three questions: What is so unusual about British Primary Schools? Why have

similar ideas failed to take root in this country? What are the major drawbacks of this sort of schooling?

178. Rogers, Vincent R. "A Macrocosmic Approach to Inquiry." **Social Education,** Vol. 34, No. 1, January 1970.

    A look at the principles underlying the "inquiry" approach to social studies curriculum, including an analysis of the recent revolution in British primary education and its implicit rationale.

179. Schlesinger, Joy. **Leicestershire Report: The Classroom Environment.** Cambridge, Mass.: Publication Office, Harvard Graduate School of Education, $ .20.

    One of the earliest (1965) reports of life in open classrooms by an American visitor to several schools in Leicestershire County.

180. Sealey, L. G. W. "Looking back on Leicestershire." **ESI Quarterly Report,** Education Development Center, Inc., Spring–Summer 1966. Reprint available from the publisher @ $ .25.

    A former advisor for Junior Schools in Leicestershire considers the function of the Advisory, defines "Integrated Day," and speaks of the interpersonal climate which fosters continued professional growth of teachers.

181. Sealey, Leonard. "Innovation and Experimentation in the Elementary School." **The Independent School Bulletin,** Vol. 29, No. 1, October 1969.

    An analysis of the skills and abilities required of the elementary teacher who hopes to effect significant change in his classroom.

182. Shanker, Albert. "The 'Open Classroom' Concept." **New York Times,** January 24, 1971.

    In the weekly **New York Times** *column sponsored by the United Federation of Teachers, the president of that organization reviews Charles Silberman's* **Crisis in the Classroom.** *Following a general statement in support of the "open classroom" idea, Mr. Shanker goes on to elaborate three basic points: "First, we must recognize that there is no single method which is best for all teachers and for all students." "Second, the evidence now available does not prove that the open classroom* *produces greater achievement in reading and math." "Third, the techniques of the open classroom cannot be easily adopted by every teacher."*

183. Tobier, Arthur J. "The Open Classroom: Humanizing the Coldness of Public Places." **The Center Forum,** Vol. 3, No. 6, May 1969.

    An account of Lillian Weber's work to establish a well-equipped, family-grouped "open corridor" in Harlem's P.S. 123. For a more comprehensive description, see the pamphlet, **Open Door** *(available from Center for Urban Education @ $1.50).*

184. Trachtman, Paul. "A Parent Endorses 'Classroom Chaos'." *Life,* Dec. 17, 1971.

    An introspective parent at the Manhattan Country School traces the evolution of many parents' thinking about informal classrooms from skepticism to enthusiasm. An excellent view of the many reasons parents object to informal methods.

185. Ulin, Donald S. "What I Learned From the British Schools." **Grade Teacher,** Vol. 86, No. 6, February 1969. Copies of entire issue available @ $1.00.

    A sixth grade teacher's account of a sabbatical year spent in several Leicestershire schools. After describing the classrooms he visited, Mr. Ulin offers—subject by subject—his impression of how British pupils compare with their American counterparts. He also offers some criticism of both American and English schools.

186. Villet, Barbara. "The Children Want Classrooms Alive with Chaos." **Life,** Vol. 66, No. 14, April 11, 1969.

    An illustrated article on American counterparts of the British infant school.

187. Walter, Marion and Brown, Stephen. "What If Not." **Mathematics Teaching,** No. 46, Spring 1969.

    Noting how most math courses emphasize the need to arrive at final, polished products to the neglect of any stress on problem posing, the authors present work on geoboards as a means of helping both students and teachers to generate new ways of thinking about mathematics.

188. Wason, Margaret. " 'My Mother Still Doesn't Believe It' " **Where**, No. 49, May 1970.

    A consideration of the consequences of issuing an open invitation for parents to visit a first-year junior class in an open educational school. Dr. Wason documents parents' reluctance, disbelief, eventual involvement, etc. with numerous examples.

189. Weber, Lillian. "Creating Tradition in English Infant Schools: The Mechanism of Dissemination." **The Center Forum**, Vol. 3, No. 7, July 1969.

    A discussion of inter- and intra-school communications.

190. Williams, Rosemary. "At the Heart of the Educational Process Lies the Child." **Independent School Bulletin**, Vol. 29, No. 1, October 1969.

    This is a talk given at the National Association of Independent Schools Annual Conference in March 1969. In it the former Headmistress of Westfield County Infant School in Leicestershire describes and defines the "Integrated Day." Miss Williams is now on the staff of the Follow Through Project at Education Development Center.

191. Yeomans, Edward. "Adapting Leicestershire Techniques." **The Independent School Bulletin**, Vol. 28, No. 4, May 1969.

    Notes on a discussion by Miss Mary Torrey of Cambridge Friends School and Miss Jane Prescott of Shady Hill School (both in Cambridge, Mass.) concerning the principal requirements for successful adaptation of the integrated day to American schools.

BIBLIOGRAPHIES AND LISTS OF CURRICULUM MATERIALS

192. Alschuler, Alfred and Borton, Terry. **A Bibliography on Affective Education.** Albany, New York: New York Educational Opportunities Forum (State Board of Education), 1969.

    "A Bibliography on Affective Education, Psychological Education, the Eupsychian Network, Curriculum of Concerns, Personological Education, Synoetics, Personal Learning, etc.," in-

cluding names of organizations concerned with open education, this view offers an important perspective on what happens in open education classrooms.

193. Association for Childhood Education, International. **Equipment and Supplies.** Washington, D.C., 1967.

    A comprehensive list of instructional materials for the elementary grades.

194. Barth, Roland S. and Rathbone, Charles H. "The Open School: A Way of Thinking About Children, Learning, Knowledge" and "Readings on British Primary Education and Its American Counterparts: A Selected Bibliography." **The Center Forum**, Vol. 3, No. 7, July 1969. Single copies available free from the publisher.

    An earlier and less comprehensive version of "A Bibliography of Open Education" (see footnote, page 236), together with a brief introductory discussion of open education.

195. Early Childhood Education Study. **Materials: A Useful List of Classroom Items That Can Be Scrounged or Purchased.** Newton, Mass.: Education Development Center, Inc., 1970. Available from Early Childhood Education Study @ $ .50.

    A 17-page helpful list of free or inexpensive materials, including addresses of suppliers.

196. Early Childhood Education Study. **Single Sheets.** Newton, Mass.: Education Development Center, Inc., 1970. Available from Early Childhood Education Study @ $1.00.

    "Here are some ideas we want to share." A packet of 8½ × 11" cards with informative photographs and accompanying comments and questions. Appropriate for primary grade teachers and children.

197. EDC Follow Through Program. **Instructional Aids, Materials, and Supplies.** Newton, Mass.: Education Development Center, Inc., 1970. Available from Follow Through Program @ $1.00.

    A 75-page list of possible curriculum materials for an open classroom compiled by the staff of the EDC Follow Through Program who consult with public schools across the country.

198. Education Development Center, Inc. **Open Education at**

EDC: Films and Books. Newton, Mass.: Education Development Center, Inc., 1971.

An annotated catalog of materials related to open classrooms that are available through EDC.

199. Elementary Science Study. **A Working Guide to the Elementary Science Study.** Newton, Mass.: Education Development Center, Inc., 1971. @ $3.00.

A booklet listing all of the materials developed by the Elementary Science Study over the last ten years, appropriate grade levels, and descriptions, prices, and availability of each. These curriculum materials, now distributed by Webster Division, McGraw-Hill, more than any others in this country, have facilitated the implementation of open education in the United States.

200. Hoffman, Jim and Tower, Phyllis. **A Bibliography for the Free School Movement.** New York: The Summerhill Society, 1971. Available from the publisher @ $1.00.

This 25-page annotated bibliography, which was prepared for the Summerhill Society and first published in its **Bulletin,** *includes fiction as well as many books on therapy.*

201. Judson, Madison E. **Books of Interest Concerning Infant, Primary and Elementary Schools in the United States and in England.** Belmont, Mass.: Dan Pinck Associates, 1969. Available from the publisher @ $2.25.

A bibliography compiled by the former headmaster of the Fayerweather Street School in Cambridge, Mass., including an introduction by Dan Pinck, director of Dan Pinck Associates/Educational and School Services.

202. National Froebel Foundation. **Education Bibliography.** London: National Froebel Foundation, 1968 (revised).

A listing of nearly 300 titles, with sections on Philosophy of Education, Curriculum, Educational Psychology and Child Development, etc.

203. Nuffield Foundation. **Nuffield Mathematics Project.** Ne⸱ York: John Wiley and Sons, Inc. **Nuffield Junior Science Series.** Available from Agathon Press, Inc.

In both sets of books, "the stress is on how to learn, not on what to teach."

204. Leitman, Allan and Churchill, Edith H. E. "Approximation No. 1." Newton, Mass.: Education Development Center, Inc., 1966. Available from the Early Childhood Education Study @ $1.00. Also reprinted in **Open Education: The Informal Classroom** (no. 81).

A list of materials and plans for equipping preschool and primary classrooms, including costs and often directions for constructing the materials.

205. Workshop for Learning Things, Inc. **Our Catalog.** 5 Bridge St., Watertown, Mass. 02171. Available from the publisher @ $.50.

This unusual organization ". . . tries to give people in education access to interesting materials and techniques unavailable elsewhere. We are still a store trying to go out of business. As commercial suppliers begin to offer comparable materials at comparable prices, we will drop them from our inventory. Meanwhile, as we develop new 'learning things,' they will be added."

In addition to offering an intriguing catalog, the Workshop runs workshops in photography, cardboard carpentry, design, etc., where teachers are aided in developing their own classroom materials.

FILMS

206. British Broadcasting Corporation. **Discovery and Experience** (film). 10 films, 30 min. each, 16mm, sound, black and white. Available in the U.S. through Time-Life Films. Purchase Price: $250.00 each (10/$2000.00). Rental Price $30.00 each (10/$250.00).

Child-centered schooling and the need for individual exploration are stressed in this BBC-TV series, which includes programs entitled "Learning by Doing," "Finding Out," and "Movement in Time and Space." etc. (A second film series called **Growth & Play** *is also available). For an introduction to these films, see the pamphlet by Margaret Spencer (available*

BBC Publications Office); child-centered schooling and the need for individual exploration are stressed.

207. British Broadcasting Corporation. **Mother Tongue** (film). 5 films, 30 min. each, 16mm, sound, black and white. Available in the U.S. through Time-Life Films. Purchase Price: $250.00 each (5/$1000.00). Rental Price: $30.00 each (5/$125.00).

A series of programs on language development produced by BBC-TV and narrated both by college professors and by primary school heads. The five half-hour programs are entitled, "First Foundations," "Language Building," "Reading and Writing," "Problems and Remedies," and "The Sensitive Tool." **Mother Tongue** *study notes are available; they include a brief bibliography for each of the five programs.*

208. Canadian Broadcasting Corporation. **What They Want To Produce, Not What We Want To Become** (film). 56 min., 16mm, sound, black and white. Available in the U.S. through EDC Film Library. Purchase Price: $225.00. Rental Price: $20.00.

A 56-minute film in two parts. Part One criticizes contemporary schools; Part Two offers three radical alternatives, including a look at Everdale Place and Summerhill.

209. Early Childhood Education Study. **I Ain't Playin' No More** (film). Newton, Mass.: Education Development Center, Inc. 61 min., 16mm, sound, black and white. Available from EDC Film Library. Purchase Price: $300.00. Rental Price: $20.00.

A 61-minute film by Michel Chalufour in two parts which highlights issues of community control and self-directed learning in the Morgan Community School of Washington, D.C.

210. Early Childhood Education Study/Allan Leitman. **I Am Here Today** (film). Newton, Mass.: Education Development Center, Inc. 43 min., 16mm, sound, black and white. Available from EDC Film Library. Purchase Price: $215.00. Rental Price: $20.00.

A morning visit to an open classroom filmed in May 1969 at Shady Hill School, Cambridge, Massachusetts. This class, composed of 5-, 6-, and 7-year olds operates on a highly individualized basis. Betsye Sargent and her two assistants have de-

*veloped a format which allows the older children to act as teacher to the younger ones while being free to follow their individual interests. The education process is built upon an individual and small group involvement in constructive processes. As a companion piece to this film, Mrs. Sargent's curriculum report for her classroom, **The Integrated Day in an American School**, is available from the National Association of Independent Schools.*

211. Early Childhood Education Study/Allan Leitman. **Making Things to Learn** (film). Newton, Mass.: Education Development Center, Inc., 11 min., 16mm, sound, black and white. Available from EDC Film Library. Purchase Price: $55.00. Rental Price: $10.00.

This film shows a workshop for teachers in which certain tensions, first brought into focus by an unstructured exploration of materials, are later released in a burst of creative productivity. An experience of open education at the level of teacher preparation.

212. Early Childhood Education Study/Allan Leitman. **They Can Do It** (film). Newton, Mass.: Education Development Center, Inc., 34 min., 16mm, sound, black and white. Available from EDC Film Library. Purchase Price: $170.00. Rental Price: $15.00.

The director of the Early Childhood Education Study at EDC documents developments over the span of one year within a first-grade classroom taught by Lovey Glen in Philadelphia. During the year, the class moves from a traditional to a more open structure.

213. Early Childhood Education Study/Allan Leitman. **Three Year Olds** (film). Newton, Mass.: Education Development Center, Inc. 16mm, sound, black and white. Available from EDC Film Library. Purchase Price: Set: $750.00; individual films from $45.00 to $125.00. Rental Price: $15.00 except "Rhythms" which is $10.00.

Conceived as "ethological," these nine short films (10–30 minutes) offer an unedited "real time" view of the interaction of these preschoolers through the subjective eye of the cameraman. Filmed at the City and Country School in New York.

214. Early Childhood Education Study/Allan Leitman. **To Find a Way** (film). Newton, Mass.: Education Development Center, Inc. 35 min., 16mm, sound, black and white (in production).

    A film showing a teacher education program based on the workshop process as a means of initiating and involving students in open education at college level. The students are from Lowell (Mass.) State College.

215. Early Childhood Education Study/Allan Leitman. **Vignettes** (film). Newton, Mass.: Education Development Center, Inc. 16mm, sound, black and white. Available from EDC Film Library. Purchase Price: individual films from $35.00 to $60.00. Rental Price: $10.00 each.

    A series of short (7–12 minute) films showing Head Start children from various communities at work within an open environment. Titles of the individual films are: "Chairs," "Wall Washing," "Marble Games," "Waterplay," "Seven-Day Itch," and "Injections."

216. Educational Facilities Lab. **Room to Learn** (film). 22 min., 16mm, sound, color. Available from Association Films. Purchase Price: $125.00. Rental Price: free.

    A film of the Early Learning Center of Stamford, Connecticut where the principles of open education have affected the physical environment of a specially designed building for preschoolers.

217. Elementary Science Study. **Another Way To Learn** (film). Newton, Mass.: Education Development Center, Inc. 12 min., 16mm, sound, black and white. Available from the EDC Film Library. Purchase Price: $65.00. Rental Price: $10.00.

    This 12 minute film of Nancy Howe's first grade classroom depicts open education in action in Wellesley, Massachusetts. Made by Charles Walcott and Allan Leitman.

218. Elementary Science Study. **Choosing to Learn** (film). Newton, Mass.: Education Development Center, Inc. 26 min., 16mm, sound, color. Available from the EDC Film Library. Purchase Price: $260.00. Rental Price: $20.00.

    This color film by Henry Felt shows life in The World of Inquiry School, an experimental Title III Demonstration project in Rochester, New York., where children choose their own activities. Most striking is a scene of a ten-year-old welding under the tutelage of a retired welder, now serving as a part-time teacher aide.

219. Elementary Science Study. **Classrooms in Transition** (film). Newton, Mass.: Education Development Center, Inc. 31 min., 16mm, sound, black and white. Available from EDC Film Library. Purchase Price: $155.00. Rental Price: $15.00.

    Mary Lela Sherburne narrates this film of classrooms in the Cardozo Model School Project in Washington, D.C. A central theme concerns the effect of manipulative (ESS) materials.

220. Felt, Henry. **Battling Brook Primary School (Four Days in September)** (film). Newton, Mass.: Education Development Center, Inc. 23 min., 16mm, sound, black and white. Available from the EDC Film Library. Purchase Price: $115.00. Rental Price: $15.00.

    Opening week in one of Leicestershire's finest primary schools; including an interview with Roy Illsley, its head.

221. Felt, Henry. **Medbourne Primary School: Four Days in May** (film). Newton, Mass.: Education Development Center, Inc. 12 min., 16mm, sound, black and white. Available from EDC Film Library. Purchase Price: $65.00. Rental Price: $10.00.

    The documentation of classroom life within an excellent rural primary school in Leicestershire.

222. Felt, Henry. **Westfield Infant School: Two Days in May** (film). Newton, Mass.: Education Development Center. In preparation. Will be available from EDC Film Library.

    In this black and white film of a Leicestershire infant school, Mr. Felt pays special attention to the role of a single teacher as she goes about in the midst of her forty pupils.

223. Fiering, Alvin. **Children as People: The Fayerweather Street School** (film). Boston: Polymorph Films, Inc. 35 min., 16mm, sound, black and white. Available from Polymorph Films, Inc. Purchase Price: $235.00. Rental Price: $30.00.

    John Holt narrates this 35 minute film of activity at the Fayerweather Street School of Cambridge, Mass., an American private school run on many of the same principles which underlie the current movement in British primary education.

224. I/D/E/A. **Primary Education in England: The English Infant School** (film). 17 min., 16mm, sound, color. Available from Information and Services Division at the Institute for Development of Educational Activities, Inc. Purchase Price: $120.00. Rental Price: $10.00.

    A 17 minute film showing open education at work in the Sea Mills Infant School in Bristol, England. Directed by John Patterson.

225. Ridgway, Lorna. **Children Are People** (film). London: Stockwell College of Education. 42 min., 16mm, sound, color. Available from Agathon Press, Inc. Purchase Price: $450.00. Rental Price: $45.00.

    Made in England, this film explores the various aspects of family, or vertical age, grouping and provides a vivid picture of open education in infant and junior schools.

226. Weber, Lillian. **Infants School** (film). Newton, Mass. Education Development Center, Inc. 32 min., 16mm, sound, black and white. Available from EDC Film Library. Purchase Price: $150.00. Rental Price: $15.00.

    Thirty nearly unedited minutes of activity in London's Gordonbrock Infant School, with concentration on children's movement in the classroom. For a transcription of an interview with Miss Susan Williams, headmistress of this school, see Cazden's "Infant School" pamphlet. Filmed by Peter Theobald.

227. Welch, Dorothy. **Balancing** (film). Newton, Mass.: Education Development Center, Inc. 20 min., 16mm, silent, color. Available from EDC Film Library. Purchase Price: $100.00. Rental Price: $10.00.

    This short teacher-made color film shows fifth and sixth graders of the Hollis Elementary School in New Hampshire working with various ESS units—a rather dramatic instance of open education in action.

228. Welch, Dorothy. **Bones** (film). Newton, Mass.: Education Development Center, Inc. 18 min., 16mm, silent, color. Available from EDC Film Library. Purchase Price: $100.00. Rental Price: $10.00.

    A film of fifth and sixth graders thoroughly involved in a study of bones.

PERIODICALS

229. **Big Rock Candy Mountain,** Portola Institute, 1115 Merrill St., Menlo Park, California 94025.

   Published six times per year, Big Rock Candy Mountain presents a fascinating variety of educational materials, all thoroughly reviewed and illustrated.

230. **Childhood Education,** 3815 Wisconsin Ave., Washington, D.C. 20016.

   The Journal of the Association of Childhood Education International maintains an active interest in open education and frequently includes timely and pertinent editorials and articles.

231. **Forum,** 86 Headland Rd., Evington, Leicester, England.

   A British periodical published three times a year at the University of Leicester's School of Education "for the discussion of new trends in education." Brian Simon, ed.

232. **Froebel Journal,** National Froebel Foundation, 2 Manchester Square, London, W.1, England.

   The Journal of the National Froebel Foundation, a foundation open to "men and women interested in the education of children up to 12 years of age," and not confined to those with a Froebel training. Articles and book reviews on various subjects concerning primary schools in Britain. The foundation also organizes in-service courses for experienced teachers on a variety of topics.

233. **Happenings,** Technology for Children Project, Division of Vocational Education, New Jersey Department of Education, Trenton, N.J. 08625.

   This project has developed an interest in open education through an unusual route—technology. In their attempt to provide manipulative experiences for children and materials appropriate for vocational education, the Project has intersected in interesting ways with the British primary school movement.

234. **IDEAS,** University of London Goldsmiths' College. Available

in North America from Agathon Publication Services, Inc., 150 Fifth Ave., New York, N.Y. 10011.

Periodical founded by Goldsmiths' College Curriculum Laboratory. Focus is on work with children aged 8 to 13. Emphasizes collaborative group experiences for both teachers and students.

235. **In Touch,** School of Education, University of Massachusetts, Amherst, Mass.

A periodic newsletter "dedicated to the education of young children," funded by the New England Programs in Teacher Education and prepared at the School of Education, University of Massachusetts, Amherst. Contains frequent, helpful ideas and articles for teachers moving toward more informal classrooms.

236. **Insights.** University of North Dakota (New School of Behavioral Studies in Education), Grand Forks, North Dakota 58201.

The newsletter of UND's New School, which was established in 1968 to produce teachers partial to the current practices and philosophies of British primary education.

237. **Manas.** Manas Publishing Company, P.O. Box 32112, El Sereno Station, Los Angeles, Calif. 90032.

*Published fortnightly, **Manas** often contains articles written in the spirit of the current reform movement in England. Of particular note is the section, "Children and Ourselves," which often reviews relevant books and articles outside the field of education.*

238. **Mathematics Teaching,** Journal of the Association of Teachers of Mathematics. Vine Street Chambers, Nelson, Lancaster, England.

Although many of the articles appearing in this Journal are aimed at the specialist in mathematics, in nearly every issue there are articles of a more general nature which show how the principles of open education apply to the teaching of mathematics.

239. **New Schools Exchange Newsletter,** 2840 Hidden Valley Lane, Santa Barbara, Calif. 93103.

This fortnightly newsletter contains descriptions of radical and experimental schools in this country. It also carries information about people seeking schools and schools seeking people. Issue No. 55 (March 1971) contains an extensive bibliography of works relating "in the broadest sense to humanistic, free, new, experimental, alternative, etc., education."

240. **Open Education Newsletter,** School-Within-A-School, Department of Education, Queens College, CUNY, Flushing, N.Y. 11367.

A new (February 1972) newsletter committed to reforming the educational system via teachers. "Our hope is to enlighten and encourage those moving in the direction of openness."

241. **Outlook.** Mountain View Center For Environmental Education, University of Colorado, 1441 Broadway, Boulder, Colorado 80302.

This new periodical invites its readers to share their ideas. The staff includes some of the pioneers in open education—Frances and David Hawkins, Tony Kallet, and Elwyn Richardson, among others. The magazine publishes pieces on all aspects of education—how children think, classroom arrangements, teaching materials and ideas.

242. **Play Area Review,** Niedermeyer-Martin Company, 1727 N.E. 11th Ave., Portland, Oregon 97212.

A quarterly publication devoted to pictures and articles relating to the playground revolution. Illustrated.

243. **Primary School Broadsheet,** Leicestershire Education Committee, Leicester, England (not distributed outside England).

An occasional publication of the Leicestershire Education Committee, often containing brief articles by practicing teachers, sometimes devoted entirely to a single subject (e.g. Broadsheet No. 4 of Summer 1967, which was all children's writing).

244. **Summerhill Bulletin,** Summerhill Collective, 137A West 14th St., New York, N.Y. 10011.

The Summerhill Collective is a new organization, one which has "both spiritually and legally" severed its ties with the Summerhill Society.

245. **Summerhill Society Bulletin,** New York: The Summerhill Society, 5 Beekman St., New York, N.Y. 10012.

The Bulletin of the Summerhill Society which holds "that when children are given a responsible freedom in a climate of understanding and non-possessive love, they choose with wisdom, learn with alacrity, and develop genuinely social attitudes." Published every other month. A regular membership in the Society costs $10; student membership $5.00.

246. **This Magazine Is About Schools,** P.O. Box 876, Terminal A, Toronto, Canada.

A radical quarterly, edited by Robert Davis and often sympathetic to the aims of open education.

247. **Trends in Education,** Department of Education and Science, Curzon St., London W.1, England.

The official quarterly publication of the Department of Education and Science containing articles on a wide variety of topics.

248. **The Urban Review,** Agathon Publication Services, 150 Fifth Ave., New York, N.Y. 10011.

The journal of the Center for Urban Education. Covers various aspects relating to education in urban areas. Generally sympathetic to open education. Published six times a year.

249. **Where,** Advisory Centre for Education, 57 Russell St., Cambridge, England.

A magazine published by the Advisory Centre, containing articles on a variety of topics in British education. Occasional "Supplements" on special topics are also published, such as No. 13 on Nuffield math and science projects and No. 12 on unstreaming the comprehensive schools.

Addresses of Publishers and Distributors

Advisory for Open Education
90 Sherman St.
Cambridge, Mass. 02140

Agathon Press, Inc.
150 Fifth Ave.
New York, N.Y. 10011

Alexander Graham Bell Association for the Deaf, Inc.
1537 35th St., NW
Washington, D.C. 20007

American Heritage Press
330 W. 42nd St.
New York, N.Y. 10036

American Journal of Physics
335 E. 45th St.
New York, N.Y.

Arena
Architectural Association Quarterly
Headington Hill Hall
Oxford OX 3 CBW, England

Association for Childhood Education International
3615 Wisconsin Ave., N.W.
Washington, D.C.

Association Films, Inc.
866 Third Ave.
New York, N.Y. 10017

Association of Teachers of Mathematics
Vine Street Chambers
Nelson, Lancaster, England

Basil Blackwell
Broad St.
Oxford, England

British Broadcasting Corporation
35 Marylebone High St.
London, W.1, England

British Information Services
Sales Section
845 Third Ave.
New York, N.Y. 10022

Cambridge University Press
32 E. 57th St.
New York, N.Y. 10022

Center for Coordinated Education
University of California
Santa Barbara, Calif.

Center for Urban Education
105 Madison Ave.
New York, N.Y. 10016

The Center Magazine
Box 4578
Santa Barbara, Calif. 93103

Chatto & Windus (Educational) Ltd.
42 William IV St.
London W.C. 2, England

Childhood Education
3615 Wisconsin Ave., N.W.
Washington, D.C. 20016

Citation Press
Scholastic Book Services
50 West 44th St.
New York, N.Y. 10036

Critical Quarterly Society
The Secretary
2 Radcliffe Ave.
London N.W. 10, England

Daedalus: The Journal of the American
   Academy of Arts and Sciences
280 Newton St.
Brookline, Mass. 02146

Dell Publishing Company
750 Third Ave.
New York, N.Y. 10017

Department of Education and Science
Curzon St.
London W.1, England

Department of Title I Programs
Boston Public Schools
2893 Washington St.
Roxbury, Mass. 02119

Early Childhood Education Study
Education Development Center, Inc.
55 Chapel St.
Newton, Mass. 02160

Education Development Center, Inc.
55 Chapel St.
Newton, Mass. 02160

Elementary School Journal
5835 Kimbark Ave.
Chicago, Ill. 60637

Elementary Science Advisory Center
603 Ketchum
University of Colorado
Boulder, Colo.

Elementary Science Study
Education Development Center, Inc.
55 Chapel St.
Newton, Mass. 02160

Faber & Faber
24 Russell Square
London W.C.1, England

Friends Committee on Education
1515 Cherry St.
Philadelphia, Penn. 19102

Forum
86 Headland Rd.
Evington, Leicester, England

Froebel Journal
see National Froebel Foundation

Happenings
Division of Vocational Education
State Department of Education
Trenton, N.J.

George G. Harrap and Co., Ltd.
182 High Holborn
London W.C.1, England

Grade Teacher
23 Leroy Ave.
Darien, Conn. 06820

Harvard Educational Review
Graduate School of Education, Longfel-
   low Hall
13 Appian Way
Cambridge, Mass. 02138

Harvard Graduate School of Education
Office of Field Activities
Cambridge, Mass. 02138

Her Majesty's Stationery Office
Sales Section, British Information Services
845 Third Ave.
New York, N.Y. 10022

Hutchinson Educational, Ltd.
178 Great Portland St.
London W.1, England

The Independent School Bulletin
Boston: National Association of Independent Schools
4 Liberty Square
Boston, Mass. 02109

I/D/E/A
Institute for Development of Educational Activities, Inc.
Box 446
Melbourne, Florida 32901

The John Day Company
62 West 45th St.
New York, N.Y. 10036

Journal of Educational Philosophy and Theory
Pergamon Press, Ltd.
Headington Hill Hall
Oxford, England

Kentucky Education Association
101 West Walnut
Louisville, Ky. 40202

Life
Time/Life Building
Rockefeller Center
New York, N.Y. 10020

Liveright
386 Park Ave. S.
New York, N.Y. 10016

Longmans, Green and Company
48 Grosvenor St.
London W.1, England

The Macmillan Co.
866 Third Ave.
New York, N.Y. 10022

Manas Publishing Co.
P.O. Box 32112, El Sereno Station
Los Angeles, Calif. 90032

Mathematics Teaching
Association of Teachers of Mathematics
Vine Street Chambers
Nelson, Lancashire, England

Methuen and Company, Ltd.
11 Fetter Lane
London, E.C.4, England

National Association for the Education of Young Children
1629 21st St.
Washington, D.C. 20009

National Association of Independent Schools
4 Liberty Square
Boston, Mass. 02109

National Froebel Foundation
2 Manchester Square
London W.1, England

The National Elementary Principal
National Education Association
1201 16th St., N.W.
Washington, D.C. 20036

New England School Development Center
55 Chapel Street
Newton, Mass. 02160

New Jersey Department of Education
Technology for Children Project
Division of Vocational Education
Trenton, N.J. 08625

The New Republic
1244 19th St., N.W.
Washington, D.C. 20046

New Schools Exchange
701 B Anacapa St.
Santa Barbara, Calif. 93101

New York Educational Opportunities Forum
(State Board of Education)
Albany, N.Y.

The New York Times
229 West 43rd St.
New York, N.Y. 10036

Niedermeyer Martin Co.
1727 N.E. 11th Ave.
Portland, Oreg. 97212

North Carolina Advancement School
Winston-Salem, N.C.

Office of the Commissioner of Education
State Department of Education
Albany, N.Y.

Ontario Institute for Studies in
  Education
102 Bloor St. West
Toronto 5, Ontario, Canada

Pantheon Books
Random House
201 E. 50th St., New York, N.Y. 10022

Penguin Books
7110 Ambassador Rd.,
Baltimore, Md. 21207

Pergamon Press
4-5 Fitzroy Square
London W.1, England

Phi Delta Kappan
Eight and Union Streets
Bloomington, Ind. 47401

Dan Pinck Associates
49 Clark St.,
Belmont, Mass. 02178

Pitman Publishing Corporation
20 East 46th St.
New York, N.Y. 10017

Polymorph Films, Inc.
331 Newbury St.
Boston, Mass. 02115

Praeger Publishers, Inc.
111 Fourth Ave.
New York, N.Y. 10003

Prentice-Hall, Inc.
Englewood Cliffs, N.J. 07632

Primary School Broadsheet
Advisory Section, Leicestershire
Education Department
County Hall, Glenfield
Leicester, England

Princeton Alumni Weekly
Princeton, N.J.

Random House
201 E. 50th St.,
New York, N.Y. 10022

Routledge & Kegan Paul
68-74 Carter Lane
London E.C.4, England

Saturday Review
380 Madison Ave.
New York, N.Y. 10017

Schocken Books, Inc.
200 Madison Ave.
New York, N.Y. 10016

The Science Teacher
National Science Teacher's Association
1201 16th St., N.W.
Washington, D.C. 20036

Simon and Schuster
630 Fifth Ave.
New York, N.Y. 10020

Social Education
National Council for Social Studies
1201 16th St., N.W.
Washington, D.C. 20036

Tavistock Publications
11 New Fetter Lane
London E.C.4, England

This Magazine Is About Schools
P.O. Box 876, Terminal 'A'
Toronto, 1, Ontario, Canada

Trends in Education
Department of Education and Science
Curzon St.
London, W.1, England

U.S. Government Printing Office
N. Capitol & H St., N.W.
Washington, D.C. 20401

University of London Press, Ltd.
St. Paul's Ho., Warwick Lane
London E.C.4, England

Vermont State Department of Education
Office of the Commissioner
Montpelier, Vt. 05602

Vintage Books
Random House
201 East 50th St.
New York, N.Y. 10022

Wheelock Alumnae Quarterly
Wheelock Alumnae Association
200 Pineway
Boston, Mass. 02215

John Wiley and Sons, Inc.
605 Third Avenue
New York, N.Y. 10016

Young Children
National Association for the Education of
    Young Children
1629 21 St., N.W.
Washington, D.C. 20009

Name Index

Numbers in *italic type* refer to entries in the Bibliography
(pages 237–288)

Subject Index